The Promotion of Education

Valerie Harwood · Nyssa Murray

The Promotion of Education

A Critical Cultural Social Marketing Approach

Valerie Harwood
Sydney School of Education and Social
Work
The University of Sydney
Sydney, NSW, Australia

Nyssa Murray
Sydney School of Education and Social
Work
The University of Sydney
Sydney, NSW, Australia

ISBN 978-3-030-25302-8   ISBN 978-3-030-25300-4   (eBook)
https://doi.org/10.1007/978-3-030-25300-4

This Palgrave Macmillan imprint is published by the registered company Springer Nature Switzerland AG
The registered company address is: Gewerbestrasse 11, 6330 Cham, Switzerland

We dedicate this book to the communities and to those that work hard and endlessly in communities to overcome disadvantage.

Preface

The Promotion of Education—A Critical Cultural Social Marketing Approach introduces critical cultural social marketing, an approach that builds on the discipline of social marketing, adapting these techniques for use in the promotion of educational futures in communities and places where there is educational disadvantage. The promotion of education that we describe is underpinned by a twofold commitment to an understanding of firstly, the effects of difficult experiences with institutions such as schools, and secondly, that learning is diverse. Involving the critical in promoting education means that we are alert to these effects and impacts of institutions of education such as schooling. Involving the cultural means that we are forced to appreciate and connect with learning in all its diversity, and this especially requires us to look beyond schooling. Using rich examples from Lead My Learning, an education promotion campaign produced using a critical cultural social marketing approach, the book provides a detailed account of new ways to promote education.

Sydney, Australia

Valerie Harwood
Nyssa Murray

Acknowledgements

We wish to acknowledge the Countries and Elders past, present and emerging. We give our thanks and deepest gratitude to the people of Bunjalung, Dharawal, Dunghutti, Gadigal, Gumbaynggirr, Kamilaroi, Ngemba, Wiradjuri, Wodi Wodi, Yaegl and Yuin.

We would like to express our deepest gratitude to the Dunghutti Elders Council, who worked with us in the development and implementation of Lead My Learning as a community-wide campaign.

Thank you to Aunty Beris and Uncle Roger. Your words of wisdom helped us to produce the campaign. We remember with gratitude our yarn in Darwin about little children learning while hanging out the washing. Thank you.

Thank you to Mandy. The insights from the yarns helped us to imagine and learn about parents and learning in Aboriginal early childhood centres.

Thank you Aunty Ange, it was you that helped us to see the valued and treasured moments of family portraits in the family home, and how photos can be incorporated into the Lead My Learning campaign.

Thank you Kelly Andrews and Professor Sandra Jones, who kindly provided mentoring and support in our engagement with social marketing.

Thank you Karen Hall from Families NSW School as Community Centres for your endless support and promotion of the Lead My Learning campaign.

Many people, in a number of communities and many services and organisations, were involved that contributed to the development of the educational futures campaign—Lead My Learning. These include: community services (especially Family and Community Services in one of the communities), voluntary and not-for-profit, non-government (especially Barnardo's), government organisations (especially the Regional Department of Premier and Cabinet), Aboriginal controlled organisations and other related services and small businesses. We are unable to name everyone that contributed and work with us on this project due to space and to protect confidentiality. We acknowledge everyone's contributions and provide our sincere thanks and gratitude.

Thank you to our families and children that supported us to work on this project and for just being who you are. This book is an outcome of the research undertaken for the Future Fellowship *Getting an Early Start to Aspirations: Understanding How to Promote Educational Futures in Early Childhood* (FT130101332), funded by the Australian Research Council's Discovery grants scheme. The views expressed herein are those of the authors of this book and are not necessarily those of the Australian Research Council.

Contents

About the Authors

Valerie Harwood is a Professor of Sociology and Anthropology of Education, Sydney School of Education and Social Work, University of Sydney, an Australian Research Council Future Fellow (2014–2019), an Honorary Professorial Fellow, Australian Health Services Research Institute (AHSRI), University of Wollongong and a Research Affiliate with Creative Research Interventions in Methods and Practice (CRIMP), Digital Ethnography Research Centre, RMIT, Melbourne. Valerie's research is centred on a social and cultural analysis of participation in educational futures. This work involves learning about collaborative approaches and in-depth fieldwork on educational justice with young people, families and communities.

Nyssa Murray is a Dunghutti woman, Ph.D. student and the research Project Manager for the ARC Future Fellowship project *Getting an Early Start to Aspirations: Understanding How to Promote Higher Education in Early Childhood.* In 2018, Nyssa commenced her Ph.D. at the University of Wollongong, Faculty of Business, investigating best practice for increasing Aboriginal employment outcomes and how to improve the understanding and acceptance of Aboriginal Australian culture through organisational policy. Her past and present professional employment has seen her in national and regional strategic management roles that focus on the inclusion of Aboriginal Australian people within education and employment.

List of Figures

List of Tables

1

Involving the Critical and the Cultural in Promoting Education

The Promotion of Education introduces critical cultural social marketing, an approach that builds on the discipline of social marketing, adapting these techniques for use in the promotion of educational futures in communities and places where there is educational disadvantage. Taking a critical cultural social marketing approach to promoting education involves bringing an engaged attitude of critique together with engaged respect and awareness of the cultural. Practically, this means looking at education and learning in ways that privileges the cultural. To do this brings a heightened awareness of the cultural and of diverse knowledges, experiences and practices of learning.

A generative way to think about critique can be drawn from the point made by Foucault, that critique is "the art of not being governed like that and at that cost" (1997, p. 29). Working with critique is beneficial as this provides a way to critically think through the complexity of processes that impact how people relate to contemporary institutional education (Harwood & Rasmussen, 2013). We refer to institutional and non-institutional learning (as opposed to formal and informal). This emphasises the institutional nature of schooling and calls our attention to institutional practices. At the heart of this approach, then, is a commitment to careful and

© The Author(s) 2019
V. Harwood and N. Murray, *The Promotion of Education*,
https://doi.org/10.1007/978-3-030-25300-4_1

sustained attention that involves a critical view and an emphasis on the cultural.

As we will outline, activity that engages with critique and the cultural are crucial when we turn to the challenge of promoting education. The promotion of education is an important practice to engage in, yet is usually confused with the efforts to market education. Marketing brings to mind glossy images and advertising that compete in the education marketplace to sell schools or universities to consumers. Throughout this book we are not referring to this type of selling of educational institutions or of education.

When we are talking about the promotion of education, we are referring to the efforts to promote the ideas and the cultural practices of learning and education. Turning to a dictionary definition, we use the word 'promotion' in the sense of "The action of helping forward; the fact or state of being helped forward; furtherance, advancement, encouragement" (Oxford English Dictionary, 2018). At the same time, by drawing on social marketing, we bring this 'action of helping education forward' together with a second meaning for promotion, "The publicizing of a product, organization, or venture so as to increase sales or public awareness" (Oxford English Dictionary, 2018), with our focus on public awareness (as opposed to 'sales').

In this book the promotion of education is based on the premise that education requires 'the action of helping forward'. This way of thinking contrasts with beliefs that cast certain groups of people as either not involved in education or learning, and as in need of remedial help. Differing from such beliefs, this starting point makes the case that it is education that needs promotion. Motivated by the action of 'helping forward', is not to imply that, overarchingly education helps others forward—but rather that education too needs assistance in the form of promotion for it to be helped forward. Relying on the assumption that always or intrinsically education 'helps others forward', cajoles us to overlook that education requires significant assistance to actually engage and involve; it is not a static magnet that enigmatically draws those who value it into its fold. Indeed, as we will outline, in the case of institutionally based education such as schools, there are many who value education. At the same time, some of these people are hesitant and wary of the very institutions that are charged with the provision of educational training and qualifications in contemporary society.

Widening Participation in Higher Education

Considerable effort continues to be made in many countries across the world to widen participation in university education for those who are described as 'non-traditional students' (Shah, Bennett, & Southgate, 2016; Shah & Whiteford, 2017). 'Non-traditional students' is a term used to describe those who are under-represented in higher education, which in a world perspective is inclusive of people from low socio-economic status (LSES) backgrounds, first in family students, Indigenous people, people with disabilities and people from ethnic minorities (Shah et al., 2016; Shah & Whiteford, 2017). Socio-economic status has been shown to be one of the strongest predictors of educational outcomes (Bradley, Noonan, Nugent, & Scales, 2008; Currie, 2009), and poor university attendance by people from low socio-economic status backgrounds from a range of cultural backgrounds is a problem faced by numerous countries worldwide (Lehmann, 2009; Shavitt & Blossfield, 1993).

People who 'fail' in educational terms often do so for practical reasons: reasons that relate to relationships between class, gender, ethnicity, geography, material needs and experience. There are also dimensions of this experience of 'failure', cultural disengagement and educational disadvantage that can be read as resistance to governmental imperatives. Yet there is much more to disenfranchisement from education.

Those who are disconnected, marginalised or disenfranchised from education are all too frequently believed to not 'value' education. Nothing however, can be further from the truth. Simply not attending institutional education does not equate to not valuing education. The very idea that some people don't value education means that systems of institutional education are, whether it be early childhood, primary school, secondary school or higher education, literally missing the point. Reasons for not attending, or not participating, are, as numerous studies in the sociology of education demonstrate, complex (Ball, Davies, David, & Reay, 2002; Bourdieu & Passeron, 1990; Reay, 1995; Slee, 1994; Smyth, 2004).

Promoting Education?

Little is known about how to promote education, and even less about how to promote it to those who are not involved in higher education. Examples of work in this space includes the projects on educational success and poverty alleviation supported by the Lucie and André Chagnon Foundation, Quebec, Canada (https://fondationchagnon.org/en/index.aspx). Another example is the Australian research commissioned to develop a social marketing strategy targeting universities to address participation in higher education by low socio-economic students (12–18 years), families and communities (Russell-Bennet, Drenan, & Raciti, 2016). The project website (https://research.qut.edu.au/servicesocialmarketing/research-projects/widening-participation-in-the-tertiary-education-sector/) includes reports on this work as well as hyperlinks to educator, parent and student persona quizzes.

Yet it seems to be the case that, despite proposals to create new ways to promote higher education, contemporary institutional education makes an extraordinary assumption; that education itself is not in need of promotion. When we look at lessons from relatively recent Western history, we can see that it was readily recognised that something had to be done to encourage people to get involved in schooling. In the nineteenth century for example, effort was made to promote the education of the poor. See for instance the work in the early 1800s for promoting the education of the poor in Ireland (Society for Promoting the Education of the Poor in Ireland, 1820). This serves as a reminder that it wasn't always assumed that education didn't require consideration of its promotion.

Many people 'sit outside' the current reaches of widening participation initiatives, which tend to be largely focussed on those in a 'proximal' relationship to university enrolment. This proximal emphasis includes programmes for high school (secondary) students or programmes to improve the retention of university students. Those not in this proximal space simply miss out on access to initiatives that might offer connections to education and the opportunities afforded by higher education. Disconnected from institutional education such as schooling or higher education, these places are felt to be impossible or are unknown (Harwood, Hickey-Moody, McMahon, & O'Shea, 2017).

Parents who have experiences of educational disadvantage and who have young children are one example of the groups that widening participation efforts neglect to include. Difficult experiences with institutional education can monopolise relationships with the beautiful experiences of learning. What is often not realised is that at the same time as experiencing these difficult feelings and relationships with institutional education, people do value institutional education, whether for their children and families or for themselves (Harwood et al., 2017). In acknowledging the difficulties and challenges of widening participation, this book argues that there is need for collaborative, respectful methods that can contribute to improving parent and children's relationships with education and their educational futures.

The promotion of education that we describe is underpinned by a twofold commitment to an understanding of firstly, the effects of difficult experiences with institutions such as schools, and secondly, that learning is diverse. Involving the critical in promoting education means that we are alert to these effects and impacts of institutions of education such as schooling. Involving the cultural means that we are forced to appreciate and connect with learning in all its diversity, and this especially requires us to look beyond schooling.

The Critical and the Cultural

The critical and the cultural force us into a twofold awareness with a critique of the production of educational inequality *and* the awareness and engagement with cultural knowledges and practices of learning. We note here that this emphasis is attuned to thinking of the cultural considerations for understanding educational disadvantages—and at the same time, draws on the rich tradition of critical work in the social sciences.

The significance and subtlety of this awareness can be glimpsed in an excerpt from a group yarning session conducted after the Lead My Learning campaign was completed. Lead My Learning (www.leadmylearning.com.au) is the education promotion campaign created using critical cultural social marketing, and is the example drawn on in this book. We provide detailed explanations of the Lead My Learning campaign in Chapter 5, and in Chapter 6, detailed description of its creation using a critical cultural social marketing approach. The Lead My Learning campaign was run for a six-month period, and after it was completed we held a number of post interviews (yarning and semi-structured) with parents and families. (Throughout the book we use pseudonyms for the names of people and identifying places.)

Kristy and Tina are two parents who participated in a group yarning session at a playgroup in regional New South Wales (NSW), Australia. This facilitated playgroup involved parents and families who were accompanying their children.

> *Kristy*: I think it's always been there but this is just a reminder. You know, a
>   tool to get ... jog your memory and go 'Okay, yeah', you know?
> *Tina*: Makes us more aware of it as well, you know.
> *Kristy*: Yeah ... probably something that we've always done but now we've
>   gone 'Oh yeah', you know? It's there, 'Oh', you know? *'This is what it's
>   called'*. (Kristy and Tina, South Midtown Aboriginal Playgroup, 2017,
>   emphasis added)

When Kristy, stated "Probably something that we've always done" (South Midtown Aboriginal Playgroup, 2017), she helped us to recognise that the Lead My Learning campaign had connected with ways of learning that *she and Tina did*. Rather than telling her what to do or insinuating that she wasn't doing something 'right', the Lead My Learning messages were "just a reminder ... a tool to jog your memory and go 'Okay, yeah'" (South Midtown Aboriginal Playgroup, 2017).

We include these comments to underscore that it was crucial that the message conveyed in Lead My Learning differed from the existing educational discourses impacting parents who have experienced educational disadvantage. Such official discourses tend to convey deficit assumptions that these parents are not engaging in learning with their children or at best, not 'in the correct' way.

The first time we heard a comment like Kristy and Tina's we realised we just might be getting close to creating a respectful way to promote education. During any research project that is seeking to try something different, questions such as 'will it work' spring to the researcher's mind. Having our research confirmed by feedback that appears to indicate nothing much 'changed' might seem surprising. But this was exactly the purpose; to somehow connect with the learning parents were doing with their young children. Due to narratives of failure and deficit, this learning is largely absent from official discourses of educational expertise. This is the expertise (in these dominant discourses at least) that is said to reside only with those who are 'educated'.

This is a point argued by Ingold who makes the compelling case of distinguishing education from the 'institution of the school':

> The practice of education and the institution of the school, in short, seem joined at the hip. You cannot apparently have one without the other. What are we to say, then, of societies without schools, or where only a minority enjoy the privilege of attending them? Is it acceptable to say of persons who have not been to school that they are uneducated, and therefore uncivilised? … Anthropologists have gone to great lengths to document this knowledge, to reveal its detail, sophistication and accuracy, and to uncover the processes by which it is acquired. They have denounced, with good reason, the division of the peoples of the world into educated and uneducated, civilised and primitive. This is no more than a reflection, they say, of ethnocentric prejudice. (2017, pp. 2–3)

The Lead My Learning campaign needed to make just such a distinction, and do so in a way that acknowledged parent expertise in learning, as well as parent involvement in learning. After all, if we are to extend the sight lines of widening participation efforts, we need to address how problems with educational injustices impact opportunities for educational futures for everyone. And these principles of addressing educational injustices need to be clever enough to be inclusive of institutions such as universities. Parents, families and their young children who are impacted by systemic educational injustices such as racism, colonisation and low socio-economic status have a right to widening participation efforts that 'think beyond the next cohort' and that are visionary in how educational futures can be productively imagined (Harwood et al., 2017; Harwood & Murray, 2019). To do so means we need to be inclusive of how young children interact with and have relationships with institutional education, and parents' involvement in their children's learning is pivotal to this endeavour.

Attention to the cultural and to critique enables us to recognise what dominant practices of education tend to render unrecognisable, that these parents were involved in learning. As we will argue, if we are to find ways to extend the efforts of widening participation to those who have had difficult experiences with schooling, we need to find ways to critique what it is that makes certain forms of learning unrecognisable. And as we shall show, this is particularly important—and especially complex—when we turn to early childhood and educational disadvantage and injustice, an area which has been largely ignored in efforts to widen participation in university education.

The question of promoting education is vexing in this context. This is because of the contested nature of the truths that are produced about parents, families and children who experience educational disadvantages. The parents who participated in our research were involved in learning; yet the dominant discourses about these parents are replete with narratives of 'not valuing education' and of not being involved or engaged in learning, or of 'not caring'. A somewhat similar problem is described by Waters in her discussion of the research collaboration with five Black mothers in Chicago:

> dominant discourses of parent involvement, mothering and government … that provide a monolithic view of middle-class norms, or paint a deficit model of working class and mothers as the primary parent, are taken-for-granted representations that can readily feed public perceptions which are crippling for Black mothers. (Waters, 2016, pp. 1–2)

The literature on parent involvement—while helpful, is as Waters argues (2016) skewed by dominant discourses, which also include classed assumptions based on mostly White middle-class perceptions of education. For instance, Waters critiques Epstein's (2009) 'widely-accepted framework' on parent involvement and education, observing that it:

> alludes to the societal construction of moral responsibilities women have to their children, which haphazardly draws a major tension with parent involvement that is largely defined by school and state requirements. (Waters, 2016, p. 22)

Similarly, Bower and Griffin (2011) show the shortcomings of the Epstein (2009) model when used in a 'high-minority, high-poverty' school context.

How parent involvement is understood is crucial, and this demands a nuanced consideration of the needs of diverse communities. How parents think about their involvement is likewise important, which as Harris and Goodall (2008) point out, takes up the issue that not all parents know just how important their involvement is and the significant positive impacts it contributes to their child's learning and education. It is crucial, therefore, to promote education in a way that is respectful to parents—and consequently, to devise a campaign that was what parents wanted. In our project, and as we outline in this book, this required communicating what they were doing, showing parents that what they were doing was great, providing encouragement to continue, and possibly, to do these activities even more.

The Critical, the Cultural and Social Marketing

Demonstrating how a critical and cultural approach to social marketing techniques can generate new approaches to the promotion of education is a core objective of *The Promotion of Education*. Exploring Foucault's (1997) idea of critique as 'an art of not being governed quite so much', it is possible to see how moving differently in dominant discourses affords new twists on discourse and potentially, on how subjectivities are constructed. Take for instance this description of critique:

> critique will be the art of voluntary insubordination, that of reflected intractability. Critique would essentially insure the desubjugation of the subject in the context of what we could call, in a word, the politics of truth. (Foucault, 1997, p. 32)

This idea pitches critique as a way, through 'voluntary insubordination' or 'reflected intractability' of involvement in desubjugation, which is to have a part in the formation of the subject. Practically, then, it is possible to use critique as an 'art of not being governed quite so much' by discourses of education that stipulate what is legitimate and recognisable as learning. This means finding ways to 'desubjugate the subject' in a politics of truth that stipulates what is recognisable as learning (and what isn't recognised), what can be learned (and what cannot), or who can learn (and who cannot) and who can lead learning (and who cannot). Promoting education with people who have experienced the difficulties, challenges, inequities and injustices of institutional education requires attention to the politics of truth in education. Intervening in the dominance of discourses is one way, as we will outline in this book, that this can be achieved.

Emphasis on the critical and the cultural together with techniques from social marketing are helpful for creating education promotion strategies for at least two reasons. Firstly, it forces us to critically engage with and better understand 'problems', such as the problems of participation in higher education. This supports improved understandings of the complexity of these problems and this can have the effect of disrupting deficit explanations of experiences such as 'failure' or 'leaving school early' or 'dropouts'. In our work with Lead My Learning, this is significant as it enabled us to look at how 'problems' and 'problem subjects' are produced. Thinking critically in this way supported the recognition of the extent to which parents valued education, as well as how they were perceived by 'authorities' in a system that disenfranchises them.

Secondly, with this new edge to understanding the complexity of how problems are produced, novel approaches can be developed. Such approaches can cleverly and respectfully contribute to addressing some of the barriers that prevent access, participation and retention in higher education. For example, deeper appreciation of the cultural and social barriers that impact people's feelings towards schooling and education can enable better informed and more collaborative designs and innovations for promoting parental engagement and participation in their children's learning (Abu-Lughod, 2014). This brings previously unsaid or marginalised discourses into the open and can assist in legitimating learning practices. In the context of promoting education, critical cultural social marketing can be used to encourage new discourses in the dominating contexts of mainstream educational practices. Practically, in the Lead My Learning campaign, the critical cultural social marketing approach enabled us to promote education in ways that connected with the learning that parents are doing with their children.

Employed together with critical and cultural practices, social marketing techniques can be used to work to support generative discourses about learning. There are very few adaptations of methodologies, such as social marketing, for use in the complex cultural and social landscape of educational disadvantage (Truong, 2014). While few in number, there is emerging work in social marketing that is drawing on approaches such as ethnography (Brennan, Fry, & Previte, 2015; Cullen, Matthews, & Teske, 2008) and using sociological conceptual work such as cultural capital (Kamin & Anker, 2014). However, at the same time critical social science scholars have questioned the motives of social marketing, for instance, the Foucauldian critiques of social marketing as forms of biopolitical governance (Crawshaw, 2012; Pykett, Jones, Welsh, & Whitehead, 2014).

Recent scholarship in social marketing has sought to think through interdisciplinary connections with the critical social sciences, such as the insightful analysis by Gordon, Russell-Bennett, and Lefebvre (2016) that makes the case for the importance of interdisciplinary efforts that engage understandings from ethnography (Brennan et al., 2015) to considerations informed by political philosophy. Other work includes social countermarketing by Bellow, Bauman, Freeman, and Kite (2017).

There are efforts at decolonising approaches in social marketing research with Aboriginal people (Madill, Wallace, Goneau-Lessard, Stuart MacDonald, & Dion, 2014). Yet a recent systematic review of social marketing research worldwide in the English language that 'targeted' Indigenous people only identified 20 papers, of which 13 were 'interventions' (Kubacki & Szablewska, 2017). We note here the issue in Australia with the term 'intervention'. The term is frequently used in social marketing (as well as other disciplines). However, we argue that the word is not suitable to use in Australia with Aboriginal people (and arguably, for some non-Aboriginal people who are aware and sensitive to this issue), given the relatively recent 2007 federal government Northern Territory Emergency Response, known as the 'Intervention'. The Intervention, which continues to impact Aboriginal communities in the Northern Territory, is widely condemned by Aboriginal people and has been critiqued for racism and paternalism and worsening the living conditions for Aboriginal people (Australian Indigenous Doctors Association, 2010; Gibson, 2017; Povinelli, 2016). Consequently, the term is not used to refer to our work, and we opted for a more culturally appropriate term 'campaign', or occasionally the term 'educational futures promotion'.

We propose that as well as informing the critique of social marketing campaigns, social science theories such as the work on governmentality by Foucault (1991, 2000) can also assist in building critical approaches that enable productive discourse techniques that can disrupt dominant deficit views. We suggest that access to and participation in educational futures—and opportunities for higher education, can benefit from such new approaches to promoting education. Indeed, efforts to widen participation in higher education may well benefit from the contribution of innovative, engaging and respectful ways of communicating with parents and families that promote education and learning. Approaches that draw on social marketing and that are informed by critical and cultural understandings have a valuable role to contribute to this effort.

As we have explained above, we use the word 'marketing' in this book in a way distinct from a framework of 'selling' schools or education to 'consumers' in the neoliberal marketplace. Working with marketing concepts doesn't mean fixing an 'image problem' with schools and institutionalised forms of education. Much more is required than simply restoring or fixing how images are made or received. The purpose is to borrow from marketing ideas that have been developed in social marketing and adapt these using critical cultural and social approaches. As scholars in the discipline of social marketing point out, social marketing differs from marketing, yet at the same time draws on specific ideas from marketing, such as 'value creation' (French, 2017). Chapter 3 includes a detailed discussion of social marketing.

One useful way to get acquainted with social marketing is to look at examples of social marketing campaigns; for instance the campaigns: Get Yourself Tested (it's your sex life) http://www.itsyoursexlife.com/stds-testing-gyt; Take the H3O Challenge—'try switching your sweet drinks with water for 30 days. You'll be surprised by what you save' http://h30challenge.com.au/. The potential for the application of marketing insights is argued by Lefevbre (2013), who states, "people's everyday lives include exposure to all types of ideas and behaviors, whether transacted directly with their family and friends or vicariously through television and the internet" (2013, p. 5). Use of the word 'transacted' alludes to the concept in marketing of exchange—based on marketing constructs.

There are, of course, many more instances of this 'exposure' such as how institutional education impacts feelings about learning and education and participation in higher education. The point is that insights from marketing and the 'marketplace of ideas' can be drawn on to think through the discourses that impact people in the 'politics of truth' of education. And further, through considering these it becomes feasible to think about forms of what we are terming 'strategic discourse production' (Harwood & Murray, 2019) as ways to engage in 'reflected intractability' and 'desubjugate' notions such as 'being uneducated' or 'can't learn or teach learning'.

One of the beneficial features of social marketing is the importance placed on understanding the 'audience'. While we discuss this in detail in Chapter 3, here we wish to draw attention to how this emphasis acts as a central conduit that drives thinking toward listening and learning from those who participated in this research project in order to produce materials that are wanted by the priority group. (This is the group of parents we focussed on for the Lead My Learning campaign; the term 'priority group' is discussed in Chapter 4). In Lead My Learning, this attention to the 'audience' was improved through our own attention and respect for Aboriginal Protocols in our research. This improved our research with *both* Aboriginal and with non-Aboriginal people.

Australian Aboriginal Protocols and Lead My Learning

Ensuring close attention to critique as well as to the cultural, in the creation of Lead My Learning, we listened and learned from Aboriginal Australian Protocols. Respect for Country and Aboriginal people's relationships with Country is integral to Aboriginal Protocols in Australia, and also internationally, as Baskin (2005) contends. We respectfully and gratefully acknowledge the significance of Country to Australia's First Nations people. Aunty Laklak Burarrwanga, a Datiwuy Elder, Caretaker for Gumatj explains:

> Country has many layers of meaning. It incorporates people, animals, plants, water and land. But Country is more than just people and things,

it is also what connects them to each other and to multiple spiritual and symbolic realms. It relates to laws, custom, movement, song, knowledges, relationships, histories, presents, futures and spirit beings. Country can be talked to, it can be known, it can itself communicate, feel and take action. Country for us is alive with story, law, power and kinship relations that join not only people to each other but link people, ancestors, place, animals, rocks, plants, stories and songs within land and sea. So you see knowledge about Country is important because it's about how and where you fit within the world and how you connect to others and to place. (Burarrwanga et al., 2013, p. 54)

The Australian Government reports that before colonisation of Australia (prior to 1776) there were over 500 Aboriginal and Torres Strait Islander clan groups (Australian Government 2015). There is debate concerning how this has been estimated. (It is likely there were actually many more clan groups.) It is also problematic to use past tense to describe the rich, diverse living cultural practices and knowledges of the continent that since colonisation has been called Australia. The Countries of Indigenous Australia may be viewed in an online map (https://aiatsis.gov.au/explore/articles/aiatsis-map-indigenous-australia). We likewise acknowledge that this map is an "attempt to represent the language, tribal or nation groups of Aboriginal people of Australia ..." and that "the information on which the map is based is contested and may not be agreed to by some landowners" (Australian Institute for Aboriginal and Torres Strait Islander Studies, 2019).

Following Aboriginal Protocols, our research was influenced by Aboriginal Australian ways of Knowing, Being and Doing (Martin & Mirraboopa, 2003). Aboriginal Australian ways of Knowing and Being are thousands and thousands of years old. Archaeological research proposes an estimate of 65,000 years (Clarkson et al., 2017), with a recent study suggesting 120,000 years (Bowler, Price, Sherwood, & Carey, 2019). However, it is important to note that there is the view that disputes 'coming to Australia theories' and states "we have always been here". The work and research we share in this book has been guided by Aboriginal Australian Protocols in research (Murray & Harwood, 2016), and informed by *The Guidelines for Ethical Research in Australian Indigenous Studies* (Australian Institute for Aboriginal and Torres Strait Islander Studies, 2012).

In describing the Aboriginal Protocols in research that we worked with, we acknowledge that this is how these protocols have been interpreted and used by us in this research project, and that we are not claiming there is 'one set' of Aboriginal protocols. Indeed, we don't want to create any misunderstanding that there is 'one set' of Aboriginal protocols. The point we are making is eloquently stated by Martin,

> The ideas in this chapter should not be considered as generic Aboriginal understandings of reality. While some universal principles may appear and there may be some common principles among us as Aboriginal peoples, I can only speak from my own understanding, experiences and realities. Therefore, one size does not fit all because the one-size-fits-all model is not respectful. (2012, p. 28)

Being guided by Aboriginal Protocols when doing research that involves Aboriginal people is paramount. As Baskin (2005) explains in her discussion of research in Canada, researching with Aboriginal Protocols influences research in a number of ways, such as how participants are recruited. Describing her own experience in recruiting participants, she explains how this could "take one visit or several" and that there are unique requirements for Elders:

> if the person being approached is an Elder, further relationship protocols are followed. Several visits will be required, with the visitor/researcher doing chores around the Elder's home, listening carefully, and following directions. (Baskin, 2005, p. 179)

Aboriginal Australian Protocols guided our work in a number of ways and the benefit to the Lead My Learning project are numerous. We learnt to understand the importance of relationships. To create ways to promote education meant taking the time to build relationships with people and communities. Contributing in different ways, listening carefully, and following directions were part of what we did in our research with Aboriginal and non-Aboriginal participants. Taking time for people to get to know us was very important, and in taking this time, we were able to connect, build relationships, and increase willingness of participation in the research project.

Guided by these protocols helped us to draw on Aboriginal methodologies such as yarning (Bessarab & Ng'Andu, 2010; Leeson, Smith, & Rynne, 2016). This methodology is beneficial since:

> Yarning then becomes the medium of interaction in the research partnership; where learning becomes a storied two-way process on a research journey for both the researcher and participant. (Geia, Hayes, & Usher, 2013, p. 16)

This guidance has encouraged us to reflect on Aboriginal practices, including Dadirri (deep listening), shared by Elder Miriam-Rose Ungunmerr (2017), which has contributed to research approaches (Miller, 2014; West, Stewart, Foster, & Usher, 2013)

By paying close attention to considerations of the cultural and relationships with Aboriginal people and with non-Aboriginal people, we were able to adapt social marketing in the Lead My Learning campaign to respectfully address issues of widening participation in ways that acknowledge the expertise of the parents and value the knowledge and practices parents have in their children's learning. Our creation of the Lead My Learning campaign drew on these protocols, using what we have termed a Critical Cultural Yarning Model, which we discuss in Chapter 5. As we have outlined elsewhere (Murray & Harwood, 2016) the guidance of Aboriginal Protocols improved our work as researchers. We were better able to build relationships with Aboriginal and non-Aboriginal participants as well as with the numerous services and organisations involved with young children, families and education.

The Research

The research for this book was conducted for Getting an Early Start to Aspirations, an Australian Research Council Future Fellowship project (FT130101332). Taking a cross-cultural approach, the participants included Aboriginal and non-Aboriginal participants. All fieldwork was conducted in compliance with the *Guidelines for Ethical Research in Indigenous Studies* (Australian Institute for Aboriginal and Torres Strait Islander

Studies, 2012). Ethics approval was secured from the Human Research Ethics Committees at The University of Sydney and the University of Wollongong. Pseudonyms are used for people and for places and identifying information has been changed or removed.

As described above, Aboriginal Research Protocols (Murray & Harwood, 2016) that emphasise respect, relationships and rights to knowledge guided the project. This approach looks to the strengths of Aboriginal people, Aboriginal Cultures and Aboriginal Communities. At the same time, this seeks to actively critique deficit and colonising approaches. Adhering to these protocols offered the opportunity to connect with deep philosophical and practical ways to undertake research processes and listen to and be guided by those involved in the research. Embedding Aboriginal Protocols provided a basis for participants and project stakeholders to see us as respectful researchers.

The writing, thinking and learning for this book happened on different Countries; Bunjalung, Dharawal, Dunghutti, Gadigal, Gumbaynggirr, Kamilaroi, Ngemba, Thungutti, Wiradjuri, Wodi Wodi, Yaegl and Yuin in South-Eastern Australia (known as New South Wales since colonisation). The fieldwork was carried out on many different Countries in Australia. To protect confidentiality, throughout the book, we do not describe specific Countries in relation to both the research sites or the biographies of the participants. We use pseudonyms for the places and for people.

Research activities for this project occurred over a four-year period (2015–2018). Data collection firstly focussed on formative research for the creation of the campaign and drew on interviews (yarning and semi-structured) with parent groups and service providers. Secondly, research to understand what the campaign might have achieved or what occurred involved interviews (yarning and semi-structured) with individuals and with groups, and a pre- and post- questionnaire survey. Thirdly, longitudinal interviews (yarning and semi-structured) with parents who have experienced educational disadvantage, live in places of socio-economic disadvantage and who have young children. The purpose of the latter was to better understand more about this cohort of parents' knowledge of education. As described above, two types of methods were used to gather interview data, yarning, which is an Aboriginal methodology, and semi-structured interviews. The type of interview technique used depended on the context, the participants and the researcher (if they were Aboriginal or non-Aboriginal). Non-Aboriginal people did participate in yarning sessions, such as for example when an Aboriginal researcher was present or in a cross-cultural interview that included Aboriginal people. Yarning occurred in some of the one-one interviews with an Aboriginal researcher when the non-Aboriginal person was familiar with or comfortable with yarning (Fig. 1.1).

Fieldwork occurred with Aboriginal and non-Aboriginal people in eight different communities with proportionally higher numbers of Aboriginal people in urban regional, and in rural-remote settings in New South Wales, Australia. Sites were selected based on the presence of considerable

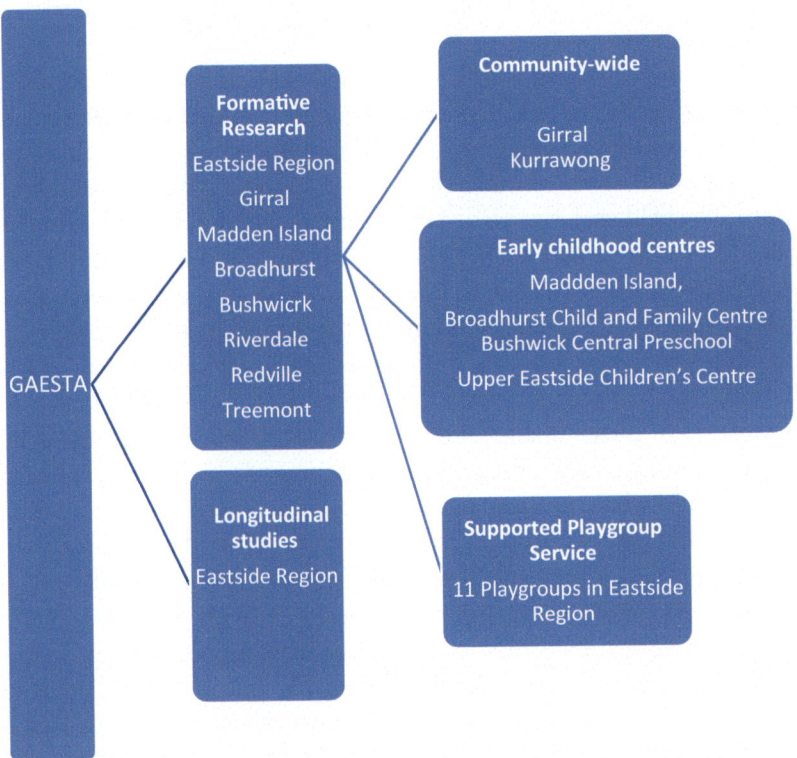

Fig. 1.1 The Getting an Early Start to Aspirations (GAESTA) Research Design

socio-economic and educational disadvantage. For a detailed discussion of educational disadvantage and place, see Harwood et al. (2017).

Our research activities incorporated consultations with community stakeholders, including Aboriginal-led services and where appropriate, Elders, and with Aboriginal and non-Aboriginal parents of young children. Non-Aboriginal participants included parents for whom English was not their first language. All participants were from sites with high representations of Aboriginal people (higher than the 3.3% national average) with for example, in the formative phase which totalled 111 participants, 22% (59 people) were Aboriginal. Our data reflects these demographics, with the number of participants who identified to us as Aboriginal higher than the national average. The number of Aboriginal participants may well be higher, as not all participants identified themselves to us as Aboriginal (either during fieldwork, in yarning sessions, in interviews or in surveys). The reporting in the data of Aboriginal or non-Aboriginal participants is based on the self-reports of the participants, the exception being in sites data collection were held only with Aboriginal participants (such as an Aboriginal parents' playgroup).

There were significantly higher numbers of female participants, very low numbers of males, and no participants identifying to us as non-binary. In the formative research, 6% were male, in the longitudinal, 2% were male, and in the post campaign interviews (yarning and semi-structured), 10% were male. In terms of the survey participants, for the pre-survey, 13.7% were male, and for the post survey, 5.2% were male. The participant profile can be explained by the gendering of both the early childhood workforce, which is predominantly women, and of the care of young children (Andrew, 2016; Van Laere, Vandenbroeck, Roets, & Peeters, 2014).

As well as extensive fieldwork visits, research activity involved data collection using pre- and post-interviews (including yarning), and surveys using a questionnaire designed for the project (pre- and post-surveys with parents, post-surveys for service providers). A total of 942 Aboriginal and non-Aboriginal people participated in these; 888 were parents of young children and 54 were childcare educators from a range of Aboriginal and non-Aboriginal services (Table 1.1).

The pre- and post-surveys were completed either on paper or online. As well as quantitative items, the survey questionnaire included open-ended

Table 1.1 Overview of interview and survey participants

Participants	Formative yarning interviews	Longitudinal interviews	Pre-survey survey (paper and online)	Post-survey (paper and online)	Post-yarning interviews	Service provider (post) survey (online)	Total
Parents	111	56 (160 interviews)	511	223 (135 of these were returning participants)	122	n/a	942
Service providers	38	n/a	n/a	n/a	n/a	16	54

questions that we found gave some insight into the learning practices in which parents were involved and recall of the campaign (in the post-survey).

The Lead My Learning campaign design was based on formative research conducted over a 14-month period with 149 people, 111 parents and 38 childcare educators. Formative research is a key stage in social marketing (French & Gordon, 2015) used to understand the 'problem' and design a bespoke social marketing strategy. This extensive time period supported us to better build relationships and develop critical insight on how parents viewed educational futures and higher education, as well as many opportunities to carefully and responsively finetune the strategy. The formative phase provided the insight to refine the research design and incorporate three approaches to be trialled as potential ways for the campaign message to reach parents.

1. A community-wide campaign in Girral, a regional NSW town with a population of approximately 29,000. The national population of Aboriginal people is 3.3%, at Girral it is 12% (with a wait-list control site in Kurrawong, a comparable location).
2. A multi-playgroup campaign in 11 sites across the Eastside Region that included Aboriginal playgroups, in partnership with a service provider in regional NSW.

3. An early childhood centre campaign in four Aboriginal owned and operated services (Madden Island, Broadhurst Child and Family Centre, Bushwick Central Preschool, Upper Eastside Children's Centre) with Aboriginal-led centres that rely on bus transport for children in regional NSW.

The campaign was rolled out for each of these modalities in September 2016 (with the exception of Kurrawong, the wait-list control site), and ran for a six-month period. After the campaign was completed, the post data collection included interviews (yarning and semi-structured), and the post-survey. Following this data collection, a modified campaign was rolled out at Kurrawong. Following this roll out, two post individual interviews and three group interviews (yarning and semi-structured) were conducted in Kurrawong, which involved 22 parents.

The community-wide campaign focused on the range of places where parents of young children might connect with campaign messages, and as such also included playgroups, childcare centres and other related services. A wait-list-control approach was run in Kurrawong, a community of similar demographics to Girral. This was done so that it might be possible to compare the delivery of the community-wide campaign against other factors that may have influenced parent involvement in their children's learning.

Playgroups proved to be the best way to meet with parents and family members of young children. Family members were usually parents, and could also as well be grandparents, aunties, uncles, brothers, sisters or cousins. Attempts to meet parents at childcare services proved difficult; parents were mostly, and understandably, focussed on picking up or dropping off their children as they move to or from activities such as work, appointments or carer duties. Playgroups were different. As a fieldwork site, we found there was time to meet and sit with parents, and have conversations that flowed with the rhythm of the children and their activities. We came to realise playgroups are significant sites for accessing parents. One of the project findings was the potential that playgroups offer as sites for strategic discourse production with parents of young children (Harwood & Murray, 2019).

Participants were involved in different aspects of the research. Considerable input was made by the 111 parents and 38 early childhood educators who were involved in the formative research to design the Lead My Learning campaign (a total of 149 participants). Another 160 interviews with 56 parents contributed to longitudinal interviews that sought to better understand how parents of young children learn about education and schooling cultures. These longitudinal interviews were not designed for feedback on the development, design or research about the contribution of Lead My Learning. Rather these interviews were conducted in order to potentially develop insight into how, over time, knowledge about education is constructed by parents who have young children. These parents, as with the other parents in the research, had also experienced educational disadvantage and lived in communities of significant social and economic disadvantage.

In an effort to provide a depth of understanding of the possible outcomes and contributions of the campaign, several methodologies were incorporated. Provision was also made in advance to be flexible and responsive with the application of methodologies and responsiveness to insights and feedback that may occur throughout this long-term project, with fieldwork that lasted over three years. Methodologies included: yarning sessions and semi-structured interviews (both individual and group); multi-site fieldwork visits that included critical ethnographic approaches; collaborative design process that involved iterative discussions and feedback loops; pre- and post-campaign surveys for parents using predominantly quantitative items (with some open-ended questions); and an online post-survey for services, across all sites, inclusive of the wait-list control site (Kurrawong).

In terms of the flexibility 'built in' to the methodological design, this was put into practice during the campaign when we reviewed the methods for collecting data on the outcomes and possible contributions to the campaign. The majority of feedback from participants and services on the survey was that it wasn't popular and that interviews (yarning and semi-structured) were the preferred modality for listening to the views of the parents on Lead My Learning. Accordingly, post-campaign research resources for data collection were prioritised to the post-interviews (yarning and semi-structured). This flexible or responsive approach to the methodologies is discussed in more detail in Chapters 6 and 7.

The Structure of the Book

Critical cultural social marketing places emphasis on taking a 'critical' approach and giving careful, sustained and respectful attention to the 'cultural'. Chapter 2 explores in detail why this emphasis is significant, making the case that there is an urgent need to focus thinking onto cultural as well as social considerations. Building on this discussion, Chapter 3 introduces critical cultural social marketing and provides a summary of some of the key features of social marketing. Chapter 4 further develops the concepts used in critical cultural social marketing, providing an expanded discussion of the theoretical underpinning. In Chapter 5 rich detail of the Lead My Learning campaign is provided. This includes images of the promotional products and activities and outlines of the campaign content. Chapter 6 offers a detailed description of how a critical cultural social marketing approach was applied to create the Lead My Learning campaign. This description is important, since is shows that to create an education promotion campaign, social marketing concepts needed to be considered using a critical cultural approach. This chapter outlines in detail how this was achieved.

An analysis and review of Lead My Learning and how the critical cultural social marketing approach was applied is the subject of Chapter 7. Here we provide discussion of the possible contributions of the Lead My Learning campaign, as well as share the 'lessons learned' in undertaking the creation of this education promotion campaign. We conclude in Chapter 8 with an overview of some of the key features of a critical cultural social marketing approach and how it can contribute to the important activity of promoting educational futures. In this final chapter we make the case that access and participation to educational futures—and opportunities for higher education, can benefit from new approaches to promoting educational futures.

References

Abu-Lughod, L. (2014). Writing against culture. In H. L. Moore & T. Sanders (Eds.), *Anthropology in theory: Issues in epistemology* (pp. 386–399). Chichester, West Sussex: Wiley.

Andrew, Y. (2016). The unavoidable salience of gender: Notes from Australian childcare work. *Gender, Place & Culture, 23*(12), 1738–1749. https://doi.org/10.1080/0966369X.2016.1249353.

Australian Indigenous Doctors Association. (2010). *Health impact assessment of the Northern Territory Emergency Response*. Canberra: Australian Indigenous Doctors' Association.

Australian Institute for Aboriginal and Torres Strait Islander Studies. (2012). *Guidelines for ethical research in Australian Indigenous studies.*

Australian Institute of Aboriginal and Torres Strait Islander Studies. (2019 [1996] 4, October). *Aboriginal Australia Map*. Available https://aiatsis.gov.au/explore/articles/aiatsis-map-indigenous-australia.

Ball, S. J., Davies, J., David, M., & Reay, D. (2002). 'Classification' and 'judgement': Social class and the 'cognitive structures' of choice in Higher Education. *British Journal of Sociology of Education, 23*(1), 51–72.

Baskin, C. (2005). Storytelling circles: Reflections of Aboriginal protocols in research. *Canadian Social Work Review/Revue canadienne de service social, 22*(2), 171–187.

Bellew, W., Bauman, A., Freeman, B., & Kite, J. (2017). Social countermarketing: Brave new world, brave new map. *Journal of Social Marketing, 7*(2), 205–222. https://doi.org/10.1108/JSOCM-09-2016-0052.

Bessarab, D., & Ng'Andu, B. (2010). Yarning about yarning as a legitimate method in Indigenous research. *International Journal of Critical Indigenous Studies, 3*(1), 37–50.

Bourdieu, P., & Passeron, J. C. (1990). *Reproduction in education, society, and culture* (1990 ed., preface by P. Bourdieu, Ed.). London: Sage in association with Theory, Culture & Society, Department of Administrative and Social Studies, Teesside Polytechnic.

Bower, H. A., & Griffin, D. (2011). Can the Epstein model of parental involvement work in a high-minority, high-poverty elementary school? A case study. *Professional School Counseling, 15*(2), 77–87.

Bowler, J. M., Price, D. M., Sherwood, J. E., & Carey, S. P. (2019). The Moyjil site, south-west Victoria, Australia: Fire and environment in a 120,000-year coastal midden—Nature or people? *Proceedings of the Royal Society of Victoria, 130*, 71–93.

Bradley, D., Noonan, P., Nugent, H., & Scales, B. (2008). *Review of Australian higher education, final report*. Canberra.

Brennan, L., Fry, M.-L., & Previte, J. (2015). Strengthening social marketing research: Harnessing "insight" through ethnography. *Australasian Marketing Journal (AMJ), 23*(4), 286–293. https://doi.org/10.1016/j.ausmj.2015.10.003.

Burarrwanga, L., Ganambarr, R., Ganambarr-Stubbs, M., Ganambarr, B., Maymuru, D., Wright, S., Suchet-Pearson, S., & Lloyd, K. (2013). *Welcome to my country*. Melbourne: Allen & Unwin.

Clarkson, C., Jacobs, Z., Marwick, B., Fullagar, R., Wallis, L., Smith, M., … Pardoe, C. (2017). Human occupation of northern Australia by 65,000 years ago. *Nature, 547*, 306. https://doi.org/10.1038/nature22968, https://www.nature.com/articles/nature22968#supplementary-information.

Crawshaw, P. (2012). Governing at a distance: Social marketing and the (bio) politics of responsibility. *Social Science and Medicine, 75*(1), 200–207. https://doi.org/10.1016/j.socscimed.2012.02.040.

Cullen, E. T., Matthews, L. N. H., & Teske, T. D. (2008). Use of occupational ethnography and social marketing strategies to develop a safety awareness campaign for coal miners. *Social Marketing Quarterly, 14*(4), 2–21. https://doi.org/10.1080/15245000802546187.

Currie, J. (2009). Healthy, wealthy, and wise: Socioeconomic status, poor health in childhood, and human capital development. *Journal of Economic Literature, 47*(1), 87–122.

Epstein, J. (Ed.). (2009). *School, family, and community partnerships: Your handbook for acgion* (3rd ed.). Thousand Oaks, CA: Sage.

Foucault, M. (1991). Politics and the study of discourse. In G. Burchell, C. Gordon, & P. Miller (Eds.), *The Foucault effect: Studies in governmentality* (pp. 53–72). London: Harvester Wheatsheaf.

Foucault, M. (1997). What is critique? In S. Lotringer & L. Hochroth (Eds.), *The politics of truth: Michel Foucault* (pp. 23–82). New York: Semiotext(e).

Foucault, M. (2000). Governmentality. In J. D. Faubion (Ed.), *Power, the essential works of Michel Foucault* (Vol. III, pp. 201–222). New York: The New Press.

French, J. (2017). *Social marketing and public health* (2nd ed.). Oxford: Oxford University Press.

French, J., & Gordon, R. (2015). *Strategic social marketing*. Los Angeles: Sage.

Geia, L. K., Hayes, B., & Usher, K. (2013). Yarning/Aboriginal storytelling: Towards an understanding of an Indigenous perspective and its implications for research practice. *Contemporary Nurse, 46* (1), 13–17. https://doi.org/10. 5172/conu.2013.46.1.13.

Gibson, P. (2017, 21 June). *10 impacts of the NT intervention.* Retrieved from https://www.sbs.com.au/nitv/article/2017/06/21/10-impacts-nt-intervention.

Gordon, R., Russell-Bennett, R., & Lefebvre, R. C. (2016). Social marketing: The state of play and brokering the way forward. *Journal of Marketing Management, 32*(11–12), 1059–1082. https://doi.org/10.1080/0267257X.2016.1199156.

Harris, A., & Goodall, J. (2008). Do parents know they matter? Engaging all parents in learning. *Educational Research, 50*(3), 277–289. https://doi.org/10. 1080/00131880802309424.

Harwood, V., Hickey-Moody, A., McMahon, S., & O'Shea, S. (2017). *The politics of widening participation and university access for young people: Making educational futures.* London: Routledge.

Harwood, V., & Murray, N. (2019). Strategic discourse production and parent involvement: Including parent knowledge and practices in the Lead My Learning campaign. *International Journal of Inclusive Education, 23*(4), 353–368. https://doi.org/10.1080/13603116.2019.1571119.

Harwood, V., & Rasmussen, M. L. (2013). Practising critique, attending to truth: The pedagogy of discriminatory speech. *Educational Philosophy and Theory, 45*(8), 874–884. https://doi.org/10.1111/j.1469-5812.2011.00834.x.

Ingold, T. (2017). *Anthropology and/as education: Anthropology, art, architecture and design.* Abingdon, Oxon and New York, NY: Routledge.

Kamin, T., & Anker, T. (2014). Cultural capital and strategic social marketing orientations. *Journal of Social Marketing, 4*(2), 94–110. https://doi.org/10. 1108/JSOCM-08-2013-0057.

Kubacki, K., & Szablewska, N. (2017). Social marketing targeting Indigenous peoples: A systematic review. *Health Promotion International, 34*, 133–143. https://doi.org/10.1093/heapro/dax060.

Leeson, S., Smith, C., & Rynne, J. (2016). Yarning and appreciative inquiry: The use of culturally appropriate and respectful research methods when working with Aboriginal and Torres Strait Islander women in Australian prisons. *Methodological Innovations Online, 9*(1), 1.

Lefebvre, R. C. (2013). *Social marketing and social change: Strategies and tools for improving health, well-being, and the environment.* Chichester: Wiley.

Lehmann, W. (2009). Becoming middle class: How working-class university students draw and trangress moral class boundaries. *Sociology, 43*(4), 631–647.

Madill, J., Wallace, L., Goneau-Lessard, K., Stuart MacDonald, R., & Dion, C. (2014). Best practices in social marketing among Aboriginal people. *Journal of Social Marketing, 4*(2), 155–175. https://doi.org/10.1108/JSOCM-08-2013-0056.

Martin, K. (2012). Childhood, lifehood and relatedness: Aboriginal ways of being, knowing and doing. In J. Phillips & J. Lampert (Eds.), *Introductory indigenous studies in education: Reflection and the importance of knowing* (2nd ed., pp. 27–40). Frenchs Forest, NSW: Pearson Australia.

Martin, K., & Mirraboopa, B. (2003). Ways of knowing, being and doing: A theoretical framework and methods for indigenous and indigenist re-search. *Journal of Australian Studies, 76*, 203–214.

Miller, K. (2014). Respectful listening and reflective communication from the heart and with the spirit. *Qualitative Social Work, 13*(6), 828–841. https://doi.org/10.1177/1473325013508596.

Murray, N., & Harwood, V. (2016*). The importance of Aboriginal Protocols in promoting educational futures.* National Centre for Student Equity in Higher Education.

Oxford English Dictionary. (2018). *Promotion, n.* Oxford: Oxford University Press.

Povinelli, E. A. (2016). *Geontologies: A requiem to late liberalism.* Durham: Duke University Press.

Pykett, J., Jones, R., Welsh, M., & Whitehead, M. (2014). The art of choosing and the politics of social marketing. *Policy Studies, 35*(2), 97–114. https://doi.org/10.1080/01442872.2013.875141.

Reay, D. (1995). The employ cleaners to do that: Habitus in the primary classroom. *British Journal of Sociology of Education, 16*, 353–371.

Russell-Bennet, R., Drenan, J., & Raciti, M. (2016). *Social marketing strategy for LSES communities: Research and strategy phase.* Retrieved from https://research.qut.edu.au/servicesocialmarketing/research-projects/widening-participation-in-the-tertiary-education-sector/.

Shah, M., Bennett, A., & Southgate, E. (2016). *Widening higher education participation: A global perspective.* Waltham, MA: Chandos Publishing.

Shah, M., & Whiteford, G. (2017). *Bridges, pathways and transitions: International innovations in widening participation.* Cambridge, MA: Chandos Publishing.

Shavitt, Y., & Blossfield, H.-P. (Eds.). (1993). *Persistent inequality: Changing educational attainment in thirteen countries.* Boulder, CO: Westview Press.

Slee, R. (1994). Finding a student voice in school reform: Student disaffection, pathologies of disruption and educational control. *International Studies in Sociology of Education, 4*(2), 147–172.

Smyth, J. (2004). Social capital and the 'socially just school'. *British Journal of Sociology of Education, 25*(1), 19–33.

Society for Promoting the Education of the Poor in Ireland. (1820). *Eighth report of the Society for Promoting the Education of the Poor of Ireland.* Dublin.

Truong, V. D. (2014). Social marketing: A systematic review of research 1998–2012. *Social Marketing Quarterly, 20*(1), 15–34. https://doi.org/10.1177/1524500413517666.

Ungunmerr, M.-R. (2017). To be listened to in her teaching: Dadirri: Inner Deep Listening and Quiet Still Awareness. *EarthSong Journal: Perspectives in Ecology, Spirituality and Education, 3*, 14–15.

Van Laere, K., Vandenbroeck, M., Roets, G., & Peeters, J. (2014). Challenging the feminisation of the workforce: Rethinking the mind–body dualism in Early Childhood Education and Care. *Gender and Education, 26*(3), 1–14. https://doi.org/10.1080/09540253.2014.901721.

Waters, B. S. (2016). *We can speak for ourselves parent involvement and ideologies of Black mothers in Chicago.* Rotterdam: Sense Publishers.

West, R., Stewart, L., Foster, K., & Usher, K. (2013). Through a critical lens: Indigenist research and the Dadirri method (Vol. 22, p. 1582, 2012). *Qualitative Health Research, 23*(12), 1708. https://doi.org/10.1177/1049732312467610.

2

Appreciating, Understanding and Respecting the Cultural and Social Contexts of Learning

Education is political (Apple, 1996, 2014; Kenway, 2013; Kirka, 2017; Matasci, 2017). The harsh realities of the politics of education gained world attention in October 2012 when the Taliban attempted to assassinate a teenage young woman, Malala Yousafzai. The shooting caused critical injuries and she was later transferred to a hospital in the UK. Three years earlier, at the age of 11, Yousafzai had begun writing and, later, speaking publicly to promote the education of girls in her region in Pakistan. Her efforts were recognised with the award of the Nobel Peace Prize. She has since gone to Oxford University, as the headline from *India-West*, a US-based newspaper reports, "Malala Yousafzai, Shot for Promoting Education in Pakistan, Earns Admission to Oxford" (Kirka, 2017). Yousafzai's struggle has brought into sharp focus the politics of education for girls and young women, who under Taliban edicts, were not permitted to attend school—and certainly not permitted to speak about their right to education.

Control of who can and who cannot access education is tied up with the political, and this connects with the cultural and the social. While we are not suggesting a comparison, 'control' over education is not limited to direct forms of violent acts. As argued by sociologists (for example,

© The Author(s) 2019
V. Harwood and N. Murray, *The Promotion of Education*,
https://doi.org/10.1007/978-3-030-25300-4_2

Bourdieu, 1986) and anthropologists of education (for example Alim, 2011; Miñana Blasco & Arango Vargas, 2011), there are numerous ways in which the politics of education influences and impacts the social and cultural contexts of the lives of people, families, groups and communities.

Critical studies have set out to show how this operates, including Dei, Mazzuca, and McIsaac's (2016) *Reconstructing 'Dropout': A Critical Ethnography of the Dynamics of Black Students Disengagement from School*; Youdell's (2011) analysis of school exclusions, inequalities and the politics of schooling; Kotlowitz's (1991) study of two boys growing up in public housing in Chicago, USA; White's (2015) *Free to be Mohawk: Indigenous Education at the Akwesasne Freedom School*; Paniagua's (2017) analysis in the evocatively titled paper "The Intersection of cultural diversity and special education in Catalonia: The subtle production of exclusion though classroom routines"; Stahl's (2018) *Ethnography of a Neo-liberal School*; and the ethnography of White British working-class boys to education and why they 'leave' secondary schooling by Willis (1977). Internationally focussed studies include the edited book by Levinson, Foley, and Holland (1996) *The Cultural Production of the Educated Person: Critical Ethnographies of Schooling and Local Practice* that draws attention to workings of educational 'production' in countries such as Mexico, France, Taiwan, Bolivia and Nepal.

To think of education as somehow intrinsically good, unbiased, democratic and fair is, while at its best optimistic, to overlook the workings of a complex politics; a politics that profoundly exercises itself on those touched by schooling. This, however, is not to say 'education via schooling is bad' or that it cannot provide ways to create opportunities. In her memoir *Becoming*, Michelle Obama tells of the opportunities of attending Princeton, one of the leading Ivy League Colleges in the United States, as well as her experience of a white, male-dominated campus and the comment when in high school of her career counsellor "'I'm not sure,' she said, giving me a perfunctory, patronizing smile, 'that you're Princeton material'" (Obama, 2018, p. 66). Malala Yousafzai's attendance at Oxford University is undoubtedly a wonderful opportunity—and at the same time, a reminder of the ongoing educational discrimination against young women. So too there are undoubtedly many stories of the opportunity of education, and these need to be read with the understanding of the ways in which the mechanisms of education favour some and do not favour others, and words that discriminate (such as those by Michelle Obama's high school career counsellor).

When thought of in this way, we can see how the social and cultural contexts of educational futures are important. And we can appreciate why understanding—or at the very least, aspiring to appreciate these, are vital to the concern of widening participation in higher education. In this chapter we outline the relevance of the problem of promoting educational futures and how this problem connects to the efforts to widen participation in higher education. In so doing, we set out the case for why this also matters for parents with young children. We begin with a discussion of thinking about the cultural and then move to outline how contemporary sociological and anthropological approaches to education provide nuanced views to how educational injustice is produced. We then discuss the efforts of widening participation in university and turn to argue why we need to remember that educational disadvantage also impacts parents, and that this has repercussions for efforts to widen participation. This leads us to argue why it is important to consider the promotion of educational futures.

Thinking About the Cultural

Thinking about the cultural demands a type of critical engagement that eschews seeking to define or locate 'culture'. This necessitates stepping away from the notion of culture as a specific entity that, from the standpoint of an 'objective observer', can be pinned down, tabulated and definitively 'known'. Underlying movement away from this notion of studying the 'exotic' are the trenchant critiques of Western imperialism. As Tanaka points out, "culture [is] already been doomed by its historical connection to a Western colonial project that assigned such romanticising notions to non-Western peoples while reserving to white people the luxury of no longer having to possess an ethnic culture" (2009, p. 85). One of (the many) problems with the historical Western 'study of culture' is the notion of culture neutrality. This has implications, as Ladson-Billings elaborates, for the objectification of others, "Most members of the dominant society rarely acknowledge themselves as cultural beings. They have no reason to. Culture is that exotic element possessed by 'minorities'" (Ladson-Billings, 2006, p. 107). Maintaining such lack of acknowledgment is achieved via a dialectical process of acknowledging culture; that is, the culture of the other (Bhabha, 2004). As Bhabha states:

> Despite the structural similarities with the play of need and desire … it effectively displays the 'separation', makes it more visible. It is the visibility of this separation which, in denying the colonized the capacities of self-government, independence, western modes of civility, lends authority to the official version and mission of colonial power. (2004, p. 118)

The otherness produced with colonisation has far reaching effects, "The colonized population is then deemed to be both the cause and effect of the system, imprisoned in the circle of interpretation" (Bhabha, p. 119).

Enchantment with culture and exoticisation of the other, while undoubtedly problematic, needs to also take into consideration how culture was used in early twentieth-century attempts to challenge racism. For instance, Boas, who is considered to have a founding influence on the development of cultural anthropology, defended diversity by emphasising culture (Boas, 1940). As Rosaldo states:

> Boas argued for the integrity of separate cultures which were equal with respect to their values. Differences between cultures with respect to technological development conferred them with neither moral superiority nor moral inferiority. The historical importance of Boasian cultural relativism and related efforts to combat racism cannot be denied. (1993, pp. xvi–xvii)

Gonzalez also notes that "The idea that something external to the human organism, something called 'culture', could contribute to perceived human diversity was at the time pivotal shift in paradigm" (1999, p. 431). Similarly, Abu-Lughod observes that "despite its anti-essentialist intent, however, the culture concept retains the tendency to make difference seem self-evident and people seem 'other'" (1993, pp. 10–11).

While the motives for positing the importance of culture might have initially set out to 'combat racism', what has occurred in uptakes of the term are another matter. As Gonzalez makes plain, the concept of culture has become problematic and "the initial power and potential of the culture concept seem to have been detoured through a reductionistic abuse of the term" (1999, p. 431). This pinpoints the problem with a certain (and popularised) ideal of culture, which Turner eloquently sets out:

> Essentializing the idea of culture as the property of an ethnic group or race: it risks reifying cultures as separate entities by overemphasizing their bounded-ness and mutual distinctness; it risks overemphasizing the internal homogeneity of cultures in terms that potentially legitimize repressive demands for communal conformity; and by treating cultures as badges of group identity, it tends to fetishize them in ways that put them beyond the reach of critical analysis. (1993, p. 412)

Through these forms of fetishisation, culture appears as though internally structurally coherent and timeless; and simultaneously, the gaze with which it is located evades notice and rebukes inspection.

It then makes sense to think through how culture is 'known'. Which is to say, we might well learn more about those doing the depiction than could ever be known about the depicted. This connects with Mamdani's critique of 'culture talk', which "dehistoricizes the construction of political identities" (2002, p. 767). Drawing on critiques of colonisation, we can see how depictions of culture are invoked to form part of the mechanisms of ongoing colonisation. Povinelli writes in her examination of late-liberalism that "In the first instance, culture had to become equivalent to an artefact – something that could be said to have specific qualities that could then be measured and evaluated" (2011, p. 26). And in this production of culture as artefact, it must be remembered it is the authorised depicters who say with legitimacy what does and doesn't count as culture as artefact.

Such actions occur in colonising depictions in Australia of 'who is a real Aboriginal person' where for example, the 'real' people are portrayed as living in the 'bush' and those in the city are 'fakes' (Fredericks, 2013). We are thus prompted to think more carefully about how the term culture is invoked and to what ends it is applied. Critique of culture needs to be a critique of the notion of something static where one can locate as a set of rules and where there is not only timelessness but the different tense of the artefact (Povinelli, 2011), and usually those doing the 'naming' or 'defining' of the culture claim neutrality. Undertaking such a critique engages in an awareness that distinguishes the use of the term (and here we need to remember the colonising uses) and the "dehistorization of the construction of political identities" (Mamdani, 2002, p. 767) from the reality it purports to know. Rosaldo cogently picks up on this point when he states "the terms culture and ideology refer more to distinct analytical perspectives than to separate realities" (1993, p. 83).

So it is to the analytical perspectives that we might do well to turn, and in so doing, we draw on the activity of critique (Butler, 2001). This means in practice an effort that sets out to understand the cultural will necessarily be vigilant to the *depictions* of culture. To do so means to engage critique in a manner that consistently questions such depictions—and seeks to grasp how these are produced. Returning to Rosaldo's discussion, our attention is drawn to culture and to power: "because culture and power are always at play with one another, social analysts have learned to inspect not only what was said but also who was speaking to whom under what circumstances" (1993, p. 214). Whilst being mindful of not imposing a Foucauldian reading of power onto Rosaldo's use of this term, Foucault is instructive for our purposes because of the way in which his activity of critique connects with power, the production of truth, the construction of the subject and the production of subjectivities (Harwood, 2006). Here we draw attention to the way in which questions about power can be formulated:

> To put it bluntly, I would say that to begin the analysis with a 'how' is to suggest that power as such does not exist. At the very least it is to ask oneself what contents one has in mind when using this all-embracing and reifying term; it is to suspect that an extremely complex configuration of realities is allowed to escape when one treads endlessly in the double question: What is power? and Where does power come from? (Foucault, 1983, p. 217)

Asking the 'how' question is instructive because it initiates a shift in emphasis from power as existing in its own right to power as existing in relation. To conceive of power as relational is generative because it forces the gaze onto the relations of power, which, when we consider this discussion of culture, encourages an analysis of the relations of power that produce certain readings of 'culture'. This can, we maintain, assist us in responding to Gonzalez's (1999) critique of the reductionist use of culture and to address the ways in which such uses occur in education. In this way, we are able to think through depictions of cultural difference with an ongoing attention to critique.

The way in which we think about the cultural in this book, then, always involves being cautious of how culture might be used in a reductionist manner and to be on the look-out for ways in which culture is depicted, such as only applying to non-dominant groups (Tanaka, 2009). With this constantly in mind, we pay careful attention to the influences and impacts of the cultural, considering how the cultural is viewed and constructed by larger forces that tend to dominate (such as an education or schooling system).

Rather than emphasising culture as an 'object', in this book, and in critical cultural social marketing, we take a focus on the cultural and seek to understand how the forces on the cultural intersect. In this regard, Comaroff, drawing on Appadurai, explains "we can use it in its adjectival form to describe a contingent practice or a process but not as an abstract noun – we may speak of the social, not of society, of the cultural, not of culture (cf.Arjun Appadurai, 1996, p. 13)" (2010, p. 526). In terms of education and culture, we can think of practices, a point that McCarthy explains:

> I conceptualize culture as a set of dynamic, productive, and generative material (and immaterial) practices in the regulation of social conduct and social behavior that emphasize personal self-management (i.e., the modification of habits, tastes, style, and physical appearance) and the expanded role of civil society in the state and vice versa in the rule of populations – "rule at a distance". (2008, p. 330)

Salient here is how this brings together the cultural and contexts that include the political, the historical, the economic, the racialising and the colonising. In terms of education, this "forces us to link the cultural and economic work of difference in education to broader dynamics operating in society at large" (McCarthy, 2008, p. 330).

Yet while drawing out these issues we are not dismissing or being dismissive of culture; rather, we are setting out to be critical of, for example, the colonising ways in which the concept of culture is used. This means, drawing on Mamdani, taking issue with the deployment of 'culture talk' and how this essentialises and 'freezes' notions of the traditional 'timelessness' of culture. As Povinelli points out, "Not only was culture made into an object that one could possess or insufficiently create, the actions of different cultures were assigned different tenses – not merely different times, as Johannes Fabian so nicely demonstrated, but different tenses" (2011, p. 26). In his discussion of 'culture talk', Mamdani points out that such culture talk "tends to think of individuals (from 'traditional' cultures) in authentic and original terms, as if their identities are shaped entirely by the supposedly unchanging culture into which they are born, in so doing, it dehistoricizes the construction of political identities" (Mamdani, 2002, p. 767). Thus, although tricky and at times challenging, we maintain it is imperative to both hold respect for how others might describe or name their culture, and at the same time, for us as researchers to not engage in culture talk about them. For this reason, we move toward thinking about the cultural.

Emphasising the cultural means looking at, for instance, the cultural production of knowledge. Critical examination of institutional education has demonstrated how schools are sites of cultural production—and that this is not necessarily inclusive of all people, but rather favours the cultural practices of the dominant group (Bourdieu, 1990; Thomson, 2000). This draws us in our thinking about the cultural toward "focusing closely on particular individuals and their changing relationships" (Abu-Lughod, 1993, p. 14). In arguing for an emphasis on "Ethnographies of the particular", Abu-Lughod makes a compelling case for being wary of generalisations, which "derives not from its participation in the authoritative discourses of professionalism but from the effects of homogeneity, coherence, and timelessness it tends to produce" (Abu-Lughod, 2014, p. 395). Appreciating this and at the same time, being alert to reductionist notions of culture, means being in a better position to identify the relations of power at play in what is and what isn't counted as, for instance, knowledge—or in our case in this book, knowledges and practices of learning and parent involvement.

Contemporary Sociological and Anthropological Work on Educational Access, Participation and Inclusion

It's very heartbreaking actually because we see the children doing so well here in the Preschool, we get feedback that the majority – the majority of the children are doing really well in primary school, get to high school and they really just fall off for so many of them. We [arrive] and just see so many children [here] - - - that we have known.

One little boy actually, I've been here for over seven years now, he was here early on. I taught him. He has hardly gone to school since he left Preschool and he now – he's in Year 6 now. We're telling you he has hardly been to school for his entire primary school education because of some behavioural issues and family issues and they just have not been able to get it together for that little boy so, you know, what – what sort of future does he have? (Alice, Early Childhood Educator, Madden Island Preschool)

The quote above is from a fieldwork yarning session with early childhood educators at an Aboriginal preschool (for a discussion of yarning, see Chapter 4). Alice, the educator described her successes with the children in preschool and turned the discussion to what they have observed as the children enter the schooling system. She begins by noting that the children 'do so well here in the Preschool' and she adds they do 'really well in primary school'. Alice's preschool takes a strengths-based approach, is inclusive of cultural and social diversity, works to challenge deficit assumptions about the children and the community. The assumption connects with what Walter, Martin, and Bodkin-Andrews (2017) term *Indigenous Children Growing Up Strong*, and with innovations such as high expectations (Sarra, 2011). That is, Alice and the preschool community approach the education of the children with a vision of children growing up strong, and with a nuanced understanding of the cultural contexts of the children's lives. Connecting with these strengths also requires an awareness of the discrimination they, their family and community encounters and the historical and political contexts of their lives and deficit accounts that are targeted at them. With this sophisticated awareness, Madden Island Preschool provided an educational environment where the young children thrived.

As an early childhood educator in this community, Alice had worked with many young children from the community and the surrounding areas. She had watched as the children who were thriving in preschool, moved on to primary and then secondary schooling. She emphasised to us the number of times she had observed the children 'fall off' in high school (secondary school). Just why the children 'fall off' as they move through the higher ages of schooling is a question of significance and one that demands a critical approach that doesn't fall prey to the clichés of 'individualised school failure', racialised and/or classed stereotypes or the easily reached for deficit accounts of students who 'fail at school'.

Taking a sociological and critical anthropological approach demands us to look both more broadly at the larger societal, historical and political mechanisms as well as at the more particular accounts of how such mechanisms wreak their havoc and sustain their impacts. Such an approach eschews an 'individual as deficit' appraisal that might depict a child or young person as having 'failed school', or of being uneducable. Thinking through disparities in education and educational outcomes therefore demands a nuanced understanding of educational disadvantage (Harwood, Hickey-Moody, McMahon, & O'Shea, 2017). This involves grasping how education itself is a cultural practice; it not neutral nor is it unbiased. Likewise too, this involves conceiving of disadvantage as multifaceted and complex (Wolff & De-Shalit, 2007). Stressing the politics of educational disadvantage situates the problem differently; rather than a deficit of the individual we are encouraged to be alert to, look for and seek to recognise how the politics of education is tied in the production of educational disadvantage.

Such views can be contrasted with viewpoints where deficit is individualised, such as, for example, in problem behaviours of students from LSES communities (Harwood et al., 2017). LSES children, particularly those living with burdens of poverty, can be impacted by medicalisation of child behaviour (Harwood, 2010; Harwood & Allan, 2014), and we note here that we are saying impacted by medicalisation of behaviour—as opposed to assuming they are behaviourally disordered. Children who become disengaged from school are affected by social, economic and health problems (Curtis & McMillan, 2008), and UK research predicts children living in disadvantaged circumstances have increased likelihood of school suspension and exclusion (HM Treasury & DEFES, 2007). While living in disadvantaged circumstances makes it four times more likely that a child will be diagnosed with borderline to abnormal social, emotional or behavioural difficulties (Barnes, Chanfreau, & Tomaszewski, 2010; Goodman, Gregg, & Washbrook, 2011; HM Treasury & DEFES, 2007), it is important to also recognise that living in these circumstances means also being subject to an increased medicalising and psychopathologising gaze (Allan & Harwood, 2013; Harwood & Allan, 2014).

Take for example a report from a study of teachers in 'disadvantaged' schools in the UK, who were reported to be interpreting parents as having 'low aspirations' since their focus for their children was on 'being healthy and good' (Holloway & Pimlott-Wilson, 2011). 'Being healthy and good' are aspirations that are not illogical given the higher rates of behavioural diagnoses parents in LSES communities encounter, and arguably aren't necessarily dismissive of parents caring about education. This underscores the need to contextualise phenomena such as 'challenging behaviour' as well as how interpretations of behaviour – by both teachers and parents is far more complex than only an individualised problem or deficit.

Socio-economic status has been shown to be one of the strongest predictors of educational outcomes, with those from high SES backgrounds three times more likely to attend university than their LSES peers (Bradley, Noonan, Nugent, & Scales, 2008; Currie, 2009). For the children at Madden Island preschool, the problem is not to do with an individual 'failing'; it is rather, the failure to successfully provide the children with their schooling education. This failure is all the more evident when we consider that these young people clearly, when they were young children, proved themselves to be thriving in their preschool educational environment. It is imperative here to reiterate this point: that the young children thrived at Madden Island Preschool and that they do have histories of success in learning both in the institutionally organised context such as preschool and in non-institutional contexts such as with family, peers and community.

This problem of an educational environment failing Aboriginal and Torres Strait Islander children in Australia is stated in the *Closing the*

Gap Report 2019 (Prime Minister and Cabinet, 2019), which shows the gap between Indigenous and non-Indigenous students "is evident from when children start school. During primary school the attendance gap was around 8 percentage points in 2018. Attendance falls when students reach secondary school – particularly for Indigenous students – and the attendance gap widens to 14 percentage points" (2019, p. 69). Significantly as well as a gap in attendance, there is a gap in 'consistent attendance' (consistently attending school), with "poor school attendance has been linked to lower achievement in numeracy, writing and reading" (Prime Minister and Cabinet, 2019, p. 73). The *Closing the Gap Report 2019*, which we quote at length below, describes the disproportionately high number of Indigenous students who don't consistently attend school.

> Levels of consistent attendance are lower again among Indigenous students – just under half (49 per cent) of Indigenous students attended school 90 per cent or more of the time, compared with 77 per cent of non-Indigenous students. This leaves a gap in the level of consistent school attendance of around 28 percentage points. In 2018, the gap in consistent attendance was 26 percentage points for primary school students compared to 32 percentage points for secondary students. (Prime Minister and Cabinet, 2019, p. 73)

Why is it that Indigenous students attend far less consistently than their non-Indigenous peers? One way to think this through is by emphasising the social and cultural contexts of the schools and of the young people, and recognising that educational failure is precisely that, failure of education (and not of the young people).

Efforts to understand or perhaps explain why this occurs and/or the patterns of such occurrences reveal the different approaches to conceiving educational injustice. In this book we draw on the work from critical sociology of education and anthropology of education that sets out to interrogate the practices that produce such educational injustice. Broadly speaking, this work considers the socio-cultural contexts, politics and histories that contribute to the production of educational injustice.

Socio-Cultural Contexts, Politics, Histories and Educational Injustice

I: What sorts of things about education are you talking about when you're around your kids?
Helen: To get the highest education they can ... To go as far as they can, hopefully they all go to Year 12.
Helen: And the teachers all say, what is it, categorise kids ... I get a lot ... 'That's the mum that had her kids taken off her'. (Helen, Eastside)

The transcript above is from the second longitudinal interview conducted with Helen, an Aboriginal mother who wanted her children "to get the highest education they can" and "to go as far as they can, hopefully they all go to Year 12" (the final year of secondary schooling in NSW, Australia). Helen is ambitious and she is engaged in education. She wants success for her children. Helen also pointed out she wanted to attend university herself. Stating the 'highest' for her children as at secondary school does not indicate a 'lack' of aspiration. Such assumptions about a child's or parents aspirations for education are problematic, and can made by educators in schools as well as by early childhood educators (Cummings et al., 2012). What is occurring is more complex, and to go to a fall-back position of 'lack' is to not only invoke deficit assumptions about Helen, but potentially says more about the assumptions of those doing the labelling—and the discourses that influence these assumptions.

When talking about her children, while Helen hasn't explicitly stated that attending university as the highest, she has clearly articulated the importance of Year 12, flagging this as the highest education. It is likely that in an interview with a parent who had completed a university degree, a different response might occur when describing 'the highest'. And this difference needs to be understood in terms of the contexts and constructions of knowledge that contribute to its production—not due to some kind of deficit that inheres in Helen. The tensions in these comments, drawn from a set of interviews with one parent, helps to illustrate the complexity of widening university participation.

In her first interview Helen described some of her feelings in relation to her own experiences of education:

I guess it is that feeling like 'Well I am good enough. Am I good enough?' That's why I'm going to go to uni and I'm going to do it. And someone's got to do it, so it's gonna to be me. (Helen, Eastside)

This complexity deepens when more sustained attention is respectfully made to the cultural contexts; a critical form of attention that casts the gaze not on Helen, but onto the processes, systems, histories and politics that are present themselves in tyrannical forms. These all contribute to the formulation of the educational implications of colonisation for Helen.

Helen explains in the quote above the way the teachers categorise her as "a mum that had her kids taken off her". Helen also talks of growing up and that "all my friends weren't Aboriginal and I didn't even feel comfortable telling them I was Aboriginal at that time. See it was terrible, I feel terrible about that" (Helen, Eastside). Helen then drives home how she acts as a mother to her son:

Which is why I always tell Cameron, 'You wear your beanie [with the colours black, yellow and red from the Aboriginal flag] if you want to and you be proud', because it's terrible feeling that way. And there's always the feeling that you're not good enough, you're below. (Helen, Eastside)

Helen is a strong Aboriginal Woman, a mother and as she shares in her interview, a keen advocate for achieving in education.

Yet viewed in deficit and colonialising frame of the dominant discourse, a different, and we argue wildly incorrect depiction, is produced. It is important, and we maintain, relevant to stop here and carefully consider this critically. This is because not only does it respect the story shared by Helen, it also brings into the light the complexity of practices that directly and in an ongoing insidious way, impact parents and children's engagement in education.

This narrative about Helen is racist and inescapably bound up with colonisation. The narrative marks the mother as 'failed' as she had 'her kids taken off her'; it de-historicises and de-politicises; and it situates this parent as devoid of not only educational success, but also of educational ambition. Helen's statements about her education ambitions for herself and for and her children quash this portrayal.

This narrative of 'kids taken off her' is based on the stealing of Aboriginal children from their parents (and families), that while in the White mainstream imagination in Australia, may be relegated to a problem of the past, is still occurring. While the report, *Bringing Them Home* (Human Rights and Equal Opportunity Commission, 1997) may have prompted a view that taking children from the families belonged to the past, the practice continues. As argued in the film documentary *After the Apology* (Behrendt, 2017) Aboriginal children continue to be taken away—even After the Apology (see below). The documentary tells of GMAR (Grandmothers Against Removals) and the continued practice of the removal of Aboriginal children from their families:

> The rate of Indigenous child removal has increased at an exponential rate since Prime Minister Kevin Rudd delivered the apology to the 'stolen generations' in 2008. Helen started GMAR as a response to the rising rates of child removal and along the way she has been joined by families across Australia in the battle to bring the kids home. Together are not only taking on the system, they are changing it. (Behrendt, 2018)

For teachers to characterise Helen as a mother who has 'had her kids taken from her' is to ignorantly take part in the colonial narrative about Aboriginal people. As stated in the early pages of *Bringing Them Home*, "Indigenous children have been forcibly separated from their families and communities since the very first days of the European occupation of Australia" (Human Rights and Equal Opportunity Commission, 1997, p. 2).

Devoid of an understanding of the cultural contexts of Helen's life, a teacher (and perhaps more than one) has uttered what could be viewed as a perlocutionary speech act (Butler, 1997). Perlocutionary acts "produce certain effects as their consequence; by saying something a certain effect follows" (Butler, 1997, p. 3) but such acts are "those utterances from which effects follow only when certain other kinds of conditions are in place" (Butler, 2010, p. 147). This is crucial to appreciate since for Helen, the speech acts by this teacher where more than simply 'words'; they connected with a raft of conditions that produced significant educational disadvantage.

Who Gets to Go, to Which University; Who Stays and Who Is Out?

There are lessons to be learned more broadly about the issue of widening participation in university. For a start, taking stock of the contexts is paramount. There is also, too, the variance in views to the notion of widening participation. As Harwood et al. (2017) point out:

> The literature in this field indicates that widening participation is a contested term that evokes both positive and negative reactions amongst sections of the educational community … Such participation goals are largely justified by the dual tenets of emancipation and economics, an uncomfortable dialectic that requires deep exploration in order to understand the ambiguities and contradictions of widening participation. (2017, p. 70)

Then there is the question of to which university is the participation being 'widened', with elite universities remaining 'out of reach' for non-traditional (also termed 'first in family') students (Harwood & Murray, 2019).

The shift in attention from the individual who *has* a problem to the education system and associated contexts (including the historical and political as well as the cultural) underpins a good deal of the efforts to widen participation in university education. Educational disadvantage occurs in the context of a range of social, cultural and economic imperatives. There is a powerful and diffuse social and cultural dynamic that is apparent in educational inequality. For students who have little or no parental or family history of university attendance or those from communities where attending university is not the norm, both students and their families have a steep learning curve (O'Shea & Stone, 2011). When no one is available at a local familial level to provide guidance, students may find themselves expected to 'navigate' the culture of this tertiary experience in isolation (Harrell & Forney, 2003, p. 155).

Internationally, low participation rates in university by students from LSES backgrounds have been an ongoing concern (Lehmann, 2009; Shavitt & Blossfield, 1993). This issue was reflected in Australian higher education reforms (Bradley et al., 2008; Gillard, 2009) when the federal

Government set out to increase school participation and retention rates and achieving 20% participation of low socio-economic status students in undergraduate university courses by 2020 (Gillard, 2010).

Schooling, then, with its link as a prerequisite to higher education, is crucially important, yet there is alarm in Australia over Indigenous student participation rates (Sarra, 2011). Not surprisingly, given these issues within education, Indigenous young people face significant barriers to university and for those that do reach higher education, there are extremely high attrition rates. The number of Indigenous students leaving university prematurely is almost double that of non-Indigenous students and hovers between 35 and 39% (ACER, 2010). The issue of participation in university education by Indigenous people is not restricted to Australia, with countries such as Brazil implementing policies that include quotas "for students of African Brazilian and indigenous origin from public schools" (Norões & McCowan, 2015, p. 63).

It is widely agreed that it is difficult for Indigenous students to get to university and it is extremely difficult for those who do enter to complete their degrees (Bradley et al., 2008; Universities Australia, 2008). Indigenous students have lower completion rates in secondary school education (MCEECDYA, 2010) and have been reported as not being aware of university participation strategies (Hossain et al., 2008). Participation rates at university are low, reported as being 1.3% with extremely low rates of Indigenous Ph.D. graduates (0.5%) (Evans & Carr, 2011). Indigenous university attrition rates are alarming, with university departure statistics powerfully highlighting the significance of this problem. Each year in the 2001–2006 period approximately 4000 Indigenous students commenced university but only 1000–1200 succeeded in completing a degree during the same period. The Australasian Student Engagement Report (ACER, 2010) highlights how a higher proportion of Indigenous and non-urban students entertain thoughts of departure when compared with their non-Indigenous or urban cohorts.

The complex nature of decision making around university attendance is highlighted by Andersen, Bunda, and Walter (2008), who argue in the case of Indigenous students: "participating in higher education is not simply a matter of deciding 'yes' or 'no' to university. Whilst enrolment occurs at the individual level, such choices are socially patterned" (p. 2). The huge investment, both personal and financial involved in attending university is multiplied for those from Indigenous backgrounds—and it may not be clear what the tangible benefits of this attendance might be.

There are, too, concerns with how notions such as aspiration for education are understood. There are recognised problems with current usage of 'aspiration' when applied to LSES people (Kenway & Hickey-Moody, 2011; Sellar, Gale, & Parker, 2011). Concern has been raised over the emphasis on neoliberal discourses (Raco, 2009) where structural factors are elided and hopes and aspirations of LSES children and families are misinterpreted.

Taking Appadurai's (2004) theory of the capacity to aspire and his notion of 'narrow aspiration windows' assumptions about aspiration (or the lack of) could be differently thought of. For instance, Appadurai's concepts can be used to re-orientate emphasis onto what is available/unavailable to those experiencing poverty. In Appadurai's view, aspiration is connected to having the requisite 'aspiration window'. Thus 'low aspiration' is better understood as a navigational capacity where the capacity to aspire is underpinned by the resources to which an individual has access; resources that are not only material but also imaginative. Other work has made the case that the problem lies in the aspiration of Aboriginal students going 'unrecognised' by mainstream school, but recognised by others, such as in the example of the Australian Indigenous Mentoring Experience (AIME) (Harwood, McMahon, O'Shea, Bodkin-Andrews, & Priestly, 2015).

In terms of younger children, in Australia and internationally, the early years of children's lives—defined as the period prior to commencement of primary school—has received comparably less attention in research and policy focused on widening higher education participation (Harwood & Murray, 2019). Efforts have predominantly focussed on secondary or upper primary children in low socio-economic status communities (Gale et al., 2010). As such, there is a strong case for efforts to develop future minded strategies of education promotion for young children and their families. One advantage of long-term strategies geared at improving LSES children's educational futures is the real short- to mid-term benefits for parents. Research attests to the benefits LSES parents' post-secondary education has on children's educational attainments

(Magnuson, Sexton, Davis-Kean, & Huston, 2009). US research (Sommer et al., 2012) has argued the value early childhood centres in LSES communities can have for *both* children and their mothers and proposes the idea of 'dual generation' education.

Parents That "Ain't Got That Education"

> Well it's like for families and lower economical things to keep their children encouraged and to stay at school because the parents ain't got that education already to understand what's happening in the schools now and like Maths and Science and all that and English and all that are so different now to what it was when we was going to school.
>
> So us parents don't know how to help our children doing subjects. So there's gotta be a way forward where you can help parents to help their children to want to stay at school – like at school now there's – they've got these new Aboriginal programmes and that's where they do one-on-one education and keep up and catch up and [if they're] a bit behind in class and that.
>
> But when the children get home and they come home up with this homework and say 'Mum what's this? Or what's that?'. I say well 'I don't know I can't help you because I don't understand what the things' – and she's there explaining it to me and then she got the answer or sometimes, you know? (Niah, Madden Island Preschool)

Niah's comments pick up on the complexity of issues of 'getting an education'; it isn't as simple as a child or young person attending the school—and the school doing the rest. There are a raft of activities and supports required for the student and studies in sociology of education have shown the concerted work middle class families perform to achieve educational aspirations (Vincent & Ball, 2007). Schooling places specific demands on parents. And these demands are differently responded to, depending a parent's own experiences of education, the cultural and historical-political contexts, their parent's socio-economic status, their identities. These factors differently impact parents' capacity to support the school in its endeavours.

When thought of in this way, it is education and its assumption that are the problem, rather than the parents who love their children, and do not all have the same educational (both knowledge and pedagogy), cultural, social and economic prerequisites to engage fully in an education system (and that means being able to participate in university education).

If we consider Niah's point, she is articulating the issues of both economic disadvantage (for instance she can't buy tutoring at home) and her background in subjects such as maths and science. As described above, in Australia there is a wide disparity between how education delivers its benefits and outcomes to Aboriginal and non-Aboriginal people. For instance while reports such as the *Close the Gap* point to some improvements in this disparity (for example, in 2019 preschool enrolments were on track, but attendance remained lower), the gap remains unacceptable, and is especially significant for parents who themselves experience educational disadvantage.

Internationally it is known that children from LSES backgrounds are far less likely to attend university, leading to lesser income, poorer health and social outcomes, and be affected by intergenerational poverty. Yet this is not a question of whether the children (or their parents for that matter) are 'capable'. Many of these children are 'smart enough' to attend university, but might not think of themselves (or their parents might not think of them or of themselves) as capable. University is arguably an alien environment for many LSES parents with no family history of higher education and is simply not a part of their families' worlds (O'Shea, May, Stone, & Delahunty, 2017). These influences are tangible in early childhood, where effects of LSES such as parental expectations of educational futures are recognised as a key factor for participation in post-secondary education (Ou & Reynolds, 2014).

Also, too, is the considerable lack of recognition by the official education system of parents' knowledge and of cultural approaches to learning that differ from the school's approach. There is a glimpse of this here when Niah describes how her child is "explaining it to me and she got the answer". While we are unable to comment on this as Niah didn't describe this further, what stands out here to us is the skill Niah has in listening to her child, and her child feeling confident to explain a particular homework problem, and to work it out with the parent involved in the listening.

That this skill goes uncommented on, and indeed, is read as deficient, is a problem caused by the dominance of the specific pedagogies and knowledge of the school that relegate certain pedagogies and knowledges to the margins. Niah's experiences of education appear to have virtually disqualified her from being an educator herself. This is because, in this regime, what occurred to her in the education system and her own educational disadvantage, produces the notion of an uneducated person and a non-educated subject position.

So What Is Learning, What Is Education and Why Not Promote It?

> *Johnny:* Hopefully good, hopefully better than mine I didn't really have a good education but hopefully they listen
> *I:* So is there some things that you like to focus on around education with your kids that you sorta go 'Yeah this is my … my space, I really enjoy it?
> *Johnny:* Not really, like I said I wasn't really interested at school so not really but because it's their initial learning it's very basic and easy so it's very easy to relate to 'em with that. (Johnny, Eastside)

Education is most commonly associated with institutions that educate, such as school. The enormity of this association is important to grasp, since one consequence is the monopoly of schooling on education. This means that schooling must necessarily and logically produce both the educated—and its binary, the notion of the 'uneducated'. We hear the reverberations of this influence in Johnny's words in the above quote. Yet earlier in the same interview he spoke of the learning in his workplace using highly specialised terms. But education remained the jurisdiction of the school and his involvement in his children's education and learning is 'easy to relate to' because it is their 'initial learning', it is 'basic'.

But different views of education and learning do exist. Here we turn to Ingold's (2017) discussion of Anthropology and/as education.

> Is education, then, something that happens to every human being, living in society, as they pass from immaturity to maturity? Might it perhaps be listed alongside those capacities, including for language and symbolic thought, which are often considered to be the distinguishing marks of humanity? (Ingold, 2017, pp. 2–3)

As Ingold suggests, perhaps we might do better to wrest education from the notion of an entity owned and legitimated by schooling and associated systems such as the university, and comprehend, instead, that "education [is] something that happens to every human being" (Ingold, 2017, pp. 2–3). Describing education as a 'practice of attention' (2017, p. 2), Ingold sets out a challenge for us to differently (and might we add here, inclusively) conceive of education as something we can all do, that we all take part in—and that, while it may not seem obvious to some of us all of the time, must necessarily be assumed to be occurring? This might well disrupt an assumption that Helen isn't educating her children—both for the school—as well as for Helen, for her children and for her family and community. Different types of conversations might then occur; conversations about how educating is happening—rather than how it is not happening in the home.

> The school may not be the only kind of institution vested with a pedagogic purpose, but alternative institutional practices ranging from storytelling to ritual initiation may still be modelled on it, at least in analysis, and credited with an equivalent function. Thus they may be said to operate in a 'school-like' way, to transmit the legacy of custom, morality and belief that adds up to what we call a 'culture' to each successive generation, such that it may subsequently be expressed and enacted in the practice of everyday life. (Ingold, 2017, p. 2)

Our purpose here is to throw into the air, even momentarily, the tightly held monopoly on not only where education and learning occurs (the officially sanctioned physical or virtual education institution) but also the raft of authenticated practices that are deemed 'educating'.

Work by Rogoff and Correa-Chevaz is significant to this task since it underscores both that learning by Indigenous people in the Americas occurs (when this is rarely 'officially' acknowledged) and that there are powerful institutionally sanctioned practices that delegitimate or in our view following Kristeva (1982), render the practices 'abject'. As Rogoff incisively argues:

> Many of the adults who populate and control mainstream settings have extensive experience in the dominant paradigm (such as Assembly-Line Instruction, in many school settings). For these adults, recognizing and becoming skilled in the repertoires of practices of another paradigm may be challenging. It is often difficult to avoid value judgments based on one's familiar paradigm and to see the paradigmatic basis of one's own cultural experience as well as of unfamiliar ways of life. (2016, p. 186)

The issue is at least twofold, not only is there a 'dominant paradigm', there is the problem of those who 'control mainstream settings' being required to step outside of what is familiar. While not digressing, it is relevant here to acknowledge the sheer importance in teacher education of training in recognition of 'one's own familiarity' and of skills in listening to what is unfamiliar. This point returns us to the discussion of 'culture' and just how pivotal it is to work against a 'culture talk' (Mamdani, 2002) that envisages the culture of the other in a timeless, traditional—and consequently, with a colonising gaze. Rogoff picks up on the issue of culture, and has

> argued for shifting our notion of culture to focus on ways of life, rather than treating culture as static characteristics of groups. Focusing on ways of life entails a paradigm shift to examine people's participation in cultural communities, across generations. This paradigm fits a transactional worldview that contrasts with the interactional worldview that is common in mainstream research and everyday middle-class life in the US. (2016, p. 186)

Culture is conceived, that is, it is constructed by the viewer and largely from a mainstream stance. In places of colonisation, such as Australia and the Americas, this stance is unavoidably implicated with the privileging of a dominant paradigm that is embedded in colonisation. There is therefore significant work and effort required to not only listen to the unfamiliar, but in the first place, to notice the familiar paradigm.

Termed 'Learning by Observing and Pitching In (LOPI)', this work emerged from collaborations with Indigenous and Indigenous Heritage Communities of the Americas (Correa-Chávez, Mejia-Arauz, & Rogoff, 2015). LOPI is a 'cultural paradigm' (Correa-Chávez et al., 2015), one that "is a coherent, multifaceted cultural tradition that can organize children's learning and the supports available to them, fostering their participation with initiative and responsibility" (Rogoff, 2014, p. 79). According to Battiste (2002, p. 11), "Indigenous pedagogy values a person's ability to learn independently by observing, listening, participating with a minimum of intervention and instruction". And as Urrieta explains, "LOPI helps to highlight the dynamic and experiential ways of Indigenous pedagogies, and views Indigenous knowing(s) as living processes to be absorbed and understood by community members throughout the life span (Battiste, 2002)" (Urrieta, 2015, p. 321).

> A participation paradigm shifts our conceptualization of culture to focus on processes, as people engage in cultural activities, rather than on static characteristics (such as ethnicity). Thus, cultural analysis examines individuals' participation in the practices of cultural communities, rather than equating culture with their belonging to a bounded ethnic, racial, or national group. (Rogoff, 2016, p. 184)

By emphasising cultural analysis rather than an examination or interrogation of culture, and by drawing on this important work, in our project we are able to pay careful and sustained emphasis to the cultural in learning. At the same time, we maintain a critical lookout for and assumptions that reify culture or that set out to 'know' it from the position of a dominant gaze.

Promoting Education in Early Childhood

> I've taken her to the ADFA Open Day for the Australian Defence Force Academy – and, you know, I've taught her that they will pay for your university, they'll pay you 40 grand a year and they'll give you a job when

you're done and they'll give you 27 per cent super –you know? Go where it's easier not harder. Work smarter.
    ... it's promoting that it's like – go into somewhere where they're going to give you a job. (Jenny, Eastside Region)

Jenny explains, she will be encouraging her child to sign up to the Australian Defence Forces because there is not only guaranteed pay for studying (and no fees), there is guaranteed employment at the conclusion of the degree. The attractiveness of the Defence Force option is set against what Jenny has determined is the uncertainty of the more commonplace university pathway, one with which she is likely unfamiliar. In this sense, the 'education promotion' by ADFA has been successful, while efforts by other higher education providers have failed.

This suggests that while it can be argued that novel strategies are needed that can "help parents from poorer families to believe that their own actions and efforts can lead to higher educational outcomes" (Goodman et al., 2011, p. 13), this is not all of the issue. Indeed, when we look at Jenny's comments, the assumption about 'parents from poorer families' doesn't hold true for her; or at least, a more nuanced approach is required that appreciates why the Defence Force tertiary option is preferred, such as the work by Kleykamp (2006) that notes LSES as a factor for post-secondary students with college aspirations in choosing the military over higher education.

The question as to whether the promotion of educational futures is appropriate in early childhood can be thought through by heeding work emerging from the sociology of education that for example, recognises the impact of class-based issues on education achievements and how education is engaged (McLeod & Yates, 2006). Social marketing has been used in early childhood—but for different reasons. For instance, it has been used to improve awareness of Autism (Daniel, Prue, Taylor, Thomas, & Scales, 2009) and has also been recommended as a method for improving information about early childhood services for vulnerable parents (Winkworth, McArthur, Layton, & Thompson, 2010).

Education promotion strategies for young children need to take account of the education services working with LSES children. As recent UK research into educational aspirations of low-income families and their primary school aged children points out, it is crucial to be aware of how schools in low-income areas interpret educational aspirations (Holloway & Pimlott-Wilson, 2011). It is therefore important to understand how LSES children and parents experience and interpret educational futures and for how new ways might be developed for education promotion.

References

Abu-Lughod, L. (1993). *Writing women's worlds: Bedouin stories.* Berkeley: University of California Press.

Abu-Lughod, L. (2014). Writing against culture. In H. L. Moore & T. Sanders (Eds.), *Anthropology in theory: Issues in epistemology* (pp. 386–399). Chichester, West Sussex: Wiley.

ACER. (2010). *Australasian Survey of Student Engagement—Australasian Student Engagement Report: Doing more for learning: Enhancing engagement and outcomes.* Camberwell, VIC.

Alim, H. S. (2011). Hip hop and the politics of ill-literacy. In *A companion to the anthropology of education.* Malden: Wiley-Blackwell.

Allan, J., & Harwood, V. (2013). Medicus interruptus in the behaviour of children in disadvantaged contexts in Scotland. *British Journal of Sociology of Education, 35,* 413–431. Published online 27 April.

Andersen, C., Bunda, T., & Walter, M. (2008). Indigenous higher education: The role of universities in releasing the potential. *Australian Journal of Indigenous Education, 37*(1), 1–8. https://doi.org/10.1017/S1326011100016033.

Appadurai, A. (1996). *Modernity at large cultural dimensions of globalization.* Minneapolis: University of Minnesota Press.

Appadurai, A. (2004). The capacity to aspire: Culture and terms of recognition. In R. Vijayendra & M. Walton (Eds.), *Culture and public action* (pp. 59–84). Stanford: Stanford University Press.

Apple, M. (1996). *Cultural politics and education.* New York: Teachers College Press.

Apple, M. (2014). Immigration, social realities, and the complex politics of education. *Race Ethnicity and Education, 17*(2), 291–298. https://doi.org/10.1080/13613324.2013.873571.

Barnes, M., Chanfreau, J., & Tomaszewski, W. (2010). *Growing up in Scotland: The circumstances of persistently poor children.* Edinburgh.

Battiste, M. (2002). *Indigenous knowledge and pedagogy in first nations education: A literature review with recommendations.* Ottawa: Indian and Northern Affairs Canada.

Behrendt, L. (Writer). (2017). *After the apology* (M. Purske, Producer). Waverley, NSW: Pursekey Productions.

Behrendt, L. (2018). *After the apology*. Retrieved from http://aftertheapology.com/.

Bhabha, H. K. (2004). *The location of culture*. London: Routledge.

Boas, F. (1940). *Race, language and culture*. New York: Macmillan.

Bourdieu, P. (1986). The forms of capital. In J. Westport (Ed.), *Handbook of theory and research for the sociology of education* (pp. 214–258). New York: Greenwood.

Bourdieu, P. (1990). *Reproduction in education, society, and culture* (1990 ed., Preface by P. Bourdieu, Ed.). London: Sage in association with Theory, Culture & Society, Department of Administrative and Social Studies, Teesside Polytechnic.

Bradley, D., Noonan, P., Nugent, H., & Scales, B. (2008). *Review of Australian higher education, final report*. Canberra.

Butler, J. (1997). *Excitable speech: A politics of the performative*. New York: Routledge.

Butler, J. (2001). *What is critique? An essay on Foucault's virtue*. Retrieved from http://eipcp.net/transversal/0806/butler/en.

Butler, J. (2010). Performative agency. *Journal of Cultural Economy, 3*(2), 147–161. https://doi.org/10.1080/17530350.2010.494117.

Comaroff, J. (2010). The end of anthropology, again: On the future of an in/discipline. *American Anthropologist, 112*(4), 524–538. https://doi.org/10.1111/j.1548-1433.2010.01273.x.

Correa-Chávez, M., Mejia-Arauz, R., & Rogoff, B. (2015). *Children learn by observing and contributing to family and community endeavours: A cultural paradigm* (Vol. 49). Waltham. MA: Academic Press.

Cummings, C., Laing, K., Law, J., McLaughlin, J., Papps, I., Todd, L., & Woolner, P. (2012). *Can changing aspirations and attitudes impact educational attainment: A review of interventions*. London.

Currie, J. (2009). Healthy, wealthy, and wise: Socioeconomic status, poor health in childhood, and human capital development. *Journal of Economic Literature, 47*(1), 87–122.

Curtis, D., & McMillan, J. (2008). *School non-completers: Profiles and initial destinations* (Longitudinal Surveys of Australian Youth, Research Report 54). Camberwell, VIC.

Daniel, K. L., Prue, C., Taylor, M. K., Thomas, J., & Scales, M. (2009). 'Learn the signs. Act early': A campaign to help every child reach his or her full potential. *Public Health, 123*(1), e11–e16.

Dei, G. J. S., Mazzuca, J., & McIsaac, E. (2016). *Reconstructing 'dropout': A critical ethnography of the dynamics of Black students' disengagement from school.* Toronto: University of Toronto Press.

Evans, C., & Carr, K. (2011). *Have your say on Indigenous higher education* [Media Release]. Retrieved from https://ministers.employment.gov.au/evans/have-yoursayindigenous-higher-education.

Foucault, M. (1983). The subject and power. In H. L. Dreyfus & P. Rabinow (Eds.), *Michel Foucault: Beyond structuralism and hermeneutics* (2nd ed., pp. 208–226). Chicago: University of Chicago press.

Fredericks, B. (2013). 'We don't leave our identities at the city limits': Aboriginal and Torres Strait Islander people living in urban localities. *Australian Aboriginal Studies, 2013*(1), 4–16.

Gale, T., Sellar, S., Parker, S., Hattam, R., Comber, B., Tranter, D., & Bills, D. (2010). *Interventions early in school as a means to improve higher education outcomes for disadvantaged (particularly low SES) students.* Underdale, Australia: National Centre Student Equity in Higher Education. Retrieved from http://dro.deakin.edu.au/view/DU:30040776.

Gillard, J. (2009). *Funding boost helps low-SES higher education places.* Canberra: Commonwealth of Australia.

Gillard, J. (2010). *Keynote address: Australia's productivity challenge: A key role for education.* John Curtin Institute of Public Policy. Canberra: Commonwealth of Australia.

Gonzalez, N. (1999). What will we do when culture does not exist anymore? *Anthropology & Education Quarterly, 30*(4), 431–435.

Goodman, A., Gregg, P., & Washbrook, E. (2011). Children's educational attainment and the aspirations, attitudes and behaviours of parents and children through childhood in the UK. *Longitudinal and Life Course Studies, 2*(1), 1–18.

Harrell, P. E., & Forney, W. S. (2003). Ready or not, here we come: Retaining hispanic and first-generation students in postsecondary education. *Community College Journal of Research and Practice, 27*(2), 147–156. https://doi.org/10.1080/713838112.

Harwood, V. (2006). *Diagnosing 'disorderly' children: A critique of behaviour disorder discourses.* Oxford: Routledge.

Harwood, V. (2010). The new outsiders: ADHD and disadvantage. In L. J. Graham (Ed.), *(De)Constructing ADHD: Critical guidance for teachers and teacher educators* (pp. 119–142). New York: Peter Lang.

Harwood, V., & Allan, J. (2014). *Psychopathology at school: Theorising mental disorders in education.* Oxford: Routledge.

Harwood, V., Hickey-Moody, A., McMahon, S., & O'Shea, S. (2017). *The politics of widening participation and university access for young people: Making educational futures*. London: Routledge.

Harwood, V., McMahon, S., O'Shea, S., Bodkin-Andrews, G., & Priestly, A. (2015). Recognising aspiration: The AIME program's effectiveness in inspiring Indigenous young people's participation in schooling and opportunities for further education and employment. *Australian Educational Researcher, 42*(2), 217. https://doi.org/10.1007/s13384-015-0174-3.

Harwood, V., & Murray, N. (2019). Strategic discourse production and parent involvement: Including parent knowledge and practices in the Lead My Learning campaign. *International Journal of Inclusive Education, 23*(4), 353–368. https://doi.org/10.1080/13603116.2019.1571119.

HM Treasury & DEFES. (2007). *Policy review of children and young people: A discussion paper*. Norwich.

Holloway, S. L., & Pimlott-Wilson, H. (2011). The politics of aspiration: Neo-liberal education policy, 'low' parental aspirations, and primary school Extended Services in disadvantaged communities. *Children's Geographies, 9*(1), 79–94.

Hossain, D., Gorman, D., Willams-Mozley, J., & Garvey, D. (2008). Bridging the gap: Identifying needs and aspirations of indigenous students to facilitate their entry into university. *Australian Journal of Indigenous Education, 37*(1), 9–17.

Human Rights and Equal Opportunity Commission. (1997). *Bringing them home: Report of the National Inquiry into the separation of Aboriginal and Torres Strait Islander children from their families*. Sydney: Human Rights and Equal Opportunity Commission.

Ingold, T. (2017). *Anthropology and/as education: Anthropology, art, architecture and design*. Abingdon, Oxon and New York, NY: Routledge.

Kenway, J. (2013). Challenging inequality in Australian schools: Gonski and beyond. *Discourse: Studies in the Cultural Politics of Education, 34*(2), 1–23. https://doi.org/10.1080/01596306.2013.770254.

Kenway, J., & Hickey-Moody, A. (2011). Life chances, lifestyle and everyday aspirational strategies and tactics. *Critical Studies in Education, 52*(2), 151–163.

Kirka, D. (2017, August 17). Malala Yousafzai, shot for promoting education in Pakistan, earns admission to Oxford. *India-West*. Retrieved from http://www.indiawest.com/news/global_indian/malala-yousafzai-shot-for-promoting-education-in-pakistan-earns-admission/article_75d65d5e-83a9-11e7-9b24-03304e5280be.html.

Kleykamp, M. (2006). College, jobs, or the military? Enlistment during a time of war. *Social Science Quarterly, 87*(2), 272–290. https://doi.org/10.1111/j.1540-6237.2006.00380.x.

Kotlowitz, A. (1991). *There are no children here: The story of two boys growing up in the other America* (1st ed.). New York: Doubleday.

Kristeva, J. (1982). *Powers of horror: An essay in abjection.* New York: Columbia University Press.

Ladson-Billings, G. (2006). It's not the culture of poverty, it's the poverty of culture: The problem with teacher education. *Anthropology & Education Quarterly, 37*(2), 104–109. https://doi.org/10.1525/aeq.2006.37.2.104.

Lehmann, W. (2009). Becoming middle class: How working-class university students draw and trangress moral class boundaries. *Sociology, 43*(4), 631–647.

Levinson, B. A., Foley, D. E., & Holland, D. C. (Eds.). (1996). *The cultural production of the educated person: Critical ethnographies of schooling and local practice.* Albany: State University of New York Press.

Magnuson, K., Sexton, H., Davis-Kean, P. F., & Huston, A. (2009). The effects of increases in maternal education on young children's language skills. *Merill Palmer Quarterly, 55,* 319–350.

Mamdani, M. (2002). Good Muslim, bad Muslim: A political perspective on culture and terrorism. *American Anthropologist, 104*(3), 766–775. https://doi.org/10.1525/aa.2002.104.3.766.

Matasci, D. (2017). Assessing needs, fostering development: UNESCO, illiteracy and the global politics of education (1945–1960). *Comparative Education, 53*(1), 35–53. https://doi.org/10.1080/03050068.2017.1254952.

McCarthy, C. (2008). Understanding the neoliberal context of race and schooling in the age of globalization. In *Transnational perspectives on culture, policy, and education: Redirecting cultural studies in neoliberal times* (pp. 319–340, Chapter 15). New York: Peter Lang.

McLeod, J., & Yates, L. (2006). *Making modern lives: Subjectivity, schooling, and social change.* New York: State University of New York.

Miñana Blasco, C., & Arango Vargas, C. (2011). Educational policy, anthropology, and the state. In *A companion to the anthropology of education.* Malden: Wiley-Blackwell.

Norões, K., & McCowan, T. (2015). The challenge of widening participation to higher education in Brazil: Injustices, innovations, and outcomes. In M. Shah, A. Bennett, & E. Southgate (Eds.), *Widening higher education participation: A global perspective* (pp. 63–80). Waltham, MA: Chandos Publishing.

Obama, M. (2018). *Becoming.* New York: Viking.

O'Shea, S., May, J., Stone, C., & Delahunty, J. (2017). *First-in-family students, university experience and family life: Motivations, transitions and participation.* London: Palgrave Macmillan.

O'Shea, S., & Stone, C. (2011). Transformations and self-discovery: Mature-age women's reflections on returning to university study. *Studies in Continuing Education, 33*(3), 273–288. https://doi.org/10.1080/0158037X.2011.565046.

Ou, S.-R., & Reynolds, A. J. (2014). Early determinants of postsecondary education participation and degree attainment: Findings from an inner-city minority cohort. *Education and Urban Society, 46*(4), 474–504. https://doi.org/10.1177/0013124512447810.

Paniagua, A. (2017). The intersection of cultural diversity and special education in Catalonia: The subtle production of exclusion through classroom routines. *Anthropology & Education Quarterly, 48*(2), 141–158. https://doi.org/10.1111/aeq.12190.

Povinelli, E. A. (2011). *Economies of abandonment: Social belonging and endurance in late liberalism.* Durham, NC: Duke University Press.

Prime Minister and Cabinet. (2019). *Closing the gap, report 2019.* Canberra.

Raco, M. (2009). From expectations to aspirations: State modernisation, urban policy, and the existential politics of welfare in the UK, *Political Geography, 28*, 436–454.

Rogoff, B. (2014). Learning by observing and pitching in to family and community endeavours. *Human Development, 57*, 69–81.

Rogoff, B. (2016). Culture and participation: A paradigm shift. *Current Opinion in Psychology, 8*, 182–189. https://doi.org/10.1016/j.copsyc.2015.12.002.

Rosaldo, R. (1993). *Culture and truth: The remaking of social analysis.* Boston: Beacon Press.

Sarra, C. (2011). *Strong and smart: Towards a pedagogy for emancipation, education for first peoples.* New York, NY: Routledge.

Sellar, S., Gale, T., & Parker, S. (2011). Appreciating aspirations in Australian higher education. *Cambridge Journal of Education, 41*(1), 37–52.

Shavitt, Y., & Blossfield, H.-P. (Eds.). (1993). *Persitent inequality: Changing educational attainment in thirteen countries.* Boulder, CO: Westview Press.

Sommer, T. E., Chase-Lansdale, P. L., Brooks-Gunn, J., Gardner, M., Rauneer, D. M., & Freel, K. (2012). Early childhood education centers and mothers' postsecondary attainment: A new conceptual framework for a dual-generation education intervention. *Teachers College Record, 114*(100305), 1–40. Retrieved from https://www.tcrecord.org, Date Accessed: 8 October 2019.

Stahl, G. (2018). *Ethnography of a neo-liberal school: Cultures of success*. Oxford: Routledge.

Tanaka, G. (2009). The elephant in the living room that no one wants to talk about: Why U.S. anthropologists are unable to acknowledge the end of culture. *Anthropology & Education Quarterly, 40*(1), 82–95. https://doi.org/10.1111/j.1548-1492.2009.01029.x.

Thomson, P. (2000). Against the odds: Developing school programmes that make a difference for students and families in communities placed at risk. *Childrenz Issues, 3*(1), 7–13.

Turner, T. (1993). Anthropology and multiculturalism: What is anthropology that multiculturalists should be mindful of it? *Cultural Anthropology, 8*(4), 411–429. https://doi.org/10.1525/can.1993.8.4.02a00010.

Universities Australia. (2008). *Advancing equity and participation in Australian higher education: Action to address participation and equity levels in higher education of people from low socioeconomic backgrounds and Indigenous people*. Canberra.

Urrieta, L. J. (2015). Learning by observing and pitching in and the connections to native and Indigenous knowledge systems. In M. Correa-Chevaz, R. Mejia-Arauz, & B. Rogoff (Eds.), *Children learn by observing and contributing to family and community endeavours: A cultural paradigm* (pp. 357–380). Waltham, MA: Elsevier.

Vincent, C., & Ball, S. J. (2007). 'Making up' the middle class child: Families, activities and class dispositions. *Sociology, 41*(6), 1061–1077.

Walter, M., Martin, K. L., & Bodkin-Andrews, G. (Eds.). (2017). *Indigenous children growing up strong: A longitudinal study of Aboriginal and Torres Strait Islander families*. London: Palgrave Macmillan.

White, L. (2015). *Free to be Mohawk: Indigenous education at the Akwesasne Freedom School*. Norman: University of Oklahoma Press.

Willis, P. (1977). *Learning to labour*. Farmborough: Saxon House.

Winkworth, G., McArthur, M., Layton, M., & Thompson, L. (2010). Someone to check in on me: Social capital, social support and vulnerable parents with very young children in the Australian Capital Territory. *Child and Family Social Work, 15*, 206–215.

Wolff, J., & De-Shalit, A. (2007). *Disadvantage*. Oxford: Oxford University Press.

Youdell, D. (2011). *School trouble: Identity, power and politics in education*. Oxford: Routledge.

3

A Critical Cultural Approach to Social Marketing?

Having outlined the importance of the cultural and social contexts of education, in this chapter we begin our discussion of a critical cultural approach to social marketing. In the previous chapter the case was made that the cultural and social contexts of education need to be at the fore-front when it comes to devising new ways to change our thinking about how education is promoted. As we discussed in Chapter 1, when it comes to promoting education we really do need to rethink assumptions about education promotion as a 'given', and embrace the proposition that there is a need to make better efforts to promote the ideas, practices and cultures of learning and education. In this regard, education promotion is underpinned by the idea of an 'action of helping forward' (Oxford English Dictionary, 2018); that is, helping education forward.

The chapter is organised into two parts. We start with a discussion of what we mean by a critical and cultural emphasis, and how we envisage that this works with concepts and techniques from social marketing. We then provide an overview of social marketing and a brief explanation of social marketing techniques. This includes a short background to social marketing, including social marketing definitions, the social marketing 'benchmarks' or 'criteria' and the processes involved in social marketing.

© The Author(s) 2019
V. Harwood and N. Murray, *The Promotion of Education*,
https://doi.org/10.1007/978-3-030-25300-4_3

We also briefly discuss some of the key characteristics or concepts in social marketing, influencing behaviour or behaviour change and the marketing mix.

A Critical and Cultural Emphasis

When we talk about critical cultural social marketing, we are not advocating that cultural considerations be added to or 'inserted' into a social marketing planning process. Nor could we just be critical 'some of the time' or at certain prescribed stages. We need to maintain an ongoing activity of critique. Indeed, in working on a project which includes people impacted by dominant education discourses that too often depict them in deficit ways (such as 'un-educated'), we need to be in tune to those practices that produce these truths about them. Doing so helps us to not only be watchful of deficit discourses; we become better able to listen and be respectful to the people with whom and for whom we are creating a social marketing campaign. Possibly, too, over time, we may better recognise the mechanisms that produce these discourses.

As such, an incorporation or 'additive' method to connecting with the cultural, does not in our view, provide for the necessary reconceptualisation of the underpinnings of social marketing required if the cultural is to be at the forefront. An additive method that simply appended a new aspect would be fragmentary, and likely to not only overlook the many facets of culture that are important for social marketing in education, but also miss the pivotal points at which community relationships are needed to create and shape a critical cultural social marketing campaign. Indeed, this would be a piecemeal approach, where a 'template' is adopted. Or as Peattie and Peattie (2011) state in their critical review of the social marketing mix and its adaptation from marketing, "can I borrow your tools" (2011, p. 152). Their point is salient; it is crucial not to uncritically adopt the tools of commercial marketing into social marketing. Likewise, it is similarly vital to not simply adopt the tools of social marketing, used widely in areas such as health, into education and the design of an education promotion strategy.

Another problem is to do with the power structures that underlie a social marketing paradigm. To an extent, Gordon Russell-Bennett, and Lefebvre (2016) note this issue, suggesting that:

> Rather than considering social marketing as a Western-dominated approach to social change, it could be viewed as a broad tent in which various ideas, debates and discourses should feature. This would mean providing platforms for different cultural and gender perspectives to be heard. (2016, p. 1069)

The reason we say, 'to an extent' is because in this tent metaphor the question is, just whose tent is it? That said, their proposal is certainly useful and likely generative. What we are expressing here is the need for a critical take, so that cultural difference is not corralled by particular kinds of Western assumptions. Bringing the cultural to the forefront places a direct emphasis on culture onto social marketing. Likewise, foregrounding the critical situates practices of critique front and centre in social marketing.

Our use of 'critical' in critical cultural social marketing differs from 'critical social marketing', which is focussed on examining the impacts of commercial meeting. As Hastings (2009) argues, since critical marketing is being used to better inform marketing, and since social marketing draws on marketing, 'why not' have critical social marketing. He points out that "Critical marketing seeks not to just determine what is 'wrong and bad' about commercial marketing, but to reflect on its nature, learn from its successes, and analyse its weaknesses" (p. 263). Gordon (2011) defines critical social marketing as, "critical research from a marketing perspective on the impact commercial marketing has upon society, to build the evidence base, inform upstream efforts such as advocacy, policy and regulation, and inform the development of downstream social marketing interventions" (2011, p. 89). Thus, critical social marketing is concerned with the impacts of commercial marketing (Gordon, 2011) and "can inform upstream activities such as advocacy and policy and regulation" (p. 85).

This differs substantially to what we are proposing with critical cultural social marketing. While the former does set out to use social theory, informed by the 'critical theory' of the Frankfurt School, and the work of Habermas (Gordon, 2011, p. 85), the focus is commercial marketing. By contrast, what we are outlining in this book is a critical focus that takes the form of an ongoing critique, and this is to critically inform all of the activities, processes and techniques in social marketing. For instance, if social marketing were to be considered in relation to the impacts of obesity discourse in education (Wright & Harwood, 2009), commercial marketing, as well as discourses about obesity in education, would be scrutinised.

An Active Critique

Our use of the word 'critical' signals our commitment to the activity that Foucault (1997) and Butler (2001) term 'critique'. Early in her essay, *What Is Critique? An Essay on Foucault's Virtue,* Butler distinguishes between critique as Foucault sets out to deploy it, and how it is used in the work of Habermas. Pointing to the very activity of critique, Butler writes:

> Critique will be dependent on its objects, but its objects will in turn define the very meaning of critique. Further, the primary task of critique will not be to evaluate whether its objects – social conditions, practices, forms of knowledge, power, and discourse – are good or bad, valued highly or demeaned, but to bring into relief the very framework of evaluation itself. (2001)

Here, we see an emphasis on not only the relationship between critique and its objects, but also on the knowledge upon which the critique might easily rely.

This point is crucial for the practices of critique we are advocating in critical cultural social marketing. This is because this style of critique is necessary for creating social marketing approaches that are respectful and attentive of culture. To do so, there is a twofold awareness: not only of culture, but also of how cultures and cultural practices (as well as the social) are subjugated. We therefore need to recognise there are mechanisms that subjugate, such as how institutional forms of education (schools, universities) produce powerful discourses about what it means to be 'educated' or 'clever'. Such discourses not only impact a young person during their experiences of schooling systems (Harwood, Hickey-Moody, McMahon, & O'Shea, 2017; McMahon, Harwood, & Hickey-Moody, 2016), the effects often continue beyond the school experience, and can effectively delegitimise the myriad ways that parents are involved in the learning of their children. This is why it is so important to prioritise a critical attitude to how discourses situate people such as parents who have experienced educational disadvantage. In critical cultural social marketing, a practice of critique weaves a critical attitude 'front and centre' into all of the various activities undertaken in social marketing.

An ongoing prioritisation of a critical attitude means engaging in the activity of critique that scrutinises knowledge, our certainties about knowledge and calls for 'an ethics of discomfort' (Harwood & Rasmussen, 2004). As Butler continues:

> What is the relation of knowledge to power such that our epistemological certainties turn out to support a way of structuring the world that forecloses alternative possibilities of ordering? Of course, we may think that we need epistemological certainty in order to state for sure that the world is and ought to be ordered a given way. To what extent, however, is that certainty orchestrated by forms of knowledge precisely in order to foreclose the possibility of thinking otherwise? (2001)

The significance here is that critique, envisaged in this way, is always concerned with the 'possibility of thinking otherwise'. To achieve this, when examining educational injustices—or those depicted as problems—critique looks to unsettle what might be assumed to be known about 'social problems'.

Undertaking practices of critique in critical cultural social marketing requires an activeness that looks for and examines 'epistemological certainties', such as for instance, the notion of 'educated'. It is important to make such certainties unsteady, for when we also think about 'who gets to say who is educated' the operations of what Foucault terms 'relations of power' become less hidden. This means that the way power interacts with truth to demarcate who is 'educated' and who is not, is not only put under scrutiny, but can, through critical cultural social marketing, be challenged. We are suggesting that, by using the techniques of social marketing, this can be challenged not only by 'telling different truths' but by also being alert to how truths impact the subjects of these truths (such as how parents might be impacted by school truths about who is and isn't educated). This is important as it: (1) enables an understanding of how deficit educational subjects are constructed ('the failure', 'the uneducated'); and (2) provides a way to grasp how the subject can have a different relationship with a dominant truth.

The activity of critique doesn't take problems at face value; it interrogates, questions and is not content with the taken for granted. By reconsidering how problems are understood, it lends a form of critical insight into the issue at hand that, for instance, doesn't accept the 'foreclose of the possibility of thinking otherwise'. In our work, this meant, for instance, not accepting the idea that the parents weren't involved or engaged in their children's learning.

Importantly, this use of a critique that carefully reconsiders 'knowledge' or which is 'true' opens possibilities for enhanced ways of collaborating with the people or communities for whom the social marketing may be designed. By not simply accepting a dominant narrative about 'a problem' (such as parent's not being engaged in their children's learning or them or their child not 'having aspirations'), we needed to pursue a different understanding. This required careful and respectful listening and respectful relationships with the people in our research. Through this in-depth approach we were able to confront the dominant deficit narratives, examine our own assumptions, and displace ourselves from the status of 'expert' researcher. This process (which was not linear, but cyclical and iterative as we improved our understanding) meant we were able to better grasp the learning practices of the parents and recognise parent involvement in learning and their deep valuing of education(Harwood & Murray, 2019).

Respecting Culture and Drawing on Critique

In critical cultural social marketing, critique is used with an appreciation and respect for the cultural. The two are relational; one informing the other. Bringing this into sharp focus, at the forefront, obligates us to be constantly aware of the cultural. Accentuating critique helps us to remain vigilant to assumptions and deficit discourses. Holding these two as guiding or steering social marketing impacted and changed the processes, and significantly influenced the campaign (as we will discuss in Chapters 4, 5 and 6). One of the conceptual outcomes was *strategic discourse production* (Harwood & Murray, 2019). Drawing on social marketing enabled us to create a way to communicate the messages about parent involvement. But—and this is crucial—we could not have reached the point of realising these messages without engaging the practices of critique and without careful attention to the cultural.

Strategic discourse production can provide opportunities for different relations to truth, and through this, different practices of subjectivation by the subject. To give an example from Lead My Learning, through critical cultural social marketing we were able to create Lead My Learning as a campaign that connected with the learning practices that parents (who have experienced educational disadvantages) are doing. These are practices, however, that largely go unnoticed or are not legitimated by the discourses of learning that dominate. Lead My Learning 'tells a different story' that connects with what the parents are doing in learning activities with their children. Doing so opens possibilities for thinking otherwise and for the parents to be subjects who recognise their involvement in their children's learning (even if the dominant practices do not). From this point of view, as we stated in Chapter 1, it is possible to use critique as an 'art of not being governed quite so much' by discourses of education that stipulates the legitimate and recognisable in learning.

Social Marketing

Our discussion of social marketing is kept relatively brief, as there are excellent social marketing publications that go into rich detail on social marketing. Recently published examples include: Dietrich, Rundle-Thiele and Kubacki's (2017) *Segmentation in Social Marketing: Process, Methods and Application*; French and Gordon's (2015) *Strategic Social Marketing*; Ladero and Alves (2019) edited book *Case Studies on Social Marketing: A Global Perspective*; Lee and Kotler's (2019) *Social Marketing, Behavior Change for Social Good*; Lefebvre's (2013) *Social Marketing and Social Change: Strategies and Tools for Improving Well-Being, and the Environment*;

and Kubacki and Rundle-Thiele's (2017) *Formative Research in Social Marketing: Innovative Methods to Gain Consumer Insights*.

Social marketing can be described as a consumer-oriented approach (Grier & Bryant, 2005) to changing behaviour 'for the good'. It should not be confused with social media marketing or marketing more generally. Similar to marketing (from which it was developed) it requires a thorough, well-researched understanding of the target market, specifically their knowledge, attitudes and behaviours relevant to the behaviour change at hand. While sharing an affinity with marketing, the relationship between the two might be better appreciated in terms of the techniques that are similar, while the purposes and specificity of approaches differ. For instance, social marketing sets out with the explicit purpose of 'social good'; it is not governed by the concept of selling for profit, but rather has its origins in exploiting techniques from marketing.

> Social marketing is a distinct marketing discipline, one that has been labeled as such since the early 1970s and refers primarily to efforts focused on influencing behaviors that will improve health, prevent injuries, protect the environment, contribute to communities, and more recently, enhance financial well-being. (Lee & Kotler, 2011, p. 7)

Since its inception in the US in the 1970s, social marketing has been used in many countries, and has been especially applied in health promotion (Johnson, Jones, & Iverson, 2009; Opel, Diekema, Lee, & Marcuse, 2009; Wong, 2002) to address health related issues. Such social marketing campaigns include: skin cancer prevention in the UK (Kemp, Eagle, & Verne, 2011) and in Australia (McLeod, Insch, & Henry, 2011); seat belt use in Russia (Zambon, Hyder, & Peden, 2012) and in the US (Bryant-Stephens, Garcia-Espana, & Winston, 2013); sexual assault prevention in the US (Potter & Stapleton, 2012); use of bike helmets in Vietnam (Hue, Brennan, Parker, & Florian, 2015); HIV/AIDS prevention in Fiji (Sewak & Singh, 2017); smoking reduction in Mexico (Thrasher et al., 2011); and underage drinking in Australia (Jones, Andrews, & Francis, 2017). While perhaps its greatest application has been health-related (Suarez-Almazor, 2011), examples of social marketing in other areas include for environmental benefits such as to decrease water consumption (Lowe, Lynch, & Lowe, 2015) and reducing litter (Almosa, Parkinson, & Rundle-Thiele, 2017), and in programmes of social change such as poverty reduction (Kotler & Lee, 2015).

These campaigns all deliver a key message to change behaviours for the social benefit of people and/or communities. While widely used to address health behaviours, and growing usage in fields such as human-environment impacts (e.g. sustainability, water use) social marketing remains a largely untapped strategy for addressing issues of educational inclusion. Examples of use in education-related fields include: with early childhood health and education professionals to improve awareness of autism (Daniel, Prue, Taylor, Thomas, & Scales, 2009) and being recommended as a method for improving information about early childhood services for vulnerable parents in the Australian Capital Territory (Winkworth, McArthur, Layton, & Thompson, 2010)

Background to Social Marketing

Social marketing is described as having 'first' presented itself (Kotler & Zaltman, 1971) when a question was raised in 1952 by G. D. Wiebe "*Why can't you sell brotherhood like you sell soap*" (Wiebe, 1951, p. 679). This question sparked the thinking of broadening marketing to include a social aspect. There has been discussion regarding broadening marketing to consider social impacts, as well as how it is defined. We mention here a few significant moments that have considerably impacted and contributed to the development of the social marketing discipline.

In the late 1960s, Philip Kotler and Sidney Levy argued in their paper *Broadening the Concept of Marketing*, that "no attempt had been made to redefine the meaning [of this social aspect and that] no attempt is made to examine whether the principles of 'good' marketing in traditional product areas are transferrable to the marketing of services, persons and ideas" (1969, p. 10). Two years later Kolter and Zaltman (1971) proposed that it was in Kotler and Levy's (1969) article that social marketing is regarded as being when it was officially formalised.

It is important to mention there has also been a history of alternatives to how social marketing has been described. From the idea of broadening the concept of marketing (Kotler & Levy, 1969) and the 'birth' of social marketing (Kotler & Zaltman, 1971), there have been for instance, contributions to the definition, domain and criteria of social marketing, as is exemplified in the work of Andreasen (1984, 1994, 1995, 2002; Andreasen & Mirabella, 2006). Proposed alternatives and frameworks put forward to the discipline, include but are not limited to community based social marketing (McKenzie-Mohr, 2000a, 2000b), critical social marketing (Gordon, 2011), macro-level social marketing (Kennedy, 2017), and social counter marketing (Bellew, Bauman, Freeman, & Kite, 2017). Other researchers have contributed in relation to broadening from individual behaviours to include social determinants of behaviour (Collins, Tapp, & Pressley, 2010); researching the social marketing concept of nudging (French, 2011) to identifying best practices among Aboriginal people (Madill, Wallace, Goneau-Lessard, Stuart MacDonald, & Dion, 2014), identifying the multiple layers of social marketing (Dibb & Carrigan, 2013); different theories (Kamin & Anker, 2014; Luca, Hibbert, & McDonald, 2016); proposing a hierarchical model of principles, concepts and techniques (French & Russell-Bennett, 2015); and putting forward an agenda for social marketing research (Rundle-Thiele, 2015).

An international journal, *Social Marketing Quarterly*, was established in 1994 that is dedicated to theoretical research and practical issues confronting social marketers, and there are annual national and international conferences devoted to social marketing where delegates from across the world come together to network, share research and expertise. Other journals include: *The Journal of Social Marketing*, with volumes commencing in 2011. Reflecting the growing interest in the discipline as well as degree specialisation, a number of textbooks have been written about social marketing. These textbooks also tend to place emphasis on how to develop social marketing interventions (Andreasen & Mirabella, 2006; French, 2017a; French & Gordon, 2015; Hastings, 2007; Lee & Kotler, 2011). Furthermore, there are social marketing training courses that have become readily available and include basic introductions to advanced specialist topics offered through dedicated training centres e.g. National Social Marketing Centre (NSMC). Currently there are two annual international social marketing conferences, the World Social Marketing conference and the International Social Marketing Association conference.

Becoming a popular approach (especially in relation to health issues), social marketing has been the subject of numerous reviews. These reviews cover areas such as: effectiveness (Firestone, Rowe, Modi, & Sievers, 2017; Stead, McDermott, & Hastings, 2007); sustainability (Brennan & Binney, 2008); involvement of stakeholders (Buyucek, Kubacki, Rundle-Thiele, & Pang, 2016); nutrition and physical health early care (Luecking et al., 2017). A systematic review of the development of social marketing by Truong (2014) provides a detailed account of the discipline. Covering the time period 1998–2012, this systematic review found the United States led the research in the field with 56.9% of research contributions. By comparison, the United Kingdom had 11.5%, Australia 5.7% and Canada 5.1% (Truong, 2014). Public health had the highest volume of research over the 14-year period (e.g. smoking and alcohol prevention/cessation, chronic illness and physical activity), and global health epidemics (e.g. use of condoms, HIV/AIDS and malaria). Other areas reported, but not at the same volume of research as public health and global health epidemics, include public safety (e.g. transportation and traffic), environmental protection (e.g. waste reduction/recycling), tourism and leisure, civil society, poverty, community outreach, and publications on social marketing such as on concepts, processes and theory. The latter include research papers on social marketing benchmark criteria and the techniques, principles, and marketing mix elements (Edgar, Huhman, & Miller, 2015; Fry, Previte, & Brennan, 2017; Huhman, Kelly, & Edgar, 2017; Kubacki & Szablewska, 2017; Truong, 2014).

Defining Social Marketing

Kotler and Zaltman (1971) emphasised that marketing techniques are simply the conduit to engage the target audience and that social marketing is about the effectiveness to communicate knowledge and how to use that knowledge in the exchange process. Their original definition is:

> Social marketing is the design, implementation and control of programs calculated to influence the acceptability of social ideas and involving considerations of product planning, pricing, communication, distribution and marketing research. (Kotler & Zaltman, 1971, p. 5)

Since this early definition there has, not surprisingly, been transformations in how social marketing is defined. Andreasen (1994) found the original definition proved problematic, and was "routinely (and often uncritically) repeated" and "an overly broad definition" (p. 5). Putting forward a new definition, Andreasen emphasised keeping social marketers focused on the outcome to influence:

> Social marketing is the adaptation of commercial marketing technologies to the analysis, planning, execution, and evaluation of programs designed to influence the behavior of target audiences in order to improve their physical and mental wellbeing and or that of the society of which they are a part. (1994, p. 110)

More recently a consensus definition was formed by a working group consisting of the Australian Association of Social Marketing (AASM), European Social Marketing Association (ESMA) and the International Social Marketing Association (iSMA). The definition was published in 2013:

> Social Marketing seeks to develop and integrate marketing concepts with other approaches to influence behaviour that benefit individuals and communities for the greater social good. Social Marketing practice is guided by ethical principles. It seeks to integrate research, best practice, theory, audience and partnership insight, to inform the delivery of competition sensitive and segmented social change programmes that are effective, efficient, equitable and sustainable. (International Social Marketing Association, 2013)

This definition of social marketing is now the most widely referred to and accepted definition within the social marketing discipline. Yet while commonly used, there are discussions of refinement, as well as social marketing work that does not strictly follow this definition. A good example of this is the work that does not use or prioritise the focus on the influence of behaviour (Fry et al., 2017). Another that does not use the behaviour focus is the definition by Saunders, Barrington, and Sridharan, (2015), who explain that their definition "implies the following":

- Social marketing's core competency is in the application of marketing principles.
- Social marketing is concerned with both the effects (efficiency and effectiveness) and the process (equity, fairness and sustainability) of social marketing programmes.
- The application of marketing principles occurs through participatory actions of all stakeholders.
- Social marketing programmes aim to enable individuals and foster collective ideas and actions that are meaningful and valuable to those they are intended to benefit.
- Social marketing programmes seek to enable a set of opportunities, or "*substantial freedoms*", which individuals and collectives may choose to act upon.
- Social marketing recognises the rights of all individuals and collectives to act and bring about change that is self-defined and self-determined.
- Social marketing's purpose is to transform society for the greater good. (Saunders et al., 2015, p. 165, emphasis added)

We discuss this description further in Chapter 6, and note that, unlike the emphasis on behaviour, these authors draw from Sen's work on 'freedoms' and the capability approach (for an in-depth discussion see Harwood et al., 2017; Wilson-Strydom, 2015).

Benchmark Criteria

In 2002, the social marketing discipline had a significant development when Andreasen (2002) proposed the six-point benchmark criteria. The proposed new 'benchmark criteria' introduced a means to determine what is social marketing, and by consequence, what it is not. With a focus on including social change, the six-point criteria provided a much needed differentiation from commercial marketing and a way to identify social marketing (Andreasen, 2002). Andreasen's (2002, p. 7) "benchmarks for identifying an approach that could be legitimately called social marketing" are:

1. Behavior-change is the benchmark used to design and evaluate interventions.
2. Projects consistently use audience research to (a) understand target audiences at the outset of interventions (i.e. formative research), (b) routinely pretest interventions before they are implemented, and (c) monitor interventions as they are rolled out.
3. There is careful segmentation of target audiences to ensure maximum efficiency and effectiveness in the use of scarce resources.
4. The central element of any influence strategy is creating attractive and motivational exchanges with the target audiences.
5. The strategy attempts to use all four Ps of the traditional marketing mix; for example, it is not just advertising or communications. That is, it creates attractive benefit packages (products) while minimizing costs (price) wherever possible, making the exchange convenient and easy (place) and communicating powerful messages through media relevant to—and preferred by—target audiences (promotion).
6. Careful attention is paid to the competition faced by the desired behavior. (Andreasen, 2002, p. 7)

Since the inception of these six benchmarks in 2002, the criteria have been refined and adapted. French and Russell-Bennett (2015) in their discussion of the background to the benchmark criteria, explain that the next revision was one of the outcomes of a "review of social marketing by the UK Government" (p. 145) conducted in 2004, and led by French. An outcome from this review was French and Blair-Stevens' (2006) benchmarks, which both revised and extended on Andreasen's (2002) benchmarks. Published by the UK National Social Marketing Centre (NSMC), with two new criteria, "Customer Orientation" and "Insight". Their revision envisaged the benchmark criteria not as a strict process, but rather as elements that integrate with each other (French & Russell-Bennett, 2015). In addition to the two new concepts, the eight-point benchmark criteria also redefined the original six concepts.

These eight-point criteria are commonly used by social marketers and advocate the foundational basis for all interventions in behaviour change—an emphasis that, as we will go on to discuss, has been the subject of debate by some social marketers (Fry et al., 2017). French and Blair-Stevens' eight benchmark criteria are:

1. Clear focus on behavior, with specific behavioural goals
2. Uses consumer and/or market research
3. Is theory based and informed
4. Is insight driven
5. Uses exchange concept
6. Uses competition concept
7. Uses a segmentation approach (not just targeting)
8. Integrates a mix of methods mix. (National Social Marketing Centre, Blair-Stevens, Slater, & French, 2006)

The NSMC provides a detailed guide to social marketing, including a comprehensive description of the benchmark criteria (see www.thensmc. com/resource/social-marketing-benchmark-criteria).

While the eight-point benchmark criteria are highly regarded and endorsed as the concept to be used when creating health focused interventions (Firestone et al., 2017), others have contested the criteria and put forward debate that the benchmarks are not validated or tested and that the benchmark criteria's are still open to change (French & Russell-Bennett, 2015; Fry et al., 2017). There are proposals to adapt, refine and extend the eight-point criteria, such as the Hierarchical Model proposed by French and Russell-Bennett (2015). This proposal emphasises a 'core principal' of 'social value creation' which they point out "reflects the central feature of the consensus definition of social marketing developed by the iSMA, ESMA and AASM" (p. 149).

In a different approach, Robinson-Maynard suggested a 19-step benchmark of variables to develop a comprehensive model (Robinson-Maynard, Meaton, & Lowry, 2013). Examples of other proposed changes include operating a more strategic intervention (Kamin & Anker, 2014) and extension of the benchmarks to have a focus on service-dominant logic (Luca et al., 2016). Rundle-Thiele (2015) compared four different benchmark criteria to find common understanding, declaring that the underlying principles are as yet untested.

Merritt Kamin, Hussenöder, and Huibregtsen's (2017) discussion of social marketing in Europe demonstrates how US or UK benchmark criteria can challenge or confirm social marketing legitimacy. Assuming legitimacy to be based on benchmark criteria, the authors reported that if German social marketing was to be assessed against Andreasen's (2002) six-point social marketing criteria, "very few would be considered social marketing" (Merritt et al.,2017). As they explain "in a review of alcohol misuse prevention campaigns in German-speaking countries (Germany, Austria, and Switzerland), the authors found out that only 1 of the 31 campaigns analysed, fulfilled all six of the criteria" (Wettstein, Suzanne Suggs, & Lellig, 2012). Interestingly, four years later, two of the authors of this paper, Wettstein & Suggs (2016) published an article comparing benchmark criteria and a tool the authors devised, the Social Marketing Indicator (SMI). As they explain:

> This tool allows visualizing, in a detailed manner, to what extent the methods used in an intervention correspond to social marketing methods. The purpose of the SMI is to provide indications about the extent to which an intervention corresponds to social marketing. (Wettstein & Suggs, 2016, p. 4)

Wettstein and Suggs (2016) conclude that the SMI proves useful for identifying processes of social marketing in a way that the benchmark criteria do not. They do note, however, the usefulness of the benchmarks, expressing a preference of utilising both the SMI and the benchmarks. As they state:

> both assessment methods complement each other quite well. On the one hand, an SMI profile highlights the specific process steps that make the difference to social marketing, and on the other hand, the benchmarks give an overall picture of conceptual social marketing resemblance. (Wettstein & Suggs, 2016, p. 15)

This is another example of how the benchmarks are drawn upon to convey a sense of what social marketing *is*.

Taking a different angle, others have pointed out that the benchmarks tend to focus on the individual and their behaviour. For instance Fry et al. (2017) point out:

> While Andreasen's and the NSMC's benchmark criteria have been well received and globally applied, they are largely interpreted from a downstream micro-managerial individual behaviour change perspective. This is despite Kotler and Zaltman's (1971) seminal article advocating for a wider application of marketing to address social change situations. (2017, p. 120)

While the six benchmarks (Andreasen, 2002) and eight benchmarks (National Social Marketing Centre et al., 2006) are commonly referred to, another useful way to capture 'what is social marketing' is Lefebvre's description of 'the characteristics of social marketing'.

Lefebvre (2013) compared five sets of characteristics of social marketing made over four decades, using work by Kotler and Zaltman (1971), Lefebvre and Flora (1988), Walsh, Rudd, Moeykens, and Moloney (1993), Donovan & Henley (2010) and French and Blair-Stevens (2006). Through this comparison, Lefebvre observes "several common features of a social marketing approach ... [and] the consistently described characteristics of social marketing draw from managerial frameworks and approaches identified by Wilkie and Moore (2003, p. 35)". These characteristics

> include a consumer orientation, exchange and customer value, market analysis and segmentation (also referred to as selectivity and concentration), the use of a marketing mix to develop and implement programs (this mix includes products, pricing, place or distribution, and promotion or communication – collectively referred to as the 4Ps), various types of market or consumer research to test and refine offerings, and monitoring and effectiveness evaluations. (Lefebvre, 2013, p. 35)

This idea of the 'characteristics' demonstrates the way in which social marketing is, perhaps, best depicted through descriptions of the aspects that come together to constitute it.

Despite the ongoing debate, as well as the discussion of a revision of benchmarks, or even eschewing them, there continues to be a tendency to refer to the benchmarks to 'legitimate' social marketing research and programmes. It could be argued that ISMA definition of social marketing, eight-benchmark criteria, or possibly the legacy of Andreasen's (2002) six-point criteria, are what is the most drawn on to demarcate what is 'legitimately' social marketing.

The Processes of Social Marketing

Social marketing puts into train a set of processes, which while used in other disciplines (especially marketing), when drawn together with its focus on 'social change' or 'social good', is arguably unique; a combination that sets apart social marketing, making it distinctive and recognisable. Planning processes are used by social marketers to develop and deliver social marketing campaigns. Articulating the processes in social marketing is not only useful for conceptualising how to carry out social marketing, it also helps to get a nuanced grasp of how social marketing can be achieved. It is also, as we will discuss in detail in Chapters 4 and 6, a way to structure a critical cultural social marketing approach.

As with the benchmarks, there are various ways advocated for the planning for social marketing. There is also debate about the utility of older planning models. French drives this point home in his discussion of social marketing planning for public health, "For a diminishing number of social marketers the 4Ps of marketing (product, price, place, promotion) are still used for social marketing planning (Kotler, 2009; Weinreich, 2011). This model is based on a somewhat outdated view of what the marketing process is" (French, 2017b, p. 9).

One of the widely used descriptions of the social marketing process was produced by two established contributors to the social marketing literature, Kotler and Lee (2011, 2016, 2019). Their book, *Social Marketing, Behaviour Change for Social Good* (Lee & Kotler, 2019) is now in its sixth edition (with a change of title from earlier editions). Lee and Kotler (2011) advocate a ten-step planning process that uses the 4Ps of marketing as the 'marketing mix' (product, price, place and promotion). In their view "you will need all of them [the 4Ps] to create and deliver the value your target market expects in exchange for a new behavior" (Kotler & Lee, 2009,

p. 185). Their ten-step process is summarised in their 'Quick Reference Guide' (Lee & Kotler, 2015) and reproduced in Box 3.1.

Box 3.1 Lee & Kotler's ten steps in the planning process

Step 1 Describe the Background, Purpose and Focus for the Planning Effort
Step 2 Conduct a Situation analysis
Step 3 Select and Describe the Target Audience
Step 4 Set Marketing Objectives and Goals (Behavior, Knowledge, Beliefs)
Step 5 Identify Audience Barriers, Benefits, Motivators, and the Competition
Step 6 Craft a Desired Positioning Statement
Step 7 Develop a Strategic Marketing Intervention Mix (The 4Ps)
    Product
    Price
    Place
    Promotion
Step 8 Determine an Evaluation Plan
Step 9 Establish a Campaign Budget and Find Funding
Step 10 Outline an Implementation Plan

Although steps appear linear in theory, they are actually spiral in reality with each step subject to revision as the process unfolds. (Lee & Kotler, 2015)

The UK National Social Marketing Centre has a six-stage process, based on French and Blair-Stevens' five-stage Total Process Planning Model. In this model the stages are: scope; develop; implement; evaluate, and follow up (French & Blair-Stevens, 2008). The additional stage in NSMC materials is 'getting started' (National Social Marketing Centre, 2011), summarised in Box 3.2.

Box 3.2 National Social Marketing Centre's six stage planning process

Getting started Initial planning. "There are four areas you should think about at this stage:
  (i) The issue or challenge you want to address
 (ii) The resources and assets you might be able to draw on
(iii) Potential risks
(iv) Initial timescales

You may also want to think about how much original research into your target audience you will need to carry out..."

Scoping "The scoping phase is where you consider which interventions to select, based on what is most likely to achieve and sustain the desired outcome, given your resources."

Development "This is where the interventions selected as a result of scoping are taken forward. By this point you should have a good understanding of your audience. You will have analysed their behaviours and set goals, engaged with key stakeholders and produced a scoping report."

Implement "This is where your social marketing intervention goes live."

Evaluation "At this stage, you formally review the intervention's impact."

Follow-up "The follow-up stage is when the results of the evaluation are considered by you and your stakeholders." (National Social Marketing Centre, 2011, pp. 79–90)

Other planning examples include Hastings (2007, p. 52) 'social marketing plan', that is adapted from Hastings and Elliot (1993). Hastings' (2007) plan is represented in a diagram that includes the components situational analysis, stakeholder analysis; who: segmentation and targeting; what: objectives; how: formulating the offer—product, price, promotion, place, implementation, monitoring. All of these steps are connected to Market/Consumer Research (Hastings, 2007, p. 52).

These different planning processes don't necessarily follow a lock-step approach. Rather as Lee & Kotler point out, "Although steps appear linear in theory, they are actually spiral in reality with each step subject to revision as the process unfolds" (Lee & Kotler, 2015). Similarly, Hastings (2007) emphasises it is a cyclical process and refers to the 'gestalt of marketing planning' (p. 52), and points out that, "As well as providing the tactical support through various marketing tools, planning also guides strategic thinking. This idea of progressive and continuous learning is absolutely fundamental to social marketing" (2007, p. 53).

Components of the social marketing benchmarks (Andreasen, 2002; National Social Marketing Centre et al., 2006) can be identified in both Lee and Kotler's (2019) and the NSMC's (2011) planning processes for social marketing. Take for instance 'segmentation'. Segmentation is included in the two benchmark criteria described above (Andreasen, 2002,

p. 7; French & Blair-Stevens, 2006). Likewise, segmentation is included in Lee and Kotler's (2015) *Step 3 Target Audience*, and in the NSMC planning process, in *Stage 2, Scoping*.

Behaviour and the Marketing Mix

We now turn to discuss two of the components or characteristics (Lefebvre, 2013) frequently argued to be required for social marketing: firstly influencing behaviour and behaviour change, and secondly the marketing mix. Before continuing, we note that again, this is a summary of selected components, and that detailed accounts are available in the social marketing literature.

Influencing Behaviour and Behaviour Change

Influencing behaviour and behaviour change is included in the Consensus Definition of Social Marketing (International Social Marketing Association, 2013) agreed to by the key social marketing associations: the Australian Association of Social Marketing (AASM); the European Social Marketing Association (ESMA); and the International Social Marketing Association (iSMA). The definition, (cited previously in this chapter), begins, "Social Marketing seeks to develop and integrate marketing concepts with other approaches to influence behaviour" (International Social Marketing Association, 2013). Yet behavioural influence is a topic of discussion and rethinking, despite the focus on it in this Consensus Definition (Wettstein & Suggs, 2016).

As well as the emphasis on behaviour not always being strictly adhered to, there is the point made by Lefebvre (2013) that "behavior change is far from being a distinguishing feature of social marketing anymore … many other change agents also claim behaviour change as their ultimate criterion of success" (p. 37). Others have made a direct charge at social marketing and its behavioural change emphasis, arguing "it was associated with a neoliberal approach that attributes responsibility for managing personal and social well-being to individuals (Crawshaw, 2012; Crawshaw & Newlove,

2011; Gould & Semaan, 2014; Gurrieri, Previte, & Brace-Govan, 2013; R. Jones, Pykett, & Whitehead, 2011)" (Luca et al., 2016, p. 196).

Such criticism includes not only examinations of social marketing as an entity—but also how it is used to govern people. For instance, Jones et al. (2011) mount an argument that heavily criticises the UK government's "libertarian paternalism", which it is able to expertly exercise with the deployment of methods such as the "softer powers" of social marketing to influence behaviour (p. 488). A critique by Mols Haslam, Jetten, and Steffens (2015) picks up on the use of 'nudging tactics' by the UK government.

These critiques are carefully considered in the Editorial for 'Advancing Theory and Research in Strategic Social Marketing', a special issue of the *Journal of Marketing Management* (Gordon et al., 2016). Here social marketers are described as responding to concerns over "individual behavioural change" that include "the emergence of systems thinking, multilevel and component intervention approaches and upstream/ecological systems level thinking" (Gordon et al., 2016, p. 1066). These approaches are noted by Mols et al. (2015) in their argument for more attention to be paid to social identity theory, and the emphasis this plays on how the identities of people connect with identity groups and how things such as group norms are influential. As they put it, "it is not so much the informational quality of a message that determines whether people will be responsive to it, but the social identity that it speaks to" (Mols et al., 2015, p. 88).

Relatively recent work by Fry et al. (2017) suggests a more 'ecological focus'. Here attention is drawn to 'value shaping' which "is the process whereby value is created and shared within the system of activities that constitutes the marketspace" (Fry et al., 2017, p. 129). They note that the emphasis on behavioural change or influence tends to be a downstream focus and concentrated on changing an individual's behaviour. Here behavioural change is conceptualised as an individualised matter. Alternately, Fry et al. describe:

> a markets-based social change purview extends conceptualisation of social marketing as a set of value-shaping activities requiring the intersection of multiple layers and actors in the ecosystem all with (different) goals and

objectives (Brennan, Previte, & Fry, 2016; Domegan et al., 2016). (Fry et al., 2017, p. 120)

They also make their case that their orientation:

> aligns with and responds to Kotler and Zaltman's (1971), as well as Andreasen's (1995), earlier conceptualisations of social marketing that advocate for engagement with more actors within the ecosystem (e.g. organisations, government and non-government service providers and policymakers), rather than focusing on individual consumers (i.e. the target audience) who exhibit or are prone to bad behavior. (Fry et al., 2017, p. 121)

Drawing on their analysis of social marketing and alcohol use, Fry et al. (2017) explain that, "A systems orientation aims to leverage the process of value sharing across individuals, institutions and organisations in the system" (Fry et al., 2017, p. 129). Value shaping could be characterised as either the value shaping of individuals or one that takes a broader perspective and considers the value shaping across interleaving connections, from individuals to institutions.

Interestingly, such ideas indicate that in the social marketing literature there are not only shifts in the conceptualization of what social marketing might be seeking to do, but also in how problems are conceptualised. As we discuss in Chapter 4, this is a crucial point; and as we have outlined, how problems are conceptualised is very much a concern of the activity of critique.

Marketing Mix

The marketing mix is another feature of social marketing. Originating in marketing, the 'marketing mix' is frequently connected with the 4Ps—product, price, place and promotion, a marketing concept that is popularly used and is also regularly debated. Lee and Kotler (2011) in their textbook refer to them as "marketing mix strategies" and the 4Ps "represent the fundamental building blocks of Social Marketing" (Lee & Kotler, 2011, p. 18). As Peattie and Peattie (2011) explain in their review, "it was McCarthy's (1964) simpler four 'P' factors of product, price, place and promotion that successfully captured the imagination, and lodged in the memory banks, of the marketing community" (Peattie & Peattie, 2011, p. 155). Based on their critical review, Peattie and Peattie suggest a 'social marketing mix':

- Social propositions—instead of products.
- Social cost of involvement—(including any financial costs) instead of price.
- Accessibility—instead of place.
- Social communication—instead of promotion; and adds.
- Stakeholder involvement—to reflect the frequent importance in delivering social campaigns of a mix of stakeholder contributions. (Peattie and Peattie, 2011, p. 168)

A fifth 'p' considered critical to the success of developing and implementing social marketing campaigns is 'partnerships' (French, 2010). In Chapter 4 we return to these suggestions in the context of creating the Lead My Learning campaign.

As stated above, the notion of 4Ps as *the* marketing mix is also critiqued and/or revised. Hastings (2007) points out that while "for some, [these are] the core tools of marketing … this construct has been criticised in the marketing literature over the last 10 years for being too mechanistic and naïve to handle complex marketing situations such as service provision … [and] the challenging behaviours typically being addressed by social marketers" (2007, p. 71). That said, Hasting's does not dismiss the 4Ps, suggesting "it needs to be used with care and subtlety" (p. 71).

Revision of the marketing mix includes explicit critique of the 4Ps in terms of sociocultural contexts. For example, based on their research in India, Wasan and Tripathi (2014) point to the Western emphasis of the 4Ps and argue for extending the social marketing mix to be inclusive of sociocultural factors. They exclude the 4Ps, replacing these with Policy, People, Process, Physical evidence, Publics, Partnerships and Policy (Wasan & Tripathi, 2014).

Thinking Differently About Social Marketing

As can be seen from the discussion in this chapter, social marketing is a relatively new discipline that while working to build an identity, continues to be revised and developed. The work to achieve a definition, as well as ongoing reference to benchmarks and criteria indicate the importance that is placed on defining the discipline.

Arguably, then, there is space for thinking differently about social marketing techniques, such as the insistence on behavioural influence—even if doing so risks being judged as not meeting the definition of social marketing. This is an important discussion to reflect on given that we have advocated prioritising the critical and cultural, and having this prioritisation steer our work in creating a social marketing campaign. This raises the question of at what point a decision can be made—or how far can a campaign go before it risks not 'fitting' the social marketing mould? Our view is that in prioritising critique and culture, we err on how this guides us, and in the following chapters we provide robust explanations for our decisions.

In Chapter 4, to which we now turn, we provide a description of critical cultural social marketing, and explain how this was used to create the Lead My Learning campaign.

References

Almosa, Y., Parkinson, J., & Rundle-Thiele, S. (2017). Littering reduction: A systematic review of research 1995–2015. *Social Marketing Quarterly, 23*(3), 203–222. https://doi.org/10.1177/1524500417697654.

Andreasen, A. R. (1984). A power potential approach to middlemen strategies in social marketing. *European Journal of Marketing, 18*(4), 56. https://doi.org/10.1108/EUM0000000004786.

Andreasen, A. R. (1994). Social marketing: Its definition and domain. *Journal of Public Policy and Marketing, 13*(1), 108. https://doi.org/10.1177/074391569401300109.

Andreasen, A. R. (1995). *Marketing social change: Changing behaviour to promote health, social development and the environment.* San Francisco: Josey-Bass.

Andreasen, A. R. (2002). Marketing social marketing in the social change marketplace. *Journal of Public Policy and Marketing, 21*(1), 3–13.

Andreasen, A. R., & Mirabella, R. (2006). *Social marketing in the 21st century* (Vol. 17, pp. 235–237). Thousand Oaks: Sage.

Bellew, W., Bauman, A., Freeman, B., & Kite, J. (2017). Social countermarketing: Brave new world, brave new map. *Journal of Social Marketing, 7*(2), 205–222. https://doi.org/10.1108/JSOCM-09-2016-0052.

Brennan, L., & Binney, W. (2008). Concepts in conflict: Social marketing and sustainability. *Journal of Nonprofit & Public Sector Marketing, 20*(2), 261–281. https://doi.org/10.1080/10495140802224951.

Brennan, L., Previte, J., & Fry, M.-L. (2016). Social marketing's consumer myopia. *Journal of Social Marketing, 6*(3), 219–239. https://doi.org/10.1108/JSOCM-12-2015-0079.

Bryant-Stephens, T., Garcia-Espana, J., & Winston, F. (2013). Boosting restraint norms: A community-delivered campaign to promote booster seat use. *Traffic Injury Prevention, 14*(6), 578–583. https://doi.org/10.1080/15389588.2012.733840.

Butler, J. (2001). *What is critique? An essay on Foucault's virtue.* Retrieved from http://eipcp.net/transversal/0806/butler/en.html.

Buyucek, N., Kubacki, K., Rundle-Thiele, S., & Pang, B. (2016). A systematic review of stakeholder involvement in social marketing interventions. *Australasian Marketing Journal (AMJ), 24*(1), 8–19. https://doi.org/10.1016/j.ausmj.2015.11.001.

Collins, K., Tapp, A., & Pressley, A. (2010). Social marketing and social influences: Using social ecology as a theoretical framework. *Journal of Marketing Management, 26*(13/14), 1181. https://doi.org/10.1080/0267257X.2010.522529.

Crawshaw, P. (2012). Governing at a distance: Social marketing and the (bio) politics of responsibility. *Social Science and Medicine, 75*(1), 200–207. https://doi.org/10.1016/j.socscimed.2012.02.040.

Crawshaw, P., & Newlove, C. (2011). Men's understandings of social marketing and health: Neo-liberalism and health governance. *International Journal of Men's Health, 10*(2), 136. https://doi.org/10.3149/jmh.1002.136.

Daniel, K. L., Prue, C., Taylor, M. K., Thomas, J., & Scales, M. (2009). 'Learn the signs. Act early': A campaign to help every child reach his or her full potential. *Public Health, 123*(1), e11–e16.

Dibb, S., & Carrigan, M. (2013). Social marketing transformed: Kotler, Polonsky and hastings reflect on social marketing in a period of social change. *European Journal of Marketing, 47*(9). https://doi.org/10.1108/ejm-05-2013-0248.

Dietrich, T., Rundle-Thiele, S., & Kubacki, K. (2017). *Segmentation in social marketing: Process, methods and application.* Singapore: Springer.

Domegan, C., McHugh, P., Devaney, M., Duane, S., Hogan, M., Broome, B. J., … Piwowarczyk, J. (2016). Systems-thinking social marketing: Conceptual extensions and empirical investigations. *Journal of Marketing Management, 32*(11–12), 1123–1144. https://doi.org/10.1080/0267257x.2016.1183697.

Donovan, R. J., & Henley, N. (2010). *Principles and practice of social marketing: An international perspective.* Cambridge: Cambridge University Press.

Edgar, T., Huhman, M., & Miller, G. (2015). Understanding "place" in social marketing: A systematic review. *Social Marketing Quarterly, 21*(4), 230.

Firestone, R., Rowe, C. J., Modi, S. N., & Sievers, D. (2017). The effectiveness of social marketing in global health: A systematic review. *Health Policy and Planning, 32*(1), 110–124. https://doi.org/10.1093/heapol/czw088.

Foucault, M. (1997). What is critique? In S. Lotringer & L. Hochroth (Eds.), *The politics of truth: Michel Foucault* (pp. 23–82). New York: Semiotext(e).

French, J. (2010). Social marketing on a shoestring budget. In J. French, C. Blair-Stevens, D. McVey, & R. Merritt (Eds.), *Social marketing and public health: Theory and practice* (pp. 248–262). Oxford: Oxford University Press.

French, J. (2011). Why nudging is not enough. *Journal of Social Marketing, 1*(2), 154–162. https://doi.org/10.1108/20426761111141896.

French, J. (2017a). *Social marketing and public health* (2nd ed.). Oxford: Oxford University Press.

French, J. (2017b). Social marketing planning. In J. French (Ed.), *Social marketing and public health: Theory and practice* (2nd ed.). Oxford: Oxford University Press.

French, J., & Blair-Stevens, C. (2006). *The big pocket guide to social marketing.* London: National Consumer Council, National Social Marketing Centre.

French, J., & Blair-Stevens, C. (2008). *The total process planning framework for social marketing.* London: National Social Marketing Centre.

French, J., & Gordon, R. (2015). *Strategic social marketing.* Los Angeles: Sage.

French, J., & Russell-Bennett, R. (2015). A hierarchical model of social marketing. *Journal of Social Marketing, 5*(2), 139–159. https://doi.org/10.1108/JSOCM-06-2014-0042.

Fry, M.-L., Previte, J., & Brennan, L. (2017). Social change design: Disrupting the benchmark template. *Journal of Social Marketing, 7*(2), 119–134. https://doi.org/10.1108/jsocm-10-2016-0064.

Gordon, R. (2011). Critical social marketing: Definition, application and domain. *Journal of Social Marketing, 1*(2), 82–99. https://doi.org/10.1108/20426761111141850.

Gordon, R., Russell-Bennett, R., & Lefebvre, R. C. (2016). Social marketing: The state of play and brokering the way forward. *Journal of Marketing Management, 32*(11–12), 1059–1082. https://doi.org/10.1080/0267257X.2016.1199156.

Gould, S., & Semaan, R. W. (2014). Avoiding throwing out the baby with the bathwater: Critically deconstructing contested positions on social and macromarketing in the health domain. *Journal of Macromarketing, 34*(4), 520–531. https://doi.org/10.1177/0276146714530165.

Grier, S., & Bryant, C. A. (2005). Social marketing in public health. *Annual Review of Public Health, 26*, 319–339. https://doi.org/10.1146/annurev.publhealth.26.021304.144610.

Gurrieri, L., Previte, J., & Brace-Govan, J. (2013). Women's bodies as sites of control: Inadvertent stigma and exclusion in social marketing. *Journal of Macromarketing, 33*(2), 128. https://doi.org/10.1177/0276146712469971.

Harwood, V., Hickey-Moody, A., McMahon, S., & O'Shea, S. (2017). *The politics of widening participation and university access for young people: Making educational futures*. London: Routledge.

Harwood, V., & Murray, N. (2019). Strategic discourse production and parent involvement: Including parent knowledge and practices in the Lead My Learning campaign. *International Journal of Inclusive Education, 23*(4), 353–368. https://doi.org/10.1080/13603116.2019.1571119.

Harwood, V., & Rasmussen, M. L. (2004). Studying schools with an ethic of discomfort. In B. Baker & K. Heyning (Eds.), *Dangerous coagulations? The uses of Foucault in the study of education* (pp. 305–321). New York: Peter Lang.

Hastings, G. (2007). *Social marketing: Why should the devil have all the best tunes?* London and Amsterdam: Elsevier/Butterworth-Heinemann.

Hastings, G. B. (2009). Critical social marketing. In J. French, C. Blair-Stevens, D. McVey, & R. Merritt (Eds.), *Social marketing and public health: Theory and practice* (pp. 263–280). Oxford: Oxford University Press.

Hastings, G. B., & Elliot, B. (1993). Social marketing practice in traffic safety. In *Marketing of traffic safety* (pp. 33–53, Chapter III). Paris: OECD.

Hue, D. T., Brennan, L., Parker, L., & Florian, M. (2015). But I am normal: Safe? Driving in Vietnam. *Journal of Social Marketing, 5*(2), 105–124. https://doi.org/10.1108/JSOCM-07-2013-0048.

Huhman, M., Kelly, R. P., & Edgar, T. (2017). Social marketing as a framework for youth physical activity initiatives: A 10-year retrospective on the legacy of CDC's VERB campaign. *Current Obesity Reports, 6*(2), 101. https://doi.org/10.1007/s13679-017-0252-0.

International Social Marketing Association. (2013). *Social marketing definition*. Retrieved from https://www.i-socialmarketing.org/social-marketing-definition#.XD1nqHozbu4.

Johnson, K. M., Jones, S. C., & Iverson, D. (2009). Guidelines for the development of social marketing programmes for sun protection among adolescents and young adults (Report). *Public Health, 123*, e6–e10.

Jones, R., Pykett, J., & Whitehead, M. (2011). Governing temptation: Changing behaviour in an age of libertarian paternalism. *Progress in Human Geography, 35*(4), 483–501. https://doi.org/10.1177/0309132510385741.

Jones, S., Andrews, K., & Francis, K. (2017). Combining social norms and social marketing to address underage drinking: Development and process evaluation of a whole-of-community intervention. *PLoS ONE, 12*(1), e0169872. https://doi.org/10.1371/journal.pone.0169872.

Kamin, T., & Anker, T. (2014). Cultural capital and strategic social marketing orientations. *Journal of Social Marketing, 4*(2), 94–110. https://doi.org/10.1108/JSOCM-08-2013-0057.

Kemp, G., Eagle, L., & Verne, J. (2011). Mass media barriers to social marketing interventions: The example of sun protection in the UK. *Health Promotion International, 26*(1), 37–45. https://doi.org/10.1093/heapro/daq048.

Kennedy, A.-M. (2017). Macro-social marketing research: Philosophy, methodology and methods. *Journal of Macromarketing, 37*(4), 347–355. https://doi.org/10.1177/0276146717735467.

Kotler, P., & Lee, N. (2009). *Up and out of poverty: The social marketing solution*. Upper Saddle River, NJ: Wharton School Publishing.

Kotler, P., & Lee, N. (2015). *Up and out of poverty: The social marketing solution*. Upper Saddle River, NJ: Pearson Education.

Kotler, P., & Levy, S. (1969). Broadening the concept of marketing. *Journal of Marketing (pre-1986), 33*(000001), 10.

Kotler, P., & Zaltman, G. (1971). Social marketing: An approach to planned social change. *Journal of Marketing, 35*(3), 3. https://doi.org/10.2307/1249783.

Kubacki, K., & Rundle-Thiele, S. (Eds.). (2017). *Formative research in social marketing innovative methods to gain consumer insights*. Singapore: Springer.

Kubacki, K., & Szablewska, N. (2017). Social marketing targeting Indigenous peoples: A systematic review. *Health Promotion International, 34*, 133–143. https://doi.org/10.1093/heapro/dax060.

Ladero, M. M. G., & Alves, H. M. (Eds.). (2019). *Case studies on social marketing: A global perspective*. Cham, Switzerland: Springer.

Lee, N. R., & Kotler, P. (2011). *Social marketing: Influencing behaviors for good* (4th ed.). Thousand Oaks, CA: Sage.

Lee, N. R., & Kotler, P. (2015). Social marketing influencing behaviours for good: Quick reference guide. In *Social marketing services* (5th ed.). Mercer Island, WA: Social Marketing Services.

Lee, N. R., & Kotler, P. (2016). *Social Marketing: Changing Behaviours for Good* New York: Free Press.

Lee, N. R., & Kotler, P. (2019). *Social marketing: Behavior change for social good* (6th ed.). Thousand Oaks, CA: Sage.

Lefebvre, R. C. (2013). *Social marketing and social change: Strategies and tools for improving health, well-being, and the environment.* Chichester: Wiley.

Lefebvre, R., & Flora, J. (1988, Fall). Social marketing and public health intervention. *Health Education Quarterly, 15*(88), 298–315.

Lowe, B., Lynch, D., & Lowe, J. (2015). Reducing household water consumption: A social marketing approach. *Journal of Marketing Management, 31*(3–4), 378–408. https://doi.org/10.1080/0267257X.2014.971044.

Luca, N. R., Hibbert, S., & McDonald, R. (2016). Towards a service-dominant approach to social marketing. *Marketing Theory, 16*(2), 194–218. https://doi.org/10.1177/1470593115607941.

Luecking, C. T., Hennink-Kaminski, H., Ihekweazu, C., Vaughn, A., Mazzucca, S., & Ward, D. S. (2017). Social marketing approaches to nutrition and physical activity interventions in early care and education centres: A systematic review. *Obesity Reviews, 18*, 1425–1438.

Madill, J., Wallace, L., Goneau-Lessard, K., Stuart MacDonald, R., & Dion, C. (2014). Best practices in social marketing among Aboriginal people. *Journal of Social Marketing, 4*(2), 155–175. https://doi.org/10.1108/JSOCM-08-2013-0056.

McKenzie-Mohr, D. (2000a). Fostering sustainable behavior through community-based social marketing. *American Psychologist, 55*(5), 531–537. https://doi.org/10.1037/0003-066X.55.5.531.

McKenzie-Mohr, D. (2000b). Promoting sustainable behavior: An introduction to community-based social marketing. *Journal of Social Issues, 56*(3), 543.

McLeod, G., Insch, A., & Henry, J. (2011). Reducing barriers to sun protection—Application of a holistic model for social marketing. *Australasian Marketing Journal (AMJ), 19*(3), 212–222. https://doi.org/10.1016/j.ausmj.2011.05.008.

McMahon, S., Harwood, V., & Hickey-Moody, A. (2016). 'Students that just hate school wouldn't go': Educationally disengaged and disadvantaged young people's talk about university education. *British Journal of Sociology of Education, 37*(8), 1109–1128. https://doi.org/10.1080/01425692.2015.1014546.

Merritt, R. K., Kamin, T., Hussenöder, F., & Huibregtsen, J. (2017). The history of social marketing in Europe: The story so far. *Social Marketing Quarterly, 23*(4), 291–301. https://doi.org/10.1177/1524500417732771.

Mols, F., Haslam, S. A., Jetten, J., & Steffens, N. K. (2015). Why a nudge is not enough: A social identity critique of governance by stealth. *European Journal of Political Research, 54*(1), 81–98. https://doi.org/10.1111/1475-6765.12073.

National Social Marketing Centre (Ed.). (2011). *Big pocket guide to using social marketing for behaviour change*. London: NSMC.

National Social Marketing Centre, Blair-Stevens, C., Slater, C., & French, J. (2006). *Social marketing benchmark criteria*. Retrieved from www.thensmc.com/file/244/download?token=S74a2YN9.

Opel, D., Diekema, D. S., Lee, N. R., & Marcuse, E. K. (2009). Social marketing as a strategy to increase immunization rates. *JAMA Pediatrics, 163*(5), 432–437.

Oxford English Dictionary. (2018). *Promotion, n*. Oxford: Oxford University Press.

Peattie, K., & Peattie, S. (2011). The social marketing mix: A critical review. In G. Hastings, K. Angus, & C. Bryant, A (Eds.), *The SAGE handbook of social marketing* (pp. 152–166). London: Sage.

Potter, S. J., & Stapleton, J. G. (2012). Translating sexual assault prevention from a college campus to a United States military installation: Piloting the know-your-power bystander social marketing campaign. *Journal of Interpersonal Violence, 27*(8), 1593–1621. https://doi.org/10.1177/0886260511425795.

Robinson-Maynard, A., Meaton, J., & Lowry, R. (2013). Identifying key criteria as predictors of success in social marketing: Establishing an evaluation template and grid (ETG). In K. Kubacki & S. Rundle-Thiele (Eds.), *Contemporary issues in social marketing* (pp. 41–58). Newcastle upon Tyne: Cambridge Scholars Publishing.

Rundle-Thiele, S. (2015). Looking back and moving forwards: An agenda for social marketing research. *Recherche et Applications En Marketing (English Edition), 30*(3), 128–133. https://doi.org/10.1177/2051570715599338.

Saunders, S. G., Barrington, D. J., & Sridharan, S. (2015). Redefining social marketing: Beyond behavioural change. *Journal of Social Marketing, 5*(2), 160–168. https://doi.org/10.1108/JSOCM-03-2014-0021.

Sewak, A., & Singh, G. (2017). Integrating social marketing into Fijian HIV/AIDS prevention programs: Lessons from systematic review. *Health Communication, 32*(1), 32–40. https://doi.org/10.1080/10410236.2015.1099500.

Stead, M., McDermott, L., & Hastings, G. (2007). Towards evidence-based marketing: The case of childhood obesity. *Marketing Theory, 7*(4), 379–406. https://doi.org/10.1177/1470593107083163.

Suarez-Almazor, M. E. (2011). Changing health behaviors with social marketing. *Osteoporosis International: A journal Established as Result of Cooperation Between the European Foundation for Osteoporosis and the National Osteoporosis Foundation of the USA, 22*(Suppl. 3), 461–463. https://doi.org/10.1007/s00198-011-1699-6.

Thrasher, J. F., Huang, L., Perez-Hernandez, R., Niederdeppe, J., Arillo-Santillan, E., & Alday, J. (2011). Evaluation of a social marketing campaign to support Mexico City's comprehensive smoke-free law (Research and Practice) (Author abstract) (Report). *The American Journal of Public Health, 101*(2), 328. https://doi.org/10.2105/ajph.2009.189704.

Truong, V. D. (2014). Social marketing: A systematic review of research 1998–2012. *Social Marketing Quarterly, 20*(1), 15–34. https://doi.org/10.1177/1524500413517666.

Walsh, D., Rudd, R., Moeykens, B., & Moloney, T. (1993). Social marketing for public health. *Health Affairs, 12*(2), 104–119.

Wasan, P. G., & Tripathi, G. (2014). Revisiting social marketing mix: A sociocultural perspective. *Journal of Services Research, 14*(2), 127.

Weinreich, N. K. (2011). *Hands-on social marketing a step-by-step guide to designing change for good* (2nd ed.). Los Angeles, CA: Sage.

Wettstein, D., & Suggs, L. S. (2016). Is it social marketing? The benchmarks meet the social marketing indicator. *Journal of Social Marketing, 6*(1), 2–17. https://doi.org/10.1108/jsocm-05-2014-0034.

Wettstein, D., Suzanne Suggs, L., & Lellig, C. (2012). Social marketing and alcohol misuse prevention in German-speaking countries. *Journal of Social Marketing, 2*(3), 187–206. https://doi.org/10.1108/20426761211265186.

Wiebe, G. (1951). Merchandising commodities and citizenship on television. *The Public Opinion Quarterly, 15*, 679.

Wilkie, W. L., & Moore, E. S. (2003). Scholarly research in marketing: Exploring the "4 eras" of thought development. *Journal of Public Policy & Marketing, 22*(2), 116–146. https://doi.org/10.1509/jppm.22.2.116.17639.

Wilson-Strydom, M. (2015). *University access and success: Capabilities, diversity and social justice.* Oxford: Routledge.

Winkworth, G., McArthur, M., Layton, M., & Thompson, L. (2010). Someone to check in on me: Social capital, social support and vulnerable parents with very young children in the Australian Capital Territory. *Child and Family Social Work, 15*, 206–215.

Wong, M. L. (2002). Can social marketing be applied to leprosy programmes? *Leprosy Review, 73*(4), 308–318.

Wright, J., & Harwood, V. (Eds.). (2009). *Biopolitics and the 'obesity epidemic': Governing bodies.* New York: Routledge.

Zambon, F., Hyder, A., & Peden, M. (2012). Increasing seat belt use in the Russian context: Tailored social marketing campaign and concerted strengthened enforcement. *Injury Prevention, 18*(Suppl. 1), A245–A245. https://doi.org/10.1136/injuryprev-2012-040590w.69.

4

Engaging a Critical and Cultural Emphasis to Create a Campaign That Promotes Education

In this chapter we begin by describing what we mean by critical cultural social marketing. We then explain what occurred when we engaged a critical and cultural emphasis in our approach to create an education promotion campaign. This is the first of the chapters in this book that brings together an overview of how a critical cultural social marketing approach was drawn on to create the Lead My Learning campaign. The Lead My Learning campaign is described in detail in Chapter 5. Chapter 6 provides a close analysis of how a critical cultural social marketing approach was used to adapt social marketing concepts and techniques to create Lead My Learning. Chapter 6 is where we get into the 'nitty gritty' of how the emphasis on the critical cultural was applied to crafting the Lead My Learning campaign. Our objectives in this chapter and the next two chapters are to firstly, discuss a critical cultural social marketing approach and secondly, to share the Lead My Learning campaign. Thirdly, we describe how we employed a critical cultural social marketing approach to produce the educational promotion campaign—Lead My Learning.

© The Author(s) 2019
V. Harwood and N. Murray, *The Promotion of Education*,
https://doi.org/10.1007/978-3-030-25300-4_4

Critical Cultural Social Marketing

Critical cultural social marketing is conceptualised with critical and cultural at the forefront; it guides, it advises, it instructs, it influences and it steers. This last word, steer, is a useful metaphor; steering conjures the image of the ongoing dependency that the processes of social marketing have on the critical and the cultural. To extend the metaphor, to assume the critical and the cultural can be dispensed with once the first steps of social marketing have been made is analogous to stop steering a boat once it has left the harbour. A description of critical cultural social marketing is offered in Box 4.1.

Box 4.1 A description of critical cultural social marketing

Critical cultural social marketing applies a critical frame that is culturally informed and intends to destabilise or challenge dominant deficit accounts that problematise people and/or their communities.

Critical cultural social marketing situates culture and critique at the forefront for gauging how social marketing concepts, techniques and practices might be used in a particular social and cultural context and with an appreciation of how dominant practices can have impacts on the contexts of people's lives and their relationships to education and learning.

Underpinning how social marketing activities are conceptualised, planned and applied, the activity of critique and attention to the cultural form an approach that problematises the production of knowledge and draws on the tradition of critical methodologies and researcher reflexivity.

To demonstrate how the critical and the cultural 'steer' the process of social marketing we turn to discuss how it was necessary for us to assiduously appraise social marketing processes and techniques. As an ongoing action, the act of appraisal is guided by the emphasis on the critical and the cultural. This meant that benchmarks or criteria, processes or planning, or even the definition needed to be subjected to review and assessment against the insights we had from critique and from culture. The results varied; some things remained the same, but many required reframing, adjusting, adapting, changing, tweaking or even omitting.

To undertake the critical cultural social marketing that produced Lead My Learning, the benchmarks could not be assumed as 'immovable', but needed to shift and change. This shifting and changing is not new. As outlined in Chapter 3, there is much debate and development in social marketing, and this includes discussion of social marketing moving from the 'benchmark era' (Fry, Previte, & Brennan, 2017). Indeed Fry and colleagues argue that the benchmarks are "utilitarian reductionist nature of the benchmark criteria as a checklist set of specific activities that fulfils the task of the programmes meeting, or not meeting, the social marketing label" (Fry et al., 2017, p. 126).

Engaging in Social Marketing with a Critical and Cultural Priority

One approach to responding to this 'utilitarian reductionist' problem is to utilise the social marketing benchmarks, criteria and planning process as a kind of touchstone for initiating a critically informed conversation about how a culturally directed social marketing project might be created. Taking this stance, the focus on assessing an alignment with meeting social marketing 'standards' can be realigned. Instead of a checklist (Fry et al., 2017), attention is placed on asking how an approach informed by critique and culture, responded to and consequently to the 'standards' as well as the wealth of literature in social marketing. The point being to not eschew the 'standards' or not to subscribe to a rigid template. But rather, to engage with social marketing standards, concepts and debate in a dynamic way that is always guided by the critical and cultural priority.

A critical cultural social marketing approach, then, does not uncritically adopt the prescribed definition of social marketing, the benchmarks or the planning processes. Rather it engages with them, with a critical and cultural priority. Drawing on our own critical cultural social marketing approach to promoting education, we discuss how a critical and cultural approach steered us in devising the Lead My Learning campaign. For our campaign development, we elected to work closely with the National Social Marketing Centre (NSMC, 2011) planning process, since this offered a clearly articulated planning process that best matched how we were thinking about creating an education promotion social marketing campaign that addressed parent involvement in their children's learning. Chapter 6 provides a detailed account of how we made the critical and cultural a priority and the impacts this had in changing this planning process. In electing to work with the NSMC (2011) planning process, we acknowledge there are other planning process that could have been used, including Lee and Kotler's (2015), Hastings (2007) and the more recent work by French and Russell-Bennet (2015).

Working with NSMC's (2011) planning process also meant considering the benchmarks and social marketing criteria, as well as other social marketing literature. Drawing on an established social marketing approach didn't mean importing a template. This required judgement, and this needs to be informed by both the critical and cultural approach. A way of illustrating the importance of this critical attitude, is by drawing on Arendt's discussion of judgement. As she explains, it means to "judge *particulars* without subsuming them under those general [universal] rules which can be taught and learned until they grow into habits that can be replaced by other habits and rules" (Arendt, 2003, p. 9, original emphasis). This means that not only do we need to be engaged in the activity of critique so that we are alert for dominant practices that would characterise, for example, people into generalities (for example, deficit accounts or racist stereotypes), we also need to have an awareness of the cultural to recognise particularities. Thus, the process that we used could be described as structured in terms of a response to the NSMC benchmarks, with continual referencing to other social marketing work, criteria, concepts and the range of publications.

Bringing Critique and a Cultural Emphasis to Campaign Conception

As we have described, we set out to design a campaign for promoting education that is focussed on early childhood in places of LSES and with people who have experienced (and many continue to experience) educational disadvantage. The Lead My Learning campaign is likely one of the few educational promotion strategies to consider the challenge of how to promote higher education in early childhood for parents and children with this set of experiences. As we have argued:

> efforts to widen participation in higher education will benefit from innovative, engaging and respectful ways of communicating with parents and families that can promote the diversity of learning parents do – but that dominant discourses have a tendency of blotting out. For us, this is not about making pitches for university degrees to toddlers. It is about comprehending the interconnections of educational disadvantages and recognising the powerful effects of avowal. (Harwood & Murray, 2019, p. 366)

This approach to including early childhood into the vision of widening participation by creating an education promotion approach is not an advertising or marketing higher education campaign targeting very young children and their families. Rather, it is concerned with appreciating the challenges, problems and dilemmas of efforts to widen university participation, and proposes a distal vision be incorporated in efforts to make higher education inclusive (Harwood & Murray, 2019).

Shifting the focus to education doesn't mean simply reproducing what is done in social marketing for health. From the outset it was clear to us that, given the limited use of social marketing in education (especially when compared with its implementation in other fields, such as health, and sustainability) we couldn't just 'import' what had been accomplished elsewhere.

A critical cultural approach is important for grasping the coalescing of influences that impact on educational inclusion in higher education, which in our view also needs to take in the experiences of education and learning of parents and their children. These influences can include, the impacts of educational disadvantage and injustices on parents, historical and political injustices, the influence of deficit accounts of parent engagement in education, and the lack of recognition by institutions of education of the diverse education and learning practices of parents. This especially impacts parents and communities that differ from the normalising practices of institutional education.

Working with and Adapting the NSMC Planning Process

It is important to specify that there was not a single template, benchmark or planning process that we could use and replicate for the creation of the educational promotion campaign—Lead My Learning. Instead, we identified the need to change and tweak the social marketing methodology and planning processes. Doing so enabled us to create a critical cultural social marketing campaign that is respectful to culture and critical of deficit accounts. Faced with this realisation, we elected to work with one of the well-known social marketing planning processes, the NSMC's (2011) Six Stage Planning Process.

Our choice to work from this established planning process was informed by the decision that this detailed social marketing planning process provided us the opportunity to critically consider the steps in the process. At the same time, we recognised we could also pay attention to considerations such as assumptions about benchmark criteria, social marketing definitions and the debate in the literature. Based on the Total Process Planning Model (French & Blair-Stevens, 2008) the NSMC stages are, "Getting Started, Scoping, Development, Implement, Evaluation, Follow-up" (NSMC, 2011, p. 79). As well as being widely used, and based on the detailed work by French and Blair-Stevens (2008), the NSMC planning process is clearly described and has extensive resources that can be consulted in order to not only comprehend their process, but also to make critically and culturally informed decision making with regard to the use or adaptation of components.

We could have certainly drawn on other planning processes—or indeed attempted to amalgamate processes. We note at the time of writing this book the discussion and proposed revisions to social marketing processes and benchmarks, such as by Fry et al. (2017) and by French and Russell-Bennett (2015) but were not available to us since our campaign planning process commenced in late 2014.

Aboriginal Protocols

Aboriginal Protocols guide the entirety of the project. Our identification of this explicit adherence to these protocols was realised early, what in the NSMC (2011) planning process is termed 'Getting Started'. We point out that in using the critical cultural social marketing approach, at the earliest of the steps we were prompted to respond to the need to be more specific about the cultural emphasis in our project. Aboriginal Protocols were vital to the project from beginning to end. These Aboriginal Protocols used specifically for the purpose of this project are: (1) the rights to maintain intellectual property; (2) building meaningful relationships; (3) establishing respect; (4) yarning; and (5) integrity.

The Rights to Maintain Intellectual Property

Intellectual property is a major element that cemented our relationship and respect with the local Aboriginal people and contributed to our success with our consultative research approach. A formal legally binding collaboration agreement was created between the university and the local Elders in the community-wide campaign (Girral). This allowed the local Aboriginal people to have ownership, control in decision making, act as advisors, and influence research processes and outcomes. We conducted a meetings with local Aboriginal Elders and Leaders, the Aboriginal Educational Consultative Group (AECG) and community members. Aboriginal Protocols informed our research and understanding. Elders who hold the Aboriginal knowledge were consulted and provided approval for the workings of the Lead My Learning campaign.

Building Meaningful Relationships

Building relationships involved establishing who should be consulted and requesting permission from the appropriate Elders and community leaders. For example, several meetings took place to learn from Aboriginal people before discussing the research project. The trust in building meaningful relationship was further developed through non-scheduled meetings and encounters that involved participating in community events and visiting the Elders, community members and other related services when visiting the community. Sharing the project design, benefits and outcomes helped create 'buy in' and built strong connections so that the project could be discussed and the subject of feedback and change from the stakeholders. These strong connections also increased the participation that is needed for disseminating the campaign in the community. Overall, building a strong relationship and trust further created the opportunity to establish respect in a *two-way* process.

Establishing Respect

Through our efforts to build meaningful relationships and trust we were able to interact with stakeholders in a way that we could be assessed and ascertain whether we acted in a way that was in accordance with respect for protocols. It was crucial that as researchers we earned the trust and respect of Aboriginal and non-Aboriginal stakeholders. Respect has supported us to connect with a wider network than we had anticipated and this has greatly improved the design and dissemination of our campaign.

Yarning

Aboriginal Protocols and practices led our research project design and was applied to respectfully connect with communities and services. We employed a culturally appropriate methodology 'yarning' to engage and be respectful of participants in the research project. Yarning was introduced to gather data and learn from the stories of parents and caregivers. This data was then further discussed in what we term Critical Cultural Yarning Sessions (CCYS)—the 'discussions about ideas' to develop and adapt the promotional educational campaign products for Lead My Learning. Yarning was applied and used to evaluate the campaign in all sites. Further details on yarning can be found in this chapter, under the section, CCYS. A Critical Cultural Yarning Model is discussed in Chapter 5.

Integrity

Integrity was essential to our research project stakeholders, the communities and participants with whom we engaged. This recognised Aboriginal people as the interpreters of their cultures and position the importance of Aboriginal parents to influence the design of the critical cultural social marketing campaign—Lead My Learning. Keeping to Aboriginal Protocols and practices we obtained approval and the representation from Elders for community members before campaign promotional products were produced.

Aboriginal Protocols in the Lead My Learning Project

1. Rights to maintain intellectual property

   a. Ownership
   b. Acknowledgement
   c. Indigenous cultural rights
   d. Consent (informed)
   e. Giving back and reciprocity

2. Building relationships

   a. Collaboration Agreement –with Aboriginal Community Corporation (legal document with the University)
   b. Consulting with Elders, community members and Aboriginal community services
   c. Non-Aboriginal community services organisations

3. Establishing respect

   a. Stakeholders (Aboriginal and Non-Aboriginal)
   b. Listening to people and Country
   c. Working together and partnerships
   d. Destabilising power imbalances
   e. Inclusive approaches
   f. Decolonising methodologies
   g. Operating within a culturally safe framework
   h. Critical awareness of Western versus Aboriginal knowledge

---

4. Yarning
   a. Culturally appropriate methodology
   b. Learning from stories
   c. Engaging and respectful
   d. Used to consult and adapt the campaign promotional products
   e. Used to evaluate the campaign in all sites

5. Integrity
   a. Recognise Aboriginal people as the interpreters of their culture
   b. Representation of Elders for community members and approval from Elders before campaign promotional products used.

Critical Cultural Yarning Sessions

To work in a manner that engaged actively with critique and with the cultural required an ongoing process that could be generative and critical. We needed to listen and be responsive to the cultures with which we were involved. And that could support connecting with the people and communities with and for whom the education promotion was being created. This last point drew us to think carefully about the kind of approach we could use for continually engaging, as a research team, in an activity of critique that was complemented by cultural attentiveness that connected with the people with whom and for whom we were working.

Initially termed 'critical thinking sessions', once it was decided we would use a yarning approach as our methodology in these sessions, these sessions became, CCYS. In our view, for these CCYS it is necessary to have an Aboriginal person with Aboriginal knowledge present in the CCYS. This is because a person with an Aboriginal ontology and epistemology and understanding of Ways of Knowing, Being and Doing (Martin & Mirraboopa, 2003) is needed for this process. It is also important to ensure that non-Aboriginal people don't mistakenly and inappropriately, construct notions of Aboriginal culture and/or engage in 'culture talk' about Aboriginal people. We suggest that non-Aboriginal people cannot engage in a CCYS without having an Aboriginal person present. This is due to the points raised above, at the same time, we acknowledge that a non-Aboriginal person may thoughtfully reflect on the ideas discussed in CCYS, and do so with an understanding these protocols listed above. This is a worthy start to engaging in the process, and may well be beneficial for the non-Aboriginal person who collaborates with an Aboriginal person in CCYS.

The initial idea of 'creative thinking sessions' was based on our early readings of the resources from NSMC. By critical yarning sessions, we mean a process where we meet to yarn together about the project, with the topics led by the particular task/s that were before us. The overall project was underpinned by a commitment to prioritising Aboriginal ways of knowing, being and doing (Martin & Mirraboopa, 2003),

> we were guided by Aboriginal people. This approach to promoting education flips 'mainstream' strategies. Aboriginal people consulted in our research were pleased that non-Aboriginal people were welcome to participate in the campaign. Thus, while our approach did incorporate consultation with non-Aboriginal people, we ensured this was in keeping with the Aboriginal guided approaches. (Harwood & Murray, 2019)

In taking this stand, we sought to work against the "colonialist indifference to Indigenous philosophy" (Watson, 2014, pp. 517–518).

Being guided by Aboriginal approaches meant that it made sense to engage in yarning, which is a well-known Aboriginal method (Bessarab & Ng'Andu, 2010). Thus, as well as using yarning as a methodology in our qualitative interviews, we used yarning in the discussions we had in our research team.

As Fredericks et al. (2011) state, "The terms 'yarn' and 'yarning' are used by Aboriginal peoples in everyday language" (p. 13). These authors state that:

> Yarning is more than just a light exchange of words and pleasantries in casual conversation. A yarn is both a process and an exchange; it encompasses elements of respect, protocol and engagement in individuals' relationships with each other. Yarning establishes relationality and determines accountability (K. L. Martin, 2008). (Fredericks et al., 2011, p. 13)

This connection with protocol and with relationships makes yarning significant to relationality, and as Towney shares, also to spirituality:

> Yarning is a very special and powerful way in which Aboriginal people connect to each other. This is, and always will be, a unique part of our culture which we have been practising for many years. It connects us to our spirituality. Our spirituality is central to our beliefs. (Towney, 2005, p. 40)

Also discussing yarning Geia, Hayes, and Usher (2013) note the connection with storytelling, and comment on the processes that occur:

> Aboriginal and Torres Strait Island storytelling, what we call yarning, is not a static process; it begins and it progresses, through loud and raucous engagement, to a sudden move into contemplation and silence. Aboriginal yarning is a fluid ongoing process, a moving dialogue interspersed with interjections, interpretations, and additions. (Geia et al., 2013, p. 15)

These brief descriptions start to, hopefully, give a sense of yarning; although participating in yarning, may be the most appropriate way to appreciate and understand this significant practice.

Yarning as a Research Methodology

Bessarab and Ng'andu (2010) take up the important discussion of yarning as a 'legitimate method in Indigenous research'. They describe yarning as a process whereby "both the researcher and participant journey together visiting places and topics of interest relevant to the research study. Yarning is a process that requires the researcher to develop and build a relationship that is accountable to Indigenous people participating in the research" (p. 38). This point about relationships is also commented on by Fredericks et al. (2011), who explain that "Through techniques such as yarning, it is possible to shift the way we research and the way we work in health towards forming relationships that are based on equal and respectful partnerships, support, cooperation and respect for us as Aboriginal peoples" (2011, p. 21).

Bessarab and Ng'andu (2010) describe, "four different types of yarning". These types are: Social Yarning; Research Topic Yarning; Collaborative Yarning and Therapeutic Yarning (p. 41). The descriptions given for each of these by Bessarab and Ng'andu (2010) are provided below as this is helpful for differentiating between the yarning we used in our research with participants and how we used yarning in our CCYS.

> *Social Yarning*: Conversation that takes place before the research or topic yarn is informal and often unstructured, follows a meandering course that is guided by the topic that both people choose to introduce to the discussion.
>
> *Research Topic Yarning*: Yarn that takes place in an un or semi-structured research interview. The sole purpose is to gather information through participant's stories that are related to the research topic.
>
> *Collaborative Yarn*: Yarn that occurs between two or more people where they are actively engaged in sharing information about a research project or a *discussion about ideas.*
>
> *Therapeutic Yarning*: Yarn takes place during the research conversation where the participant in telling their story discloses information that is traumatic or intensely personal. (Bessarab & Ng'andu, 2011, p. 40, emphasis added)

The relationship between these different types of yarning are also represented diagrammatically in the original article (Bessarab & Ng'andu, 2011, p. 40). We have emphasised the phrase 'or a discussion about ideas' to draw attention to the point that yarning in research is not restricted to a methodological practice with participants. Just as there are different forms of yarning, so too there are different forms of yarning in a research project. Hence in our research, yarning was a methodology used in data collection as well as a form of communication used in our 'discussions about ideas'. One of our formalised processes where this occurred was in our CCYS. Here we used the Critical Cultural Yarning Model, which set out the following processes: value the knowledge; deference; recognition; learn; privilege; and apply. See Chapter 5 (Fig. 5.2) for a diagram and detailed discussion of this model.

As well as a research methodology, work using yarning includes creating 'yarning places' online for sharing resources about Indigenous health (Burrow & Thomson, 2006); healing yarns with Aboriginal men (Towney, 2005); and clinical yarn for use work in health practice with Aboriginal people (Lin, Green, & Bessarab, 2016). Yarning is also emphasised in a project reporting on a literacy programme initiated by the mothers in a remote community. As they describe it was instigated "in 2001 by Aboriginal and Torres-Strait Islander mothers when approached the non-Indigenous preschool teacher/director, seeking support for them to assist in their children's literacy development" (Fluckiger, Diamond, & Jones, 2012, p. 57). Initiated by the mothers, the programme connected with the 'yarning space' of the parents.

A Place in Our Research

Yarning, then, can be seen to have a place in our research in a number of ways. Or to put this differently, we didn't see yarning as only to be a methodology approach for data collection. Given the cultural emphasis of the project, the focus of our work as an Aboriginal guided approach that was inclusive of Aboriginal and non-Aboriginal people, and the skills of one of us, Dunghutti Woman Nyssa Murray, we were able to use yarning for *"the discussion of ideas"* (Bessarab & Ng'andu, 2011, p. 40, emphasis added). It is relevant to note here that, where it was appropriate, and depending on the settings, we extended yarning beyond both research methodology and the CCYS. This was inclusive of Aboriginal and non-Aboriginal people, and our respect for this approach reflects the prioritisation of the Aboriginal guided approach used in this cross-cultural project (Harwood & Murray, 2019).

Our Critical Cultural Yarning Sessions

CCYS were a formalised part of our process as a research team. Our CCYS were regular meeting sessions where we focussed on the various stages of the NSMC planning process. Steered by a critical and cultural approach, we examined this published planning process, devised in England, in terms of our activity of critique and our attention to the cultural context of our project. The CCYS were employed to touch on points throughout the life of the project. We used a yarning approach to all talking points as we worked together as the research team in CCYS. This helped us to design and create the campaign. From the beginning, steps of identifying communities that experience educational disadvantage across New South Wales, through to the development, and the rollout of the campaign, the CCYS ensured an ongoing and systematic approach to the whole campaign process.

Topics for these sessions included yarning about the formative study and learning from the conversations had with the different stakeholders throughout the entirety of the project. As well as the parents, the campaign recognised key project stakeholders that support parents, caregivers and family members. These stakeholders included childcare educators, service providers, not-for-profit organisations, community workers, Aboriginal organisations, Elders and other related services that support and influence parents with their children's learning. There were a number of stakeholders to listen to and the yarning approach provided a culturally guided way to yarn about our yarns and conversations with these different people. Using the critical cultural approach demanded going through a rigorous process of appraisal and assessment of how social marketing might be adapted for our purpose (and for our project we worked closely with the NSMC planning process). The CCYS proved to be an effective way for us to engage in this difficult task.

A Twofold Process of Critique and of Recognition

Applying a critical cultural social marketing approach demanded undertaking critique, especially of deficit discourses of learning and education and of recognition of cultural practices, especially of learning. One way to demonstrate this activity of critique is our decision not to use terms such as 'problem behaviour' even though these are commonly used in social marketing and may well not be intended to connote 'deficit'. When critically examined assumptions about 'problem behaviour' in education not only includes the way some children are depicted (Harwood, 2006; Harwood, Hickey-Moody, McMahon, & O'Shea, 2017), it is also commonly tied to assumptions about social class and cultural difference. Discourses of 'the problem' in education are strongly implicated with notions of people *being* the problem (Harwood & Allan, 2014) and this includes parents (Harwood & Murray, 2019). From this standpoint, it is vital to interrogate the dominant discourses that contribute to the construction of certain people (as well as communities) as 'a problem' or 'having problems'. This is important to call out, since one of the challenges with this 'discourse of problems' in education is that it masks systemic issues that includes, colonialism, racism, classism and ableism.

How 'problems' are constructed in education has implications and consequences that include particular people and communities and their wealth of knowledge and practices going unrecognised in official (and legitimating) educational discourses. The term 'problem behaviour' has connotations of a deficit account of the Aboriginal and non-Aboriginal people who have experienced educational disadvantage. As outlined in Chapter 2, such deficit accounts create 'truths' about certain people and their relationship to education. Examples of such truths include the notion of 'uneducated parent', the 'uncaring parent' or 'parent that does not value education'.

Rogoff et al. (2017) underscore how deficit orientated conceptualisation influence 'interventions' in education. In the example cited below, these authors examine an intervention that they maintain was based on deficit assumptions. This intervention, implemented in 2016, directly impacted how Mexican mothers understood 'their child-reading practices':

> Interventions based on a deficit model also undermine aspects of parent-child relations that are important for children's development and family functioning (Dudley-Marling & Lucas, 2009; González, Moll, & Amanti, 2005). For example, last year an intervention by the Initial Education Program in Mexico made Indigenous Mexican mothers doubt their child-rearing practices and values, by insisting that children must achieve autonomy by doing chores mostly by themselves, based on Western ideology valuing individual solitary achievement. In contrast, autonomy in the participants' Indigenous ideology is a progressive capacity to collaborate, to assume social responsibilities, and to be involved in family and community activities (Bertely-Busquets, 2016). The autonomy that is involved in

collaborative initiative is an important skill, one to build on and even model from, not one to be replaced by the Western version. (Rogoff et al., 2017, p. 878)

This example clearly demonstrates how deficit views, premised on a Western model not only missed *what activities were happening*, and simultaneously imposed a 'right' way of doing these parent–child activities (the Western way), it negatively affected the mothers, causing them to doubt what they were already doing.

Rather than aiming to influence behaviours, the objective in our project was shifted onto the very discourses that contribute to the constitution of subjectivities of learning. Using what we have termed 'strategic discourse production', our theorisation that this could have some influence is premised on Foucault's work on subjectivation (Foucault, 2011, 2014a, 2014b, 2016, 2017) and on his discussion of subjugated knowledge (Foucault, 1980). Strategic discourse production operates to deliberately produce discourses of subjugated knowledge that can interrupt dominant procedures of truth. In our study, subjugated knowledges are the learning practices of parents, while the procedures of truth we are seeking to interrupt are the truths that "educationally disadvantaged parents are not involved in children's learning" (Harwood & Murray, 2019, pp. 353–354).

This idea, that "dominant procedures of truth" can be interrupted, works with a conceptualisation of subjectivities as constituted, and discourses of truth, such as a parent being uneducated and unable to lead their child's learning contribute to these subjectivities. While we might say, for instance, that subjectivities are constituted in this way, this is not to say the self is not involved. Indeed, for Foucault, through practices of subjectivation, the self can have a relationship with a different discourse. As we have argued, "such a discourse might invite avowals and practices of subjectivation that overtly and deliberately identify involvement in their children's learning" (Harwood & Murray, 2019, p. 361).

Approaching this from another angle, we could say that identity becomes produced via the relationship a subject has to discourses (but this identity is never fixed or inherently stable). Butler articulates this relationship, "The subject is a consequence of certain rule-governed discourses that govern the intelligible invocation of identity" (1990, p. 198). We might then envisage seeing identity as pointed out by Zembylas, who explains "In Foucault's writings, the unified self is challenged and fragmented; he uses the term 'subjectivity' instead of 'selfhood' or 'self-identity' to describe the manifold ways in which individuals are historically constituted" (2002, p. 113). Following this line of thought, we could say that the identity of the 'uneducated parent' or the 'unengaged parent' is similarly constituted.

Returning to the idea that identity is not fixed or stable, nor does it speak to something that inheres within us, it is possible to picture how identity is constituted (even if it feels real). This is compelling because it opens out a plethora of possibilities for doing things with that identity. Take for instance this comment by Butler:

> If the identity we say we are cannot possibly capture us, and marks immediately an excess and opacity that fall outside the terms of identity, then any effort made 'to give an account of oneself' will have to fail in order to approach being true. (2001, p. 28)

This is tantalising and prompts us to see the fault in asking parents to 'give an account of oneself' in any 'true' sense where the claim is mounted that a particular identity 'fully captures us'.

Discourse, then, is pivotal to grasping an understanding of the constitution of the many deficit identities that paradoxically education produces, such as the 'uneducated parent who is less equipped to support a child's learning'. As Zembylas makes plain:

> Only by interrogating the discursive place from which questions of identity are posed can we trace how identity is subjected to the social and historical context of practices and discourse. For Foucault, discourses do not simply reflect or describe reality, knowledge, experience, self, social relations, social institutions, and practices; rather, they play an integral role in constituting (and being constituted by) them. (2002, p. 114)

In this quote we see accentuated the significance of 'interrogating the discursive place' from where, in our case, deficit knowledge about parents and their learning practices arise. The second point, that of constitution and discourses, accentuates that discourse isn't merely a describer, it does, to put it clumsily, *do things*.

As we have outlined (Harwood & Murray, 2019), subjectivation, what Foucault describes as "the formation of a definite relationship of self to self" (2014a, p. 231) is impacted and influenced by relationships with truth, such as the discourses of what it means to be educated. As a consequence, to mark out influencing discourse as an objective is to focus on something that is certainly consequential in terms of impacting identities and actions.

The Lead My Learning Campaign Creation Process

Describing the 'Lead My Learning' campaign planning process is about explaining the way social marketing methods and techniques as well as definitions were interacted with in the terms of a critical cultural emphasis. As we have stated, the approach that we took drew on one of the well-known planning processes by the NSMC (2011). Working with one planning process, we then used Critical Cultural Yarning Sessions (CCYS) to systematically appraise how a social marketing approach could be created that could respectfully promote education with parents of young children, parents who had experienced educational disadvantage and lived in areas of high socio-economic disadvantage. Significantly, this 'appraisal tactic' enabled us to formulate how we *theorised* Lead My Learning in an iterative fashion that moved between a different set of understandings that at times connected well, such as when we tackled segmentation or quite the opposite, just couldn't be connected, such as 'behaviour change'.

The focus on behaviour change in social marketing is dominated by psychologically based behaviour change theories (Luca & Suggs, 2013). These behaviour change theories include: Prochaska and DiClemente (1983) stages of change model; Bandura's (1986, 2001) social cognitive theory; Rosenstock, Strecher, and Becker's (1988) health belief model; and the theory of planned behaviour (Ajzen, 1991). Such theories have an "emphasis [on] the cognitive, self-reflexive decision making surrounding a behaviour, rather than hidden cultural influences which underpin these seemingly rational decisions (Nigg, Allegrante, & Ory, 2002; Rothman, 2000)" (Tapp & Spotswood, 2013, p. 276).

Tapp and Springwood set out the case for 'socio-cultural change', pointing out the aim is to "enable, rather than persuade, people to change their behaviour. This approach is not offered as a simplistic alternative to classical social marketing, but rather as a possible way of expanding the scope of social marketing" (2013, p. 286). While this is a significant shift, an attentiveness to behaviour remains, and although not necessarily a problem in and of itself, what we see as the issue is the dominance of behaviour. The difficulty being that, as Tapp and Spotswood go on to explain, "The present emphasis in the definitions of persuasion social marketing runs the risk of limiting both research and intervention development to taking a cognitive, individualist approach to behaviour change" (Tapp & Spotswood, 2013, p. 287).

For this reason it is relevant to look beyond the focus on behaviour in social marketing, and we note there is "an expansion of theoretical perspectives beyond the individual psychology of behavior and rational economic theory, to engage in the social, cultural and critical theory in social marketing" (Gordon, Russell-Bennett, & Lefebvre, 2016, p. 1065). Saunders, Barrington, and Sridharan (2015) for instance, propose a definition of social marketing that is not premised on behavioural change, "Social marketing is the application of marketing principles to enable individual and collective ideas and actions in the pursuit of effective, efficient, equitable, fair and sustained social transformation" (p. 165). Drawing on the work of Sen (1999) and his Capability Approach, they emphasise the idea of 'freedoms', as opposed to 'behaviour change', and their "the approach assesses societies (and social marketing programmes) on their abilities to promote a set of opportunities, or 'substantial freedoms', which individuals may or may not act upon" (Saunders et al., 2015, p. 166).

Formative Research

Taken together with the other angles we employed, we realised that the formative research could be extended, and played a vital role in our relationships and the feedback in the development and design of Lead My Learning. Reading widely in the social marketing literature gave us ideas for increasing the amount of formative research with our priority group

(Lefebvre, 2013). The semi-structured sessions ensured parents, caregivers and family members could talk freely and engage in conversations. These were used not only to help us to understand the issue and complete tasks such as segmentation; but also, as they continued with these over a 14-month period, provided critical guidance from representatives of the priority group on the development and design of the campaign.

Thus, the formative research involved exploring the knowledge, attitudes and feelings towards education and educational futures. Equally important too was to consult and build meaningful partnerships with childcare educators, playgroup facilitators, government and non-government bodies, and local Elders. We did this as we recognised the importance of learning from local Elders and ensuring that the campaign rollout would not impact on community or service delivery.

Providing an overview of the Lead My Learning Campaign process is therefore more to do with explaining how we used a critical cultural approach to adapt social marketing, rather than the putting forward of a specified template. As such, we offer the following reflections on key activities that were undertaken.

Creating and Being Guided by Aboriginal Protocols

Adhering to the Aboriginal Protocols offered the opportunity to connect with deep philosophical and practical ways to undertake research processes and listen to and be guided by those involved in the research. Embedding Aboriginal Protocols provided a basis for participants and project stakeholders to see us as respectful researchers (Harwood & Murray, 2019). The importance of the Aboriginal Protocols informing the research cannot be underestimated. These protocols informed our behaviours, assisting us to be respectful and to listen better and learn with Aboriginal and with non-Aboriginal people.

The protocols informed how we yarned, both in the formalised research data collection activity, throughout the fieldwork visits, as well as in the yarns amongst the researchers and with a range of collaborators (stakeholders). Yarning had impacts that improved our own understanding. And it had particularly important impacts for non-Indigenous people involved in the range of facets of the project. As Geia et al. (2013) make clear:

> The non-Indigenous researcher, after listening to the yarns, will no longer consider Indigenous people as a number or statistic; they will no longer remain a nameless face or just another patient in the ward. (2013, p. 16)

A decolonising angle throws light on this power of yarning, as it upturns the dominance of Western-centric methods of data collection, and positions Aboriginal ways of knowing, being and doing not only at the forefront, but in 'command' of the process. This notion of 'in command' is used to highlight the deliberate shift to destabilise and challenge Westernised demands of what 'counts as knowledge', of who is 'in charge' and who is the 'expert'.

There were numerous positive outcomes from placing prominence on respecting culture. One of these were the beautiful images that were produced of Aboriginal and non-Aboriginal parents involved in leading learning with their young children (see Chapter 5). As our formative research with our priority group showed us, what was wanted in the campaign design and images are *Real Photos of Real People Doing Real Activities*.

What Does the Campaign Really Need to Be About? Learning About Learning

Our motive for engaging with social marketing was to figure out how it could be used to promote education and educational futures with people who experience significant educational and socio-economic disadvantage. While this motive remained, as we conducted the formative research we recognised the need to better appreciate the subtleties of educational disadvantages for parents of young children. This required a nuanced understanding of new forms of educational disadvantages that are produced in the early childhood space in concert with normalising learning practices of institutional education. By prioritising culture, we were forced to critically look at how parent learning practices were perceived by institutional forms of education (such as pre-schools, schools, universities), by other institutions and not-for-profits associated with parents and children, by the parents, by their peers and communities, and by us as researchers. This examination threw light on the 'problem' of parent involvement. We found on the one hand that it had a central role in a child's educational successes at school and beyond. But on the other, the parents in our priority group were oftentimes stereotyped as not involved or not engaged in their learning.

When we listened carefully *with* the cultural emphasis and the awareness formed from a continuing critique, a quite different account manifested. The parents were very much involved in their children's learning; but the parents, and forms of official institutional education didn't seem to recognise these practices as 'involvement' or 'engagement' in education. This insight prompted us to deepen our fieldwork and to yarn with community members, Elders, parents and services about learning with children, their families and community. These questions about learning led us to the rich literature about Learning by Observing and Pitching In (LOPI) (Correa-Chávez, Mejia-Arauz, & Rogoff, 2015; Rogoff, 2014). Detailed information about LOPI is available on this website: http://www.learningbyobservingandpitchingin.com/icp-overview-english (Barbara Rogoff). This work offers insight into the diverse learning practices of Indigenous Communities in the Americas, describing the social processes that *involve the learner.* As Urrieta explains, "LOPI is a heuristic model for IKS [Indigenous Knowledge Systems] and for understanding how Indigenous communities organise learning" (Urrieta, 2015, p. 368). Not only was the LOPI literature helpful for our thinking about the learning activities that Aboriginal parents might be doing but that institutional education failed to recognise, it also prompted us to consider what else might be being missed. Or more exactly, we came to the position that, while the parents had different learning practices, there was a similarity of experience insofar as their involvement was being 'missed', 'overlooked' or beyond the comprehension of legitimate education knowledge. What appeared to be the connection was the experience of educational disadvantage, and how this variously played out in a process that served to delegitimise the learning practices of the parents.

Conceptualising Segmentation

Essentially, segmentation is the identification of different segments in the priority group (or target group). Conducting segmentation enables a detailed understanding of the 'segments' in the group, or what we could call the variations in the group, and based on this, determining an appropriate design that is suitable. Segmentation can be employed to be beneficial in several ways, as French outlines, "Segmentation is an important technique in social marketing because in addition to helping focus and tailor social marketing intervention strategies, it informs and shapes responses to ethical considerations" (2017b, p. 26).

There are difficulties and consequences with segmentation, since after segmenting has been completed, there is the decision to be made of which segment is the priority group and will receive the social marketing campaign (or intervention as it is often termed). In the Lead My Learning campaign, we determined that, of the different groups, the one that required the campaign more was the Happiness vs Learning segment. This segment or priority group was larger, including the group that was employment focused. There are arguments for and against this process, especially in terms of its ethics (Newton, Newton, Turk, & Ewing, 2013). Notwithstanding the need to be mindful of this issue—and have a considered and informed approach to this decision making, one compelling reasoning is that a better, carefully crafted campaign can be produced if it is orientated to the particularities of the segment.

So, while there is this point of hesitation, and certainly a need for a critically and culturally informed analysis of how segmentation is performed and how decisions are made on the choice of segment for a campaign, segmentation can offer significant benefits. Segmentation is essential to the design and development of communication messages and subsequent interventions designed to achieve the goals of a social marketing project. Segmentation can be based, for example, on demographic factors, attitudinal factors (what can be termed 'psychographic', cultural factors, or in the specific case of our project, educational factors). French offers a detailed list of these, which we include below:

- Demographics such as age, gender, marital status, employment, income, socio-economic status
- Cultures/subcultures including ethnicity, religious beliefs, subcultures of consumption behaviours (e.g. night clubbers, bikers)
- Attitudes such as acceptability towards smoking or drinking
- Psychological, including motivations, personality, interests, and opinions
- Value perceptions such as perceived functional, economic or social value of using energy efficiently
- Psychographics such as lifestyle, knowledge, activities
- Behavioural, for instance people who are gamblers, smokers or drinkers. (2017b, p. 28)

Segmentation relies on a finer analysis and this can result in messages and strategies that more accurately connect with a specific priority group. For instance, this could mean that different messages and strategies are used for parents who have never considered university as an option for their children, as compared with what is required for parents who are opposed to university education.

Conceptualising the Exchange

The idea of exchange is also a distinctive concept in social marketing, with the concept again drawn from the discipline marketing, where it conveys the concept of the value-in-exchange. For instance, to put it simply, the value seen in paying a certain amount of money for particular items (goods). But in social marketing, there is a different proposal; it is not goods, but rather 'social good' such as positive changes in health (doing more exercise to improve fitness or decreasing alcohol consumption to improve wellness). Or it could be for environmental actions, for example, water saving practices that reduce time showering to decrease water consumption or switching from plastic bag use to reusable bags to reduce landfill and effects on marine life. In each of these instances social value creation is occurring, and it is based on this principle of exchange. In social marketing, this can be thought of as "social value creation through the exchange of social offerings in the form of ideas, products, service, experience, environments, and systems" (French, 2017a, p. 10).

In a discussion of their proposed use of 'Interactive Management' as a 'systems methodology' as an alternate means for understanding the complexity of exchanges, Duane, Domegan, McHugh, and Devaney (2016) put forward the case that "social marketing has two fundamentally different behavioural change states" (Duane et al., 2016, p. 872). As they explain:

> the first [change state] is a behavioural change state characterised by the individual, four P's of the marketing mix, an intervention, segmentation and targeting. It pays attention to restricted or generalised exchanges, though sometimes these are assumed or not understood. (Duane et al., 2016, p. 872)

This 'behavioural change state' could, arguably, be attributed to a good deal of social marketing. The above comments by Duane et al. (2016) draw attention to the reason why the concept of the exchange needs to be theorised both in terms of adoption of the concept from marketing into social marketing, as well as from the standpoints of different theoretical perspectives, socio-cultural contexts and places.

For instance, can a notion of exchange premised on capitalistic assumptions be applied uniformly, not only throughout the world, but within subcultures, even in places characterised as an expression of capitalism, such as New York City? This example raises just some of the problems with the premise of the exchange. Duane et al. (2016) then outline 'a second change state':

> The second change state, social change, is characterised by strategies incorporating the individual and environment. In this change state, strategies encompass webs, chains and influence clusters of complex exchanges demanding long-term relationships across networks, sectors, actors and values. All move beyond once off transactions towards interagency partnerships and social learning through complex exchange analysis and mapping. (Duane et al., 2016, pp. 872–873)

While we did not use this second change state (not only would it not suit our work, it was not available at the time we were planning the project), we include it here since it offers a different way for imagining 'the exchange'.

Our reframing of exchange was concerned to not categorise parents as though they are not involved or engaged in their children's learning, or 'lack education'. To conceptualise exchange, we needed to consider how the objective on influencing discourses of parent involvement in learning has translatable changes that could be beneficial enough that parents may engage with them. From this angle, while not working with behavioural change theory, we did work with and adapt strategies from what Duane et al. (2016) describe as 'the first change state' (for example, the marketing mix). However, because we did this with the prioritisation of critically interrogating how the deficit discourses were constructed, we were attentive to the discourses of specific 'systems' (in our case legitimating educational systems) and the interactions that these have in contributing to the construction of parent subjectivities of learning.

Conceptualising the Marketing Mix

As we have mentioned, the 4P marketing mix concept is widely used in social marketing and as such, we carefully considered how this might be implemented. The outcome was to adapt this by adding more components: Partnerships, Critique and Protocols. By protocols we are referring to the Aboriginal Protocols guiding the project. We include critique, since being a cornerstone of the process and exerting such an influence on our activities, we felt it needed to be explicitly situated in how we conceptualised the 'marketing mix'.

We also looked at the literature to see if there were other ways to describe the marketing mix that might better fit with our critical cultural emphasis. Peattie and Peattie (2011), as we noted in Chapter 2, describe a 'social mix':

- Social propositions – instead of products.
- Social cost of involvement—(including any financial costs) instead of price.
- Accessibility—instead of place.

- Social communication—instead of promotion; and adds[advertisements].
- Stakeholder involvement—to reflect the frequent importance in delivering social campaigns of a mix of stakeholder contributions. (Peattie & Peattie, 2011, p. 168)

We have adapted the above suggestions to suit our project and the critical and cultural emphasis. Below is the critical cultural and social mix created for this project:

Critical Cultural Marketing Mix

1. **Social and cultural propositions (Products)**: The core proposition was that the priority group would feel good about activities that they are doing.
2. **Social and cultural cost of involvement (Price)**: This is the cost of involvement, which included time as well as the challenge of engaging in an alternative discourse.
3. **Accessibility (Place)**: Range of places and avenues for dissemination of the propositions that are informed by the priority group as appropriate.
4. **Social and cultural communication (Promotion)**: These are the forms of social and cultural communication that are used to promote the campaign.
5. **Partnerships (Stakeholder involvement)**: Adapt to a range of situations that include formal and informal partnerships; Aboriginal and non-Aboriginal stakeholders; listening to people and Country; working together in an inclusive approach, control, decisions, power relationships.
6. **Critique (Position of discourse)**: Alertness to the discourses impacting the priority group; alertness to colonising practices; alertness to classed (social class) practices; care not to engage in acts of repetition of these; tactic of disrupting these as part of the mix.
7. **Protocols (Philosophical and practical ways)**: Adhering to cultural protocols, sharing this in our relationships, ensuring the protocols guide the marketing mix and method for the campaign. (Adapted from Peattie & Peattie, 2011)

We elected to retain the term partnerships (rather than Peattie and Peattie's suggestion of stakeholders) as this emphasis was of importance to our project. We do use 'stakeholders' in this book due to the clarity that term conveys. The definition of partnerships and relationship we use is different to 'partnership and relations for business' often used by institutions for personal or monetary gain.

Partnerships and protocols interconnect, because for us the understanding of partnerships we employed differs from a meaning that connotes business transactions. For example, it includes relating to people at a more personal level and there is no personal gain as a motivator. These partnerships require listening to people and Country that is involved. (See Chapter 1 for an explanation of Country.) Partnerships meant working together, an inclusive approach, being aware of power relationships and striving to disrupt hierarchies, particularly of colonising hierarchies and practices. There is a commitment to yarning and where feasible, for decisions to be made together. Protocols relate to the cultural protocols of the group of people. As we have stated, we were guided by Australian Aboriginal Protocols, and these were important for relationships between Aboriginal and non-Aboriginal people. The inclusion of critique is important because this component of the mix is required to ensure that.

Review Research Design, Methodologies and Theoretical Frameworks

Early insights from formative research, stakeholder discussions and literature review enabled us to look critically at the initial research design and review and change as required. One example of such a change is our approach to the marketing mix. In the work that produced the grant application and the initial research design, it was envisaged that we would apply the 4Ps of social marketing. The intention was to work with LSES families and childcare workers to identify the four 'P' marketing components. This plan involved asking: how can we position university education so that it is seen as something of value and relevance to the priority group (product); how can we reduce the perceived barriers and increase the perceived benefits (price); who are the most appropriate intermediaries and communication channels (place); and how do we best communicate with children and their families in a way that increases their aspirations (promotion).

However, as a result of further literature reviews and importantly, the formative research, we came to differently understand the challenges and issues for promoting education that could widen participation. For example, the parents expressed how they valued education:

It's the start of the future I suppose. (Connie, Redville West Public School Preschool)

I think it is important. (Johann, Eastside Region)

It's good. No I think it's incredibly important for – especially for the early years so up until, I don't know, a certain age that it's incredibly important so that there's some form of education. (Lara, Eastside Women's Health)

At the same time as holding a value for education, the parents also set out to prioritise the happiness of their children. This meant, for them a disjuncture between education and happiness, because, as they would explain to us in many yarning sessions, an emphasis on education for their young children did not meet *their* criteria for ensuring their children were happy. This was further reinforced when we discussed the words used for the campaign and the design concepts. Here the parents in the formative research emphasised that we must not use the word 'education', or even associations to education, such as university or school. For these parents, too much education is wrong because young children should be happy and playful, and education is the antithesis of this happiness.

This insight, and indeed, directive from the parents meant 'letting go' of our own ambitions for the content and design of a social marketing approach to promoting education. We had to literally go back to the drawing board in the form of our CCYS. After working through these significant revisions, not only were the messaging concepts and design changed, but so too was the research design.

In terms of the research design, instead of an emphasis on early childhood educators and long-day childcare centres, we reconceptualised the design to include a playgroup focussed approach (Eastside), a community-wide campaign (Girral) that included playgroups and childcare centres, and a third modality where we trialled placing our campaign messaging on the windows of buses used to transport the Aboriginal children to and from childcare centres. This was done because our formative research showed the parents and children in the priority group did not always attend childcare centres. For those that did use long-day childcare, we realised it was very difficult to create an education promotion campaign that could connect with the parents in our priority group.

References

Ajzen, I. (1991). The theory of planned behavior. *Organizational Behavior and Human Decision Processes, 50*(2), 179–211. https://doi.org/10.1016/0749-5978(91)90020-T.

Arendt, H. (2003). Thinking and moral considerations. In J. Kohn (Ed.), *Responsibility and judgment* (1st ed., pp. 159–189). New York: Schocken Books.

Bandura, A. (1986). *Social foundations of thought and action: A social cognitive theory.* Englewood Cliffs, NJ: Prentice-Hall.

Bandura, A. (2001). Social cognitive theory: An agentic perspective. *Annual Review of Psychology, 52*(1): 1–26.

Bertely-Busquets, M. (2016). *Análisis y propuestas para el fortalecimiento del programa de educación inicial no escolarizada de CONAFE* [Analysis and proposals for strengthening the informal early education program of CONAFE]. Mexico City.

Bessarab, D., & Ng'Andu, B. (2010). Yarning about yarning as a legitimate method in Indigenous research. *International Journal of Critical Indigenous Studies, 3*(1), 37–50.

Burrow, S., & Thomson, N. (2006). Yarning places: Using web resources and electronic yarning to promote Indigenous health. *Aboriginal and Islander Health Worker Journal, 30*(4), 17.

Butler, J. (1990). *Gender trouble: Feminism and the subversion of identity.* New York: Routledge.

Butler, J. (2001). Giving an account of oneself. *Diacritics, 31*(4), 22–40. https://doi.org/10.1353/dia.2004.0002.

Correa-Chávez, M., Mejia-Arauz, R., & Rogoff, B. (2015). *Children learn by observing and contributing to family and community endeavours: A cultural paradigm* (Vol. 49). Waltham, MA: Academic Press.

Duane, S., Domegan, C., McHugh, P., & Devaney, M. (2016). From restricted to complex exchange and beyond: Social marketing's change agenda. *Journal of Marketing Management, 32*(9–10), 856–876. https://doi.org/10.1080/0267257X.2016.1189449.

Dudley-Marling, C., & Lucas, K. (2009). Pathologizing the language and culture of poor children. *Language Arts, 86*(5), 362–370.

Fluckiger, B., Diamond, P., & Jones, W. (2012). Yarning space: Leading literacy learning through family-school partnerships. *Australasian Journal of Early Childhood, 37*(3), 53–59.

Foucault, M. (1980). Two lectures. In C. Gordon (Ed.), *Power/knowledge: Selected interviews and other writings 1972–1977* (pp. 78–108). Sussex: Harvester Press Ltd.

Foucault, M. (2011). *The courage of the truth (the government of self and others II): lectures at the Collège de France, 1983–1984.* New York and Houndmills, Basingstoke, Hampshire, UK: Palgrave Macmillan.

Foucault, M. (2014a). *On the government of the living: lectures at the Collaege de France, 1979–1980* (G. Burchell, Trans.). Basingstoke, UK: Palgrave Macmillan.

Foucault, M. (2014b). *Wrong-doing, truth-telling: The function of avowal in justice* (F. Brion, B. E. Harcourt, & S. W. Sawyer, Eds.). London, Chicago, and Louvain-la-Neuve: University of Chicago Press.

Foucault, M. (2016). *About the beginning of the hermeneutics of the self: lectures at Dartmouth College, 1980* (H.-P. Fruchaud, D. Lorenzini, L. Cremonesi, A. I. Davidson, O. Irrera, & M. Tazzioli, Eds.). London and Chicago: University of Chicago Press.

Foucault, M. (2017). *Subjectivity and truth: Lectures at the Collège de France, 1980–1981* (F. Gros, F. Ewald, & A. Fontana, Eds.). London, UK: Palgrave Macmillan.

Fredericks, B., Adams, K., Finlay, S., Fletcher, G., Andy, S., Briggs, L., Briggs, L., & Hall, R. (2011). Engaging the practice of Indigenous yarning in action research. *ALAR: Action Learning and Action Research Journal, 17*(2), 12–24.

French, J. (2017a). Key principle, concepts, and techniques of social marketing. In *Social marketing and public health: Theory and practice.* Oxford: Oxford University Press.

French, J. (2017b). The importance of segmentation in social marketing strategy. In T. Dietrich, S. Rundle-Thiele, & K. Kubacki (Eds.), *Segmentation in social marketing: Process, methods and application* (pp. 25–40). Singapore: Springer.

French, J., & Blair-Stevens, C. (2008). *The total process planning framework for social marketing.* London: National Social Marketing Centre.

French, J., & Russell-Bennett, R. (2015). A hierarchical model of social marketing. *Journal of Social Marketing, 5*(2), 139–159. https://doi.org/10.1108/JSOCM-06-2014-0042.

Fry, M.-L., Previte, J., & Brennan, L. (2017). Social change design: Disrupting the benchmark template. *Journal of Social Marketing, 7*(2), 119–134. https://doi.org/10.1108/jsocm-10-2016-0064.

Geia, L. K., Hayes, B., & Usher, K. (2013). Yarning/Aboriginal storytelling: Towards an understanding of an Indigenous perspective and its implications for research practice. *Contemporary Nurse, 46*(1), 13–17. https://doi.org/10.5172/conu.2013.46.1.13.

González, N., Moll, L. C., & Amanti, C. (Eds.). (2005). *Funds of knowledge: Theorizing practices in households, communities and classrooms.* Mahwah, NJ: Lawrence Erlbaum Associates.

Gordon, R., Russell-Bennett, R., & Lefebvre, R. C. (2016). Social marketing: The state of play and brokering the way forward. *Journal of Marketing Management, 32*(11–12), 1059–1082. https://doi.org/10.1080/0267257X.2016.1199156.

Harwood, V. (2006). *Diagnosing 'disorderly' children: A critique of behaviour disorder discourses.* Oxford: Routledge.

Harwood, V., & Allan, J. (2014). *Psychopathology at school: Theorising mental disorders in education.* Oxford: Routledge.

Harwood, V., Hickey-Moody, A., McMahon, S., & O'Shea, S. (2017). *The politics of widening participation and university access for young people: Making educational futures.* London: Routledge.

Harwood, V., & Murray, N. (2019). Strategic discourse production and parent involvement: Including parent knowledge and practices in the Lead My Learning campaign. *International Journal of Inclusive Education, 23*(4), 353–368. https://doi.org/10.1080/13603116.2019.1571119.

Hastings, G. P. (2007). *Social marketing: Why should the devil have all the best tunes?* London and Amsterdam: Elsevier/Butterworth-Heinemann.

Lee, N. R., & Kotler, P. (2015). Social marketing influencing behaviours for good: Quick reference guide. In *Social marketing services* (5th ed.). Mercer Island, WA: Social Marketing Services.

Lefebvre, R. C. (2013). *Social marketing and social change: Strategies and tools for improving health, well-being, and the environment.* Chichester: Wiley.

Lin, I., Green, C., & Bessarab, D. (2016). 'Yarn with me': Applying clinical yarning to improve clinician–patient communication in Aboriginal health care. *Australian Journal of Primary Health, 22*(5), 377–382. https://doi.org/10.1071/PY16051.

Luca, N., & Suggs, L. (2013). Theory and model use in social marketing health interventions. *Journal of Health Communication, 18*(1), 20. https://doi.org/10.1080/10810730.2012.688243.

Martin, K. L. (2008). *Please knock before you enter: Aboriginal regulation of outsiders and the implications for researchers.* Teneriffe, QLD: Post Pressed.

Martin, K. L., & Mirraboopa, B. (2003). Ways of knowing, being and doing: A theoretical framework and methods for Indigenous and indigenist re-search. *Journal of Australian Studies, 76,* 203–214.

National Social Marketing Centre (Ed.). (2011). *Big pocket guide to using social marketing for behaviour change.* London: NSMC.

Newton, J. D., Newton, F. J., Turk, T., & Ewing, M. T. (2013). Ethical evaluation of audience segmentation in social marketing. *European Journal of Marketing, 47*(9), 1421–1438. https://doi.org/10.1108/EJM-09-2011-0515.

Nigg, C. R., Allegrante, J. P., & Ory, M. (2002). Theory-comparison and multiple-behavior research: Common themes advancing health behavior research. *Health Education Research, 17*(5), 670–679.

Peattie, K., & Peattie, S. (2011). The social marketing mix: A critical review. In G. Hastings, K. Angus, & C. Bryant (Eds.), *The SAGE handbook of social marketing* (pp. 152–166). London: Sage.

Prochaska, J. O., & DiClemente, C. C. (1983). Stages and processes of self-change of smoking: Toward an integrative model of change. *Journal of Consulting and Clinical Psychology, 51*(3), 390–395. https://doi.org/10.1037/0022-006X.51.3.390.

Rogoff, B. (2014). Learning by observing and pitching into family and community endeavours. *Human Development, 57,* 69–81.

Rogoff, B., Coppens, A. D., Alcalá, L., Aceves-Azuara, I., Ruvalcaba, O., López, A., & Dayton, A. (2017). Noticing learners' strengths through cultural research. *Perspectives on Psychological Science, 12*(5), 876–888. https://doi.org/10.1177/1745691617718355.

Rogoff, B. (2014). *Learning by observing and pitching in overview.* Retrieved from http://www.learningbyobservingandpitchingin.com/icp-overview-english. 5 October, 2019.

Rosenstock, I. M., Strecher, V. J., & Becker, M. H. (1988). Social learning theory and the health belief model. *Health Education Quarterly, 15*(2), 175–183. https://doi.org/10.1177/109019818801500203.

Rothman, A. J. (2000). Toward a theory-based analysis of behavioral maintenance. *Health Psychology: Official Journal of the Division of Health Psychology, American Psychological Association, 19*(1S), 64–69. https://doi.org/10.1037/0278-6133.19.Suppl1.64.

Saunders, S. G., Barrington, D. J., & Sridharan, S. (2015). Redefining social marketing: Beyond behavioural change. *Journal of Social Marketing, 5*(2), 160–168. https://doi.org/10.1108/JSOCM-03-2014-0021.

Sen, A. K. (1999). *Development as freedom.* Oxford: Oxford University Press.

Tapp, A., & Spotswood, F. (2013). Beyond persuasion: A cultural perspective of behaviour. *Journal of Social Marketing, 3*(3), 275–294. https://doi.org/10.1108/JSOCM-01-2013-0006.

Towney, L. M. (2005). The power of healing in the yarns: Working with Aboriginal men. *International Journal of Narrative Therapy & Community Work 2005*(1), 39–43. Peer Reviewed Full content available at https://search.informit.com.au/documentSummary;dn=244322186941673;res=IELFSC.

Urrieta, L. J. (2015). Learning by observing and pitching in and the connections to native and Indigenous knowledge systems. In M. Correa-Chevaz, R. Mejia-Arauz, & B. Rogoff (Eds.), *Children learn by observing and contributing to family and community endeavours: A cultural paradigm* (pp. 357–380). Waltham, MA: Elsevier.

Watson, I. (2014). Re-centring first nations knowledge and places in a terra nullius space. *AlterNative: An International Journal of Indigenous Peoples, 10*(5), 508–520. https://doi.org/10.1177/117718011401000506.

Zembylas, M. (2002). Structures of feelings. *Educational Theory, 52*(2), 187–208.

5

The Lead My Learning Campaign

In this chapter we describe the educational promotion campaign—Lead My Learning, which was delivered across New South Wales, Australia in three modalities: childcare centres, a community-wide setting and in playgroups. As well as a detailed overview of the Lead My Learning campaign, the discussion also includes how the marketing mix was extended to include critique and cultural protocols. We also provide details of: the intellectual and creative concepts; strategic goals; the strength-based framework and what we term *critical cultural yarning model*. The second part of the chapter points out detailed accounts of different strategies and promotional products used in the Lead My Learning campaign. Here we discuss the social and cultural communication (promotion) of this educational promotion campaign. The chapter is written to provide a complete overview of the Lead My Learning campaign, and consequently there is some minor repetition of points described earlier in the book.

© The Author(s) 2019
V. Harwood and N. Murray, *The Promotion of Education*,
https://doi.org/10.1007/978-3-030-25300-4_5

Rationale for the Lead My Learning Campaign

Children from low socio-economic status backgrounds are, for a range of reasons, far less likely to attend university, leading to lesser income, poorer health and social outcomes, and be affected by intergenerational poverty. Many of these children are 'smart enough' to attend university, but there are barriers to attending that include a number of factors associated with schooling, perceptions and experiences of education institutions. Parent involvement is important to children's experiences and engagement in education, yet not all parents have their involvement in their children's learning recognised as a legitimate learning practice. Improving the recognition of these different learning practices is important for parents since it connects what they do with the education of their children. The promotion of education often starts at secondary school when it is too late, and is normally promoted by an educational institution for the sole purpose of increasing student numbers. A different form of promoting education is therefore required that can address the issue of the lack of recognition of the diversity of ways parents are involved in their children's learning.

The Lead My Learning Campaign

Lead My Learning is a critical cultural social marketing campaign that has been produced from the Australian Research Council Future Fellowship project '*Getting and early start to aspiration: Understanding how to promote higher education in early childhood*' (project number: FT1301011332). Lead My Learning promotes educational futures in early childhood in places impacted by disadvantage and particularly, educational disadvantage. The campaign objective is to enhance parents' recognition of their involvement in their children's learning through sharing and encouraging learning strategies. The campaign recognises parents are involved in their children's learning, and these activities are endorsed and promoted.

The Lead My Learning campaign was rolled out in urban regional and rural settings in New South Wales, Australia to reach parents, caregivers and family members with children aged 0–6 years. We use the term 'parents' to refer to people involved in parenting, which is inclusive of, for example, parents, grandparents, aunties and uncles, and caregivers. For our priority group we identified three modalities that we wanted to trial with Lead My Learning promotion products. These different modalities were based on the formative work, which identified the need for: a community-wide campaign; a playgroup campaign; and an Aboriginal early childhood centre campaign in places that relied on a bus service to transport children to and from home. These are summarised below:

1. A community-wide campaign in Girral (pseudonym), a regional NSW town with a population of approximately 29,000. The national population of Aboriginal people is 3.3%, at Girral it is 12%. This campaign focused on the range of places where parents of young children might connect with campaign messages, and as such also included playgroups, childcare centres and other related services. A waitlist-control approach was incorporated in Kurrawong (pseudonym), a community of similar demographics. This was done in order to compare the delivery of the campaign against other factors that may have influenced parent involvement in their children's learning (such as a different campaign).

2. A multi-playgroup campaign that included Aboriginal playgroups, in partnership with a service provider in regional NSW (11 sites). The playgroups involved parents who regularly attend with their children, and employed playgroup facilitator/s.

3. An early childhood centre campaign in four Aboriginal owned and operated services that rely on bus transport for children in regional NSW.

The Lead My Learning campaign commenced on September 2016 and was finalised in March 2017 (six months). The budget for the campaign was $AUD76,000, with $AUD60,000 for the campaign and campaign promotional products, and $AUD16,000 for the formative and design research with participants. Research costs have not been included in this budget, given that this activity formed part of the larger research project.

Across the three different modalities, we worked with childcare centres, preschools, playgroups and other child related services that would benefit from having the campaign resources. It was important to ensure that the campaign marketing promotional products did not impact on service delivery, but rather was an add on value to their service.

Lead My Learning is about turning everyday activities into opportunities to lead a child's learning, to find fun, easy and imaginative ways to share and encourage learning with young children. Parents, caregivers and family members who are around young children the most are in a great place to share and encourage learning with children each day. The priority group spend a lot of time with young children, and are with them during many ordinary daily activities. Sharing and encouraging learning can be included in everyday activities to create a fun learning relationship to build a child's future. It only takes a minute to create a learning moment that can happen in everyday activities. The Lead My Learning campaign was designed to appeal to the priority group parents, caregiver and family members with young children. The aim was to offer ideas for how to integrate sharing and encouraging learning into daily life and by providing resources of clever ways for the priority group to respond to a young child's request to 'Lead My Learning'.

The campaign was inclusive of Aboriginal and non-Aboriginal people and is an educational promotional strategy designed from discussions with parents, caregivers, families and early childhood educators across NSW. Available to Aboriginal parents and non-Aboriginal parents, we were guided by Aboriginal people. This approach to promoting education flips 'mainstream' strategies. Aboriginal people consulted in our research were pleased that non-Aboriginal people were welcome to participate in the campaign. Thus, while our approach did incorporate consultation with non-Aboriginal people, we ensured this was in keeping with the Aboriginal guided approaches. Cultural knowledge is recognised as being valuable and a privilege to learn from Aboriginal parents.

The educational promotional strategy purposely was a parent-led design by parents for parents. All promotional and printed products and the messages were developed and tested through multiple discussions with the priority group. Assessment of any contribution of the Lead My Learning campaign was likewise attentive to parent feedback. Introducing Lead My Learning when children are young could mean that they and their parents, caregivers and families, and early childhood educators start to assume educational futures are possible and that there are opportunities for them (and their families) for further education such as university.

Segmentation

Identification of different segments in a priority group is essential to the design and development of communication messages and subsequent campaigns designed to improve education outcomes. This may involve, for example, segmentation based on demographic variables (such as different messages and strategies for different cultural and language groups) or different approaches for those who have never considered university as an option for their children than for those who are actively opposed to university education.

Segmenting the priority group identified four key areas (see Table 5.1). We identified the 'happiness vs education' segment as the priority group to focus on for the delivery of the Lead My Learning core message. The 'happiness vs education' priority group viewed happiness as more important than education. Parents described getting involved in education as 'pushy' and that, because of the importance of their children's happiness, they preferred to enjoy fun playtime when their children were young and focus

Table 5.1 Segmentation

Segment	Segment description
Involvement in education	• Letting children drive the situation
	• Kids directing when they choose/want to do something
Employment focus	• Having been brought up with values that a job is more important than education
	• Securing low-skilled employment positions
Educational system	• Dislike educational system
	• Cultural/intergenerational history
	• It's school's responsibility (norm)
Happiness vs education	• Kids need to be kids
	• Will help encourage in the future only if the child wants to
	• Happy time is not when you are learning or doing homework

on education when they are older. This did not mean parents did not value education. The parents were clear that they valued education. Rather, due to their own experiences with education, schooling was not equated with happiness. For these parents, from their own perceived capacity, to be a 'good' parent meant prioritising the happiness of their children over the demands of education. Major barriers were firstly, having little time due to being busy with other daily duties, and this would take the time away from them having enjoyable fun playtime. Secondly, a major barrier was their perceived capacity to be involved in learning due to their own histories with institutional education (for example, not completing schooling or difficult schooling experiences) and dominant discourses of education that hold to a narrow version of what it 'means' to be involved in a child's learning (see Chapter 6).

Identifying the 'happiness vs education' segment and taking into account the barriers described of time limitations and perceived capacity of 'educatedness', meant it was important to produce a strategic educational futures campaign that allowed 'kids to be kids' and where parents could identify how learning is involved and is enjoyable and fun. We note here that aspects of the other segments such as cultural/intergenerational history occur in the 'happiness vs education' segment, but that the emphasis on happiness versus education was especially prominent for this segment. Following segmentation of the priority group, we developed a proposition statement, an 'offer' that has greater benefits for a child's educational futures and fewer barrier than the existing perceived capacity, action or engagement to convey the importance of integrating learning into their daily duties.

Proposition Statement

In social marketing a proposition statement is the offer to a target segment. It describes 'the behaviour' as having greater benefits and lower costs, fewer barriers than the existing behaviour. As we have outlined in Chapter 4, in our work this has been twisted to seek, acknowledge and build on practices of learning, and is not associated with changing behaviour. Lead My Learning strived to appreciate the practices that are happening, and work with these, and do this against the grain of dominant practices that erase what parents *know* and *do* in learning with their children. The Lead My Learning proposition statement is:

> **It is possible to lead your child's learning**. It only takes a little time and it can fit in with everyday activities. You can encourage your child's learning without having a specific knowledge of a topic and it gives a child the happy experiences of valuing and enjoying learning.

Importantly the statement depicts sophisticated learning relationships, how they are connected and can introduce Lead My Learning to welcome it into their families' daily lives. The proposition statement became the foundation for developing the intellectual and creative concepts, promotional products, as well as ideas for activities such as local sponsorship of community activities in Girral (the community-wide setting).

The Exchange

The concept of exchange in social marketing is about the exchange of value. The value needs to inform the priority group that to give up one behaviour will be beneficial to take up another behaviour. Lead My Learning is a critical cultural social marketing campaign that stepped away from the behaviour-based focus in social marketing principles and focused on an exchange that increases recognition of parent involvement and revealing that parents are *already doing* leading learning their children.

Although awkward to describe as it is not simply 'behaviour change', the exchange of value is that there has not been an actual name, label or language provided to the priority group, and Lead My Learning is offering this recognition. This exchange of value takes on a strength-based approach to parents' capacities and knowledges, and exposes parents viewing themselves in the learning and education space with their children. As was mentioned when we discussed segmentation, parents have a perceived capacity of where they are positioned in their 'educatedness'; the exchange of value helped parents to not think of themselves as uneducated and highlights that they are leading learning, and importantly, through the language and concepts Lead My Learning provides, to think in possibly more 'legitimated' ways about their relationship to their children's learning.

The critical cultural social marketing approach applied uses the notion of 'change state' (Duane, Domegan, McHugh, & Devaney, 2016) as a way of conceptualising the exchange concept. The *change state* that we sought to create was one where the discourses of parent involvement in learning of our campaign are taken up over and above any discourses that portray the parents as not being involved in their child's learning. Described in the reorientating scoping section of Chapter 6, the Lead My Learning educational futures campaign articulates and reinforces discourses of parent involvement in leading their children's learning. Lead My Learning is a preference over deficit discourses. The question of why parents might want to engage in such a change state needs to be differently conceptualised than a straightforward or commonplace interpretation of a marketing 'exchange'. This education promotion campaign is underpinned by the assumption that a parent can do something that has an effect on leading their children's learning, that this connects with building a future in education, and that parents can change how they perceive their involvement in learning. This creates 'a space' where parents can talk about leading learning and challenge how they identify in relation to their involvement in their children's learning.

Lead My Learning seeks to enhance parents' relationships towards education, educational engagement and participation in leading their children's learning through sharing and encouraging educational learning strategies.

Lead My Learning Marketing Mix

The marketing mix is the basis for 'getting the message out' to the priority group. As discussed in Chapter 3, the marketing mix from Peattie and Peattie (2011) offers five elements. Lead My Learning introduces two additions to this, Critique and Protocols, to form the critical cultural social marketing mix (see Chapter 4) tailored for a critical cultural social marketing campaign. The Lead My Learning marketing mix is shown below:

1. **Social and cultural propositions (Products)**: The core proposition was that parents would feel good about the learning activities that they are doing. Promotional products that communicated the Lead My Learning messages are described in detail below.
2. **Social and cultural cost of involvement (Price)**: This was the cost of involvement, which included time as well as the challenge of engaging in an alternative discourse about learning.
3. **Accessibility (Place)**: A range of places and avenues for disseminating the proposition, which are informed by the priority group as appropriate.
4. **Social and cultural communication (Promotion)**: The forms of social and cultural communication that are used to promote the campaign.
5. **Partnerships (Stakeholder involvement)**: Adapt to a range of situations. Includes formal and informal partnerships; Aboriginal and non-Aboriginal stakeholders. The definition of partnerships and relationship we use is different to partnership and relations for business or personal gain. Listening to people and Country, working together to establish an inclusive approach, control, decisions, power relationships (researcher/participants/services).
6. **Critique (Position of discourse)**: Alertness to the discourses impacting parents and their children; alertness to colonising practices; alertness to classed (social class) practices; care not to engage in acts of repetition of these; tactic of disrupting these as part of the mix.
7. **Protocols (Philosophical and practical ways)**: Adhering to cultural protocols, sharing this in our relationships, ensuring the protocols guide the marketing mix and method for the campaign (Adapted from Peattie and Peattie, 2011).

The addition of Critique and Protocols provides collaborative and respectful methods. Implementing the new elements ensured that the intellectual and creative concepts were delivered to the priority group in a dynamic way that was always guided by the critical and cultural emphasis.

Intellectual and Creative Concepts

The Lead My Learning educational futures campaign is made up of intellectual and creative concepts developed from the priority group's knowledge, ideas and experience of education. These all contributed to the: name of the campaign, Lead My Learning; campaign clear message; and to Share and Encourage learning; the key concepts used to deliver the messages.

The campaign name Lead My Learning relays a message from a child that talks to parents; it is a call to action. The purpose is to communicate that the campaign integrates leading learning into daily life and that it is accessible and free to include in daily activities. It was important that the name of the campaign demonstrates that everyone can 'Lead My Learning' and contribute to children's educational futures for a lifetime. The campaign delivers the clear message:

> Everyday Activities are opportunities to Share and Encourage Learning.

Everyday Activities was important to convey in this message, and associated promotional products incorporated the clarification that 'it only takes a little time to lead your child's learning and it can fit in with daily activities parents do each day'. This clear message is inclusive of the two key concepts: Sharing learning and Encouraging learning. Separate messages were developed for each of these. The Share Learning message is:

> You can share learning when you are doing your 'Everyday Activities': Cooking, Washing, Shopping, Out & About.

The Encourage Learning message is:

> Everyone's an expert at learning. You can encourage my learning by giving me: High fives, Fist bump, Thumbs up or even a big smile.

Explanations of the Share Learning message and the Encourage Learning message were provided in some of the promotional products and on the Lead My Learning website. A description of the Share and Encourage learning moments that was included in these promotional products is provided below:

> Sharing and Encouraging learning moments helps children enjoy learning, to feel strong about learning, and importantly, be keen to learn and explore learning relationships. Sharing learning is to talk about the 'how' to learning, describing things as you see them, sharing information, children watching you learn. Sharing can be as simple as asking a question to spark curiosity. Encouraging learning is about giving acts of encouragement like smiling, giving a thumbs up, when you child attempts to learn or has learnt what you are leading. It is about giving positive reinforcement and praise for trying. The trick here is to lead a child to feel good about learning. (Murray & Harwood, 2018)

These messages were incorporated into the Lead My Learning promotional products, the campaign sponsorship and the paid advertisement of the campaign messages in the community. Intellectual and creative concepts were based on the proposition statement. The creative concepts are designs of visual and audio promotional products that include local parents, artwork designs and the images that depict child-led cues for parent involvement in learning. Our formative research had shown that parents would respond to child-led cues to become involved in learning, and not cues from other sources, for instance, an 'education expert' such as a school teacher, which has also been reported by others (Green, Walker, Hoover-Dempsey, & Sandler, 2007).

Logo

The Lead My Learning logo portrays the nurturing and caring relationships between a parent and a child, and illustrates the existing supportive and protective learning involvement. This was developed based on the formative study that indicated the priority group are caring and protective towards their children and while parents believe education is important, they see their role as being supportive of the child and not directive.

The style of the logo represents the proposition statement of the campaign and gives the feeling of a happy experience of leading, valuing and enjoying learning between a parent and a child. The artwork depicts a parent's feet placed safely around the bright colours of a child's feet. This image demonstrates that parents are leading their children's learning. The colours in the logo represent and relate to being a fun learning moment. Its shows a powerful image, and is a non-verbal form to communicate the meaning of Lead My Learning's message.

The Lead My Learning logo uses five branded colours: golden yellow; light blue; orange; lime green; and purple. These are used to create and stimulate emotions for happiness and warmth, calming and trusting, playful and youthful, and living relationships that are strong. Within the logo there are multiple colours surrounding both the child's and the parent's feet that represent the diversity of cultures, nations and people. The Lead My Learning logo symbolises the relationship of parents leading their children's learning (Fig. 5.1).

During the formative research, a design brief for the logo was devised that was based on discussion and feedback with representatives from the

Fig. 5.1 Lead My Learning logo

priority group. The Lead My Learning logo was created based on this design brief by artist John Raymond Johnson, a Warumungu/Wombaya Man employed by the graphic designer.

Strategic Goals and Objectives

As described in Chapter 3, Lead My Learning was created using a critical cultural social marketing approach that adapted social marketing techniques to create an educational promotion campaign for use with parents who have experienced educational disadvantage and who have young children. The need for such a campaign was identified based on the very limited work that has been done on widening participation with this cohort of parents and their young children.

Social marketing strategies were utilised in the Lead My Learning campaign to deliver 'education promotion' to LSES families with young children, and in some places, indirectly to childcare professionals. The strategic goals and objectives of the Lead My Learning campaign are to better understand how these parents view education, and to devise innovative strategies for educational engagement by focussing on parents' participation in their child's learning.

Lead My Learning had a strategic goal to promote educational futures. One of the key strategies built into all campaign promotional products was to increase parents' recognition of their capacity to support their children's learning. This was communicated using supportive learning tools such as to be confident with learning strategies. The learning tools included provision of two online resources: Lead My Learning Facebook Page (a public page) and the Lead My Learning website. Strategies also involved the following activities.

Talking about parent involvement in learning
The campaign sought to create opportunities for parents to have conversations with other parents about their children's learning. The mechanism for this was by saturating the sites in each of the modalities (childcare, community-wide, playgroup) with campaign and promotional products. This included for example, online competitions via the Facebook page,

Lead My Learning promotional products in services, childcare centres and in playgroups.

In the community-wide modality, alignment with existing community strategies

In the community-wide setting, Lead My Learning was aligned with a specific Community Strategy Plan (not named to protect confidentiality). Lead My Learning aligned with this strategy by introducing community activities that connect and celebrate parents and families participating in leading their children's learning. This included free family photos and posters in services.

Differently describing parent involvement in learning

Lead My Learning differently described parental involvement in their children's learning. Parents were strongly positioned as being involved in their children's learning. This included resources/messages that depicted parents as involved in learning in a range of activities that are largely unrecognised as leading learning.

Contributing to a young child's education

As explained in Chapters 1 and 2, Parent involvement in learning is of great significance to a child's learning, to their education and consequently, can positively contribute to their educational futures. Lead My Learning sought to enhance educational opportunities in the future for children and their parents by introducing the necessary tools to inspire and build confidence around parents' involvement in their young children's learning. This was included across all of the promotional products, in all of the modalities and sites.

Design, Review and Modification of Campaign Modalities

Our initial plan, prior to the formative research and before Lead My Learning was created, was to place the educational futures campaign only at early childhood centres. However, after our fieldwork where we visited communities we soon learned that not only is there an issue with the children in our priority group not attending childcare, the childcare environment itself was not an *accessible* site for the campaign. This is because contact with parents is extremely limited in childcare settings (see Chapter 1)

Consequently, we had to ask where are the children that do not attend? And we needed to consider how can we get our campaign message to reach the priority group. This problematic prompted the design of the three modalities: Community-wide; Playgroup only setting; and Childcare centres that use a bus to transport the children to and from home.

> **Community-wide modality** included both playgroups and childcare centres, as well as other relevant services such as libraries, neighbourhood centres, cultural centres and health centres to disseminate the promotion products and information.

> **A service that provides multi-site playgroups (11 sites).** Playgroups are easily accessible environments for the campaign, with parents present with their children during the learning activities. Families have easy access to being supported with a range of information and promotional products.

> **Childcare centres** are places where parents are not always present. The childcare centres we worked with utilised buses to transport children to and from the childcare service. Lead My Learning had to get creative and innovative to ensure the information and promotional products were present in their homes.

As well as a playgroup only modality for the campaign, we also accessed playgroups in the community-wide modality. We observed that, when the campaign was taken up by parents, playgroups were the most effective environment to implement Lead My Learning. This was because playgroups have a focus to provide activities between parent and child.

Strength-Based Framework

Lead My Learning is based on a strength-based framework (see Chapters 2 and 6). Recognising what people, culture and communities do and the impacts of dominant deficit discourses that influence how one thinks about others is critical to ensuring that a non-deficit approach is constructed.

The strength-based framework highlights the fact that learning is occurring between parents and their children. Lead My Learning is about ways to show how parents are involved, how they engage with leading learning, to celebrate leading learning, and importantly, for leading learning to be recognisable for parents and families. This is a fundamental of the strength-based approach about parents leading their children's educational futures. Parents have sophisticated, deep, insightful knowledgeable ways of learning and learning practices, yet parents and families may experience negative perceptions of themselves because of how institutional education has ways of knowing that dominate and delegitimate. Institutional education does not necessarily recognise the parents' sophisticated ways of learning, learning practices, learning knowledges and learning relationships.

Referring back to the notion of valuing education and feeling uncomfortable about education, parents who have not experienced higher education, still strongly value educational futures for their children. We need to listen and become informed about the complexity of disadvantage and to actively question the hierarchy of knowledge (especially in institutional settings) and the assumptions underpinning this problematic hierarchy.

We describe later in this chapter the outcomes from our post-campaign interviews (yarning and semi-structured) with parents. In these interviews the parents described not having a name or way to say what it is that they are doing with their children and learning. The Lead My Learning campaign provided a language for parents to describe leading their children's learning.

Critical Cultural Yarning Model for Lead My Learning

Using the critical cultural social marketing approach, we complemented the strength-based framework with what we term a Critical Cultural Yarning Model for Lead My Learning. This Critical Cultural Yarning Model of Lead My Learning, illustrated in Fig. 5.2, provided a basis for describing and applying the yarning model (discussions about ideas) that we used for Lead My Learning. We outline the components of this model below.

Fig. 5.2 Critical Cultural Yarning Model

Value the knowledge and practices parents have

Firstly, to *Value the knowledge and practices parents have*, is the foundation for the yarning model. This required critical questioning such as:

> How do I value the knowledge and practices of learning that parents and families have?

Explicitly asking this question helped us to think critically about how we can be respectful of a parent's knowledge and their involvement in learning. This enabled us to recognise the parents' involvement in their children's learning through what they do in their everyday activities. Such learning from the priority group can be achieved by critically questioning our own assumptions.

Deference

Deference implies a yielding and respectful submission to valuing parents' cultural knowledge. We use the word submission here to convey the need to disrupt the power dynamic of the researchers by the submission of assumptions and knowledge of the researchers to *listen* to another. Applying critical listening techniques and being critical and reflective can assist in rejecting dominant discourses and particularly, deficit discourses about the parents, learning and education. Here we used questions such as:

How can I show respect and esteem to another?

Reminding ourselves about sharing and respectful ways, being guided by the Aboriginal Research Protocols, helped us to remember it is a privilege to be able to listen and learn from parents and families. This helped us to recognise the value of cultural knowledge.

Recognise
The status of our position and institutional affiliations can deliberately or inadvertently create barriers to strength-based approaches. To recognise the value of these knowledges and practices it is vital to first, understand and appreciate the complexity of educational disadvantage and secondly, continually adjust our thinking away from a deficit approach. Questions we asked included:

How do I recognise the value of these knowledges and practices parents have?

Learn
Thinking through methods to learn from the priority group can be achieved by understanding to critically question our own assumptions. Questions we asked included:

How do I enter into an ongoing relationship of learning from and with parents about knowledge and practices? and How can I contribute to a two-way learning process?

Privilege
It is a privilege to learn from the parents, and emphasising this brings a heightened awareness of the cultural and of diverse knowledges, experiences and practices of learning. In applying critique, we were able to

critically view deficit discourses that might 'discredit' the parents' knowledge of learning—and be on the alert for assumptions that we (or others) might have. Through understanding the value of parent knowledge and practices, deference, recognising, learning, and being sympathetic to that is a privilege. We can ask questions such as:

> How do I honour the privilege I have of experiencing the knowledges and practices that parents have? and How do I maintain relationships to have the privilege?

Apply

At this point, it is important to think about how the elements of this framework is applied to images, promotional products and to the messages that are created. This prompts the questions:

> How do I respectfully create opportunities to apply what I am learning? and Am I learning to create initiatives that value the knowledge and practices parents have? and What can I implement?

The application of the creation of a critical cultural social marketing campaign required an activity of critique that took account of these concepts, and a strength-based approach. It is through this Critical Cultural Yarning Model that we were able to create the education promotion campaign, Lead My Learning (www.leadmylearning.com.au).

Social and Cultural Communication (Promotion)

The promotion of Lead My Learning took on multiple forms of social and cultural communication using a critical cultural social marketing approach. The culturally appropriate term 'campaign' is used (see Chapter 4), or occasionally the term 'educational futures promotion'. This education promotion campaign drew on social and cultural communication. It was not an advertising programme or simply a communication strategy. Neither was it a marketing strategy for a particular university, or of higher education in general. Rather, it was a campaign that was created based on the needs identified for this priority group of parents who, to a significant extent, have their involvement in their children's learning delegitimated by discourses of institutional education (for example, that they are 'uneducated' or that the school is the only site of expertise on learning).

The campaign was created using the critical cultural social marketing approach, setting out to promote education in a way that was respectful to parents, easily accessible and non-disruptive to parents, educators and services. The social and cultural communication of the campaign was designed by parents (see Chapter 4). The design specifically was to communicate what parents were doing, show that what the parents were doing was 'great', for parents to keep going with what they were doing, and possibly, to do these activities even more. The education promotion strategies were disseminated across several modalities: childcare centres; multi-playgroup setting; and a community-wide setting.

The promotional channels for this critical cultural social marketing campaign are: the promotional products; paid advertisements; sponsorships; and the everyday activities idea resources. Using the 4P language often used in the marketing mix, each of these creates attractive benefit packages (products) while minimising costs (price) wherever possible, making the exchange convenient and easy (place) and communicating powerful messages through media relevant to, and preferred by, the priority audience (promotion). Promotion involved disseminating the social and cultural communication (promotion) benefits. These promotional products are outlined in the following section.

Promotional Products

Lead My Learning used promotional products that communicated the Lead My Learning messages (see the section in this chapter, "Intellectual and Creative Concepts") to deliver the educational futures campaign. Promotional products included: printed materials; special promotional items; signage and displays; and social media. These promotional products were designed to achieve the exchange (see earlier discussion).

The variety of promotional products were branded with the Lead My Learning logo and core messages. These products where provided to the priority group for free. The accessibility (placement) of these products was within childcare centres, playgroups, in related services, in the community-wide modality and across communities. The aim being to create a 'value add' opportunity with little to no disruption to the services or to parents. Each of these promotional products are described below. Table 5.2 provides an overview of the roll out of these promotional products. Images of the products are shown in Fig. 5.3.

Balloons
A popular promotional product. Each balloon is branded with the Lead My Learning logo, printed in the five Lead My Learning colours.

Corflute signs
External material signs positioned around the community, at the front of childcare centres, preschool, playgroups, sports grounds and in business windows. The print on the corflute sign is Lead My Learning clear message.

Drink coasters
An additional product placed external to childcare centres and playgroups. These products were distributed in local hotels, clubs and cafes. The drink coasters were a promotion product that helped increased the frequency of the message to parents.

Large greenscreen photos at the campaign launch for the community-wide modality
Free family photos presented as a great opportunity to disseminate the Lead My Learning logo and message into family homes. The free photos were branded with the Lead My Learning logo and message. Greenscreen photos allowed people to select from five different backgrounds: a beach setting, a backyard, a fruit shop, a football sports field, and a Lead My Learning magazine cover. Dress up and play items were available at the photo booth for parents and children. A print copy was made of the photo after the photographs were taken by the professional photographer. Parents and families were able to take home a hard copy print on the day and were able to access the photograph electronically via social media and by email (if they supplied an email address).

We used a professional greenscreen photography service that hired local people to assist the photographer. These free photographs were offered to parents over a five-day period. The first day was at the campaign launch, which we had aligned to be at a large annual community event. This was followed by four days open to everyone at a local and trusted family service.

Information Booklet

A six panel 'Z fold design' information booklet provided a method for parents to have easy access to Lead My Learning information. Due to the small size, parents could easily pick up this Z fold card, and keep it readily available. The information booklet provided parents with details of the campaign, creative concepts and messages and was an information resource for parents to refer to about sharing and encouraging learning through every day activities. In addition to being a useful resource for parents, this product allowed for childcare educators (including voluntary playgroup facilitators) to engage in conversations about the Lead My Learning campaign with families and community members. These conversations were reported to us as often taking place on the Lead My Learning playmat. With the exception of the image of a child having a bath, (where a stock image was sourced for child protection reasons), all images used in the information booklets were of local families leading their children's learning. The photographs were also taken by local people, including members from the services involved in the campaign.

Magnetic photo frames

In a discussion with an Aboriginal Aunty in one of the communities, we learned that photos were treasured items in their home. This insight prompted us to create magnetic photo frames with an inner part of the frame that separates to offer a second magnet branded with the Lead My Learning clear message. This photo frame was a successful promotional product that entered into families' homes and was proudly placed on their family fridge.

My name is sticker

The name stickers were a popular product at events and within childcare centres (in both the community-wide modality, and in the childcare only modality). The stickers were 9 × 6 cm in size. Children that could write their name, did so proudly. This product was also offered in two Aboriginal languages in wait-list control community-wide setting (Kurrawong).

Paint sheets

A pre-printed paint sheet (A5 size) was created, which included paint palettes and an image of a local family. These can be 'painted' by adding water to the pre-printed paper. The paint sheet also had a worksheet to engage conversation about leading children's learning, and promoted parents to talk, draw or write with their children what is happening in the image. While possibly a novel idea, the concept failed as the paint sheet was too small for the young children.

Pens

Pens with the Lead My Learning website address were a main promotional product that was accessible for everyone to use and keep. It was a popular promotional product that was widely spread for easy accessibility for our priority group.

Photobooth photos

Photobooth photos were used as a promotion product that was offered to childcare centre modality to help get the message into the family home. The photo booths were offered at events that were already in the childcare centre's event calendar (for example, end of year celebration/graduation day). The photo booth provided small print-outs that were branded with the Lead My Learning Logo.

Playmats

A 3-metre Lead My Learning branded playmat that could be used both outside and inside was provided to multiple sites in all three of the modalities (community-wide, childcare services and all the playgroup sites). The playmat can be considered the most effective and useful promotion product created for the campaign for a number of reasons that include not only how it was received by parents, but also the ease with which it could be 'used' and the value add it gave to services and to parents.

This promotional product did not impact on service delivery and provided childcare educators and voluntary playgroup facilitators with the opportunity to gather parents and their children to talk about Lead My

Learning with their families. Discussions of Lead My Learning could be both planned, and impromptu, with the design on the playmat prompting conversation.

The playmat was also offered to engage the online community parent community on the Lead My Learning Facebook page. We provided many giveaways via this online environment for parents as a mechanism for parents to promote their comments about how they are Sharing and Encouraging their children's learning. Parents would also get in contact with us (via telephone or email) to ask about purchasing the playmats. We didn't sell the playmats—these were free, and we had a finite amount of playmats that had been produced within our budget.

Posters

A3 sized posters were professionally printed and made freely available. The posters were designed with images of local people and explained the concepts of Sharing and Encouraging learning. There were three categories of posters: Sharing Learning; Encouraging Learning; and a clear message poster.

In keeping with attention to the cultural differences of the different locations in the project, as well as the different people in the priority group (Aboriginal and non-Aboriginal) 17 different posters were printed and distributed. In total, four posters were produced for each campaign rollout area. The posters were promoted in all playgroups, childcare centres and in the community-wide setting. This also included related services such as libraries, neighbourhood centres, cultural centres and health centres.

Song button

The idea of a Lead My Learning song was first raised during the formative research. Later during the Lead My Learning campaign this idea was developed, with the result of the creation and production of a Lead My Learning child-led design song. The song was created by 40 children under six years of age at one of the campaign rollout sites. The song was recorded and uploaded to the sound buttons. The buttons could be started and paused at any time when the big button was pressed. Some of the wording from this song was later used in a children's book that was produced by community members from a different campaign rollout area.

Online Products: Lead My Learning Website and Lead My Learning Facebook Page

Lead My Learning had a dedicated public website that could be accessed by parents and educators (www.leadmylearning.com.au). The website has a home page that highlights the messages and descriptions of the Sharing and Encouraging learning concepts. The 'Lead' page provides resources that could be accessed for leading learning. These resources include activities at home or 'out and about'. Topics covered include: maths and science for little kids; transition to school; as well as information about literacy and reading, speech and language, and disability. The website was the main source to access information for resources on Everyday Activities (see below for more detail on these resources).

The Lead My Learning Facebook page was a public page, where promotional products from the website was incorporated, and updates and information was shared. The Facebook page was used to communicate information when the Lead My Learning competitions were run (such as back to school).

Images of Lead My Learning Promotional Products

Images of the range of Learning promotional products are provided in Figs. 5.3, 5.4, 5.5, 5.6, 5.7 and 5.8.

Advertisements

Advertisements, both paid and unpaid, provided an additional avenue of promotion. We purchased paid advertisement channels to place the campaign messages in bus shelters, childcare bus window stickers, pre-school t-shirts, radio segments and on a taxi service. Advertising the educational promotion strategy was useful to get the messages out to the priority group and to increase the frequency of the campaign being seen. The paid advertisements are described below, and the rollout and imagery used is summarised in Table 5.3.

Table 5.2 Lead My Learning promotional products

Multi-site playgroup (Eastside services)	Childcare service (Madden Island, Broadhurst, Bushwick, Upper Eastside)	Community 1 (Girral)	Community 2 (Kurrawong)	Educators/services	Priority group	Lead My Learning promotional products
x	x	x	x	x	x	Balloons
x	x	x			x	Corflute signs
x	x	x	x	x	x	Drink coasters
		x			x	Greenscreen photos
x	x	x			x	Information booklets
x	x	x	x		x	Magnetic photo frames
x	x	x	x	x	x	My name is sticker
x				x	x	Paint sheets
x	x	x	x	x	x	Pens
x	x			x	x	Photo booths
x	x	x	x	x	x	Playmats
x	x	x	x	x	x	Posters
x	x	x	x	x	x	Song button
x	x	x	x	x	x	Online products (website and Facebook page)

Fig. 5.3 Lead My Learning promotional products

Fig. 5.4 Lead My Learning promotional products

Fig. 5.5 Clear message poster

Fig. 5.6   Share poster

Fig. 5.7 Encourage poster

Bus windown stickers

Bus shelters

Taxi service advertisement   *Preschool T-shirts*

Fig. 5.8   Paid advertisements

Bus Shelters

A paid advertisement used to promote a campaign in a community approach, placed strategically at the main bus stop near the local shopping centre and along the main busy road that community members accessed to go to and leave the centre of town. The advertisement was a larger version of the A3 sized posters. Two bus shelters displayed the posters. The bus shelter advertisements were paid to be displayed for a 12-month period, which provided the main community with visual advertising to increase the frequency of the campaign message and reinforce the educational futures campaign.

Bus Window Stickers

While not strictly a paid advertisement in the sense of hiring of a commercial advertising space, we have chosen to include the one-way vision stickers used on the windows in childcare buses as 'advertisements' given

Table 5.3 Advertisements

Lead My Learning advertisements	Multi-playgroup (Eastside)	Childcare (Madden Island, Broadhurst, Bushwick, Upper Eastside)	Community 1 (Girral)	Community 2 (Kurrawong)	Educators/services	Priority group
Bus shelters			x			x
Bus window stickers		x	x		x	x
Preschool t-shirts		x	x		x	x
Radio segment			x			x
Taxi service			x			x

(1) this technique is a commonly used paid advertising approach; and (2) the high cost of this item in terms of both production and its application onto the buses. The stickers were used on buses in the childcare centre modality, where a centre operated bus service was used to transport the young children to and from the centre.

These one-way vision window stickers provided the opportunity to ensure the campaign messages was being delivered to parents that did not attend the centre. As it turned out, it was also was another opportunity for community advertisement (although we were only able to collect informal discussions about the reactions to these in the community). The bus window stickers were only applied to four childcare bus services, creating an advertisement for the Lead My Learning campaign as the bus travelled in and around the region transporting the young children.

Preschool T-shirts

This was used in one of the community-wide modalities (Girral), where one of the Aboriginal childcare organisations that operated preschools suggested that we co-produce a children's t-shirt that was co-branded with the preschool name on the front and the Lead My Learning logo on the back. This created an opportunity to increase the campaign message in the home and around the community of the priority group. All of the children attending the preschools were given a new school t-shirt; 75 t-shirts were produced and provided to each child enrolled. The preschools later requested to have the Lead My Learning logo on their staff t-shirts.

Radio segment

A paid local radio sponsorship was arranged in the community-wide modality (Girral) for a 30 second advertisement of Lead My Learning. The radio advertisement script was based on the Lead My Learning messages and was developed with local community members; an Aboriginal Aunty and two young children. This radio segment delivered the campaign messages about sharing and encouraging learning while doing everyday activities. This local community radio station reaches listeners receptive to local events, products and services.

Taxi Service

One taxi service in the community-wide campaign had an image of the local people and the clear message on the advertising board at the rear of one of the vehicles. This advertisement was used to promote the campaign and increase the frequency of the campaign. The local taxi service provided us with a no-fee service for this advertising.

Sponsorship

Sponsorships were used in Girral, the community-wide modality and were only distributed to groups or events that provided the opportunity to disseminate the Lead My Learning message on a larger scale than placement in, for example, playgroup settings. Sponsorships were used in a variety of community groups. This technique was used as a way to spread the campaign message to places in the community that might reach the priority group.

Placement of sponsorships included:

- women's and youth sport teams;
- a women's sport team;
- an Aboriginal Elders group;
- Baby Bounty Bag that were given to parent/s when they gave birth in a local hospital;
- at a community Christmas party event at a local Aboriginal health service.

Sponsorship was used as we wanted the campaign message to be readily available to parents and those family members that influence children's learning, and not just within the childcare centres, playgroups and related child services.

Everyday Activities' Resources

As we have explained, Lead My Learning emphasised the significance of everyday activities and parent involvement in their children's learning. To support this emphasis, the Lead My Learning campaign provided resources about Everyday Activities, and drew on the expertise of an early childhood educator, who worked as a research assistant with the team in the formative and design stages of the project. This research assistant reviewed some of the early childhood literature that was used to inform the resource rationale and design. This review, for instance, highlighted the importance of mathematics and the everyday. This is discussed by Ginsburg, who terms this everyday mathematics (EM) and proposes it is "a significant aspect of children's play" (2006, p. 146). This observation by Ginsburg (2006) connected with the emphasis that we had noted from our formative work. The resources have suggestions for how parents can integrate leading learning with their children while they are doing their daily duties. The ideas that are described are free (there is no cost associated with doing them), and they are designed to reduce perception of time as a barrier to involvement in a child's learning, as well as to offer the concepts of encouraging learning to create an enjoyable learning moment that builds a child's future.

The resources created provides parents with ideas while they are cooking, washing, shopping, out and about, in the loungeroom or in the backyard, and at bath time to share learning, spark curiosity and thinking, and words of encouragement. For example, a sharing moment can take place while parents are doing their grocery shopping and asking or showing a child to compare the weights of different shopping items such as a bag of potatoes (heavy) to a box of cereal (light). A simple question while still pushing the trolley down the aisle of '*What is the biggest animal you can think of? Could you weigh it on the scales in the shop?*', allows a parent to 'fit in' Lead My Learning. Responding with words of encouragement such as '*Great thinking*' or responding with encouraging words even if the child is too young to respond with words reinforces and contributes to children's educational futures for a lifetime.

Resources for Everyday Activities are accessible via the Lead My Learning promotional products and online on the Lead My Learning website (www.leadmylearning.com.au). This website has a dedicated page to prompt moments of Sharing and Encouraging learning that are spontaneous and can occur anywhere. We now turn to provide the details of the everyday activities outlined in these resources. Everyday activities are where parents can readily engage with their children's learning. The resources give examples for each that are simple, no cost and naturally can be integrated in their everyday activities to become intentional. An example with 'washing' is 'matching a sock', where a parent could lead the learning in an enjoyable way getting the child to throw paired socks into the washing basket. Sharing learning while hanging out the washing could be as simple as:

Give the pegs to your child, get them to stand a short distance from the peg container and see if they can throw them into the container. They could try counting as they play, or ask your child to get you four green pegs. You can change it a bit by asking for different colours. Now can I have six blue pegs? If the child is a little older have the child sell the pegs to you (with imaginary money of course). If one green peg is $1, and I need two pegs, how much money will I need?

Other ways to share learning could embrace a child to help sort out piles of clothes based on who owns the clothing items, the washing will be organised and ready for folding. Examples of these activities from the Lead My Learning resources are provided below:

Washing
Washing clothes is a daily task that can provide engagement of children to learn. This could be as simple as involving the child to name the clothes going on and off the clothesline or identify who owns the clothing items. You could ask your child to match socks or sort out by colours or even discuss the process of washing the clothes. Questions to spark curiosity lead to conversation that engage learning involvement for example, 'I wonder how many different games we can think of where you have to throw a ball? Like, footy or netball. What can you think of?'

Cooking
Cooking in the kitchen is always seen as a busy time for parents. There are lots of numbers to talk about with cooking such as counting food together while holding up fingers and pointing as you say each one. You could discuss measurements while doing preparation for baking. Children love learning to measure out the items and it can be helpful too.

Sharing learning moments while cooking with kids can fit in while getting dinner prepared. Such as if you are cooking sweetcorn, you could have your child to hand you sweetcorn and count how many there are. You could ask them to help peel the sweetcorn—and talk about all the little pieces inside! Wow there's lots there! If you need to cut the sweetcorn in half, after you have done it, you could ask them how many pieces are there now. There are also opportunities to talk about spelling. Spelling out the first letter of items you are using e.g. S is for sweet, C is for Corn. Or Y for Yellow, G for Green. Or W is for Water when filling up the pot to boil the sweetcorn.

Shopping

Doing the shopping usually is a time where parents want to get in and out of a store quickly especially when their children can become restless. By creating opportunities of simple involvement, the shopping activity can become fun and a learning activity. Involving children in the smallest task such as asking your child to name items that you put in the trolley or have them tick off their own list. Or talk about each shopping item to your child; they will love the attention and you get your shopping done. Identifying if shopping items are soft or hard, biggest to the smallest, naming the shopping items as they go in the trolley or on the checkout, or if your child is a little older, letting your child become involved in paying. You could give the item to the seller and let the child give the money and receive the change. This could start a great conversation about the value of money.

Out and about

When you and the family are out and about town, there are great opportunities to get your child learning while you doing your everyday activity such as when you are at the doctor, weekend football, or you are out as a family in the park. Doing memory games such as using magazines or books while in the doctor's waiting room, car games such as I Spy using letters or colours, having your child find the numbers on the back of the football jerseys or simply talking about what you see in the park.

In the loungeroom

The lounge room is usually a place parents want to stop and put their feet up to relax. There are numerous ideas for how to Share and Encourage learning even while you are relaxing, such as using items in the loungeroom to play a mystery game. You could ask your child to find five items from around the house and lay them out on the floor. You close your eyes and have your child remove one item. Take turns trying to find the missing item. If your child gets stuck when it's their turn to work out what is missing, give them some clues – such as the colour of the item or what it is used for, or even the letter it starts with. You can change the items to make it more challenging. Here's a tricky question: What can we do when we have lots and lots of jobs to do so we can remember to do them?

If your child is a little younger, you can make cubby houses with chairs, cushions and sheets. You can talk about how they are building their structure! Mention colours and, of course, there are letters and numbers as well! How many cushions have you got? What letter does two start with? Or have your child build something with blocks, cushions or other items. This is a great activity to discuss balancing and weight.

In the backyard
While in the backyard doing the gardening or hanging out the washing you can Share and Encourage learning by using items in the garden or around the house and ask the child to create something. Encourage the child to create, and you be the helper. Questions to spark curiosity: Could we make a tower out of just grass? What about if we used just leaves? Why not? You could talk about the flowers, herbs or veggies in the garden. Their colours, what grows and when – and if you know the names of some of them. It can also be fun to show children how you find out the names. Working on the car is interesting. You can talk about what needs to be done. Explaining processes is a great way for a child to learn.

Bath time
Bath time is a great opportunity to Share and Encourage learning. Some ideas involve singing a song, trying a counting rhyme using your fingers to show the number, tell a story or play a game. Name or talk about colours you see in the bathroom, use the bath toys to demonstrate actions such as washing or swimming, or simply talk about water and hot, cold and warm.

These resources provided rich descriptions of involvement in a child's learning while doing everyday activities. For some of the parents, these may have been new ideas, or perhaps a different description of these learning activities. For those parents that did interact with Lead My Learning, it appears that describing the activities was not only beneficial as a resource to assist parents with ideas for how to lead learning, describing the activities proved to also assist in the parents recognising the various ways in which they were involved in learning.

We now turn to Chapter 6 where we describe in detail how a critical cultural social marketing approach was deployed to adapt social marketing techniques and create the Lead My Learning.

References

Duane, S., Domegan, C., McHugh, P., & Devaney, M. (2016). From restricted to complex exchange and beyond: Social marketing's change agenda. *Journal of Marketing Management, 32*(9–10), 856–876. https://doi.org/10.1080/0267257X.2016.1189449.

Ginsburg, H. P. (2006). Mathematical play and playful mathematics: A guide for early education. In *Play = learning: How play motivates and enhances children's cognitive and social-emotional growth.* New York: Oxford University Press.

Green, C. L., Walker, J. M. T., Hoover-Dempsey, K. V., & Sandler, H. M. (2007). Parents' motivations for involvement in children's education: An empirical test of a theoretical model of parental involvement. *Journal of Educational Psychology, 99*(3), 532–544. https://doi.org/10.1037/0022-0663.99.3.532.

Murray, N., & Harwood, V. (2018). *Lead My Learning.* Retrieved from leadmylearning.com.au.

Peattie, K., & Peattie, S. (2011). The social marketing mix: A critical review. In G. Hastings, K. Angus, & C. Bryant (Eds.), *The SAGE handbook of social marketing* (pp. 152–166). London: Sage.

6

Describing the Critical Cultural Social Marketing Approach Used in the Lead My Learning Campaign

In this chapter we provide a description of the application of the critical cultural social marketing approach used to create the Lead My Learning campaign. As explained in Chapter 4, a critical cultural emphasis was engaged to create an educational promotion campaign (Lead My Learning). We elected to work with a well-known planning process, the National Social Marketing Centre's (NSMC), (2011, pp. 79–90) *Six Stage Planning Process*. These six stages are: Getting started; Scoping; Development; Implement; Evaluation; Follow-up, and, as we go on to describe, were not straightforwardly adopted, but rather, were subjected to careful analysis to appraise the use to create the campaign.

Accordingly, the chapter is organised to respond to this planning process, and structured into the following six headings: reframing 'getting started'; reorienting 'scoping'; recognising knowledge in 'development'; regardful 'implementation'; respectful 'evaluation'; resourceful 'follow up'. The titles of these subsections are chosen to convey the critical and cultural emphasis we deliberately sought *to place onto* the adaptation of this planning process. Each subsection begins with a table summary that (1) overviews the key NSMC steps; (2) indicates what we did not use; and (3) describes our adaptions. In this description we refer in the main to

© The Author(s) 2019
V. Harwood and N. Murray, *The Promotion of Education*,
https://doi.org/10.1007/978-3-030-25300-4_6

NSMC processes, and where relevant, to other social marketing literature as we found that this enabled us to enhance the design.

Reframing 'Getting Started'

The first stage of the NSMC planning process 'Getting Started', is focussed on preparation. In the NSMC's (2011) *Big Pocket Guide to Using Social Marketing for Behavioural Change* it states, "Before you start your social marketing project it is useful to do some initial planning" (2011, p. 80). This is an additional stage added to the NSMC planning schema. By contrast, the Blair-Stevens five-stage Total Process Planning Model (on which the NSMC planning process is based) as the name indicates, has five stages. We mention these changes and adaptions because, in setting out to adapt this process it is relevant to recognise that this is discussed in the social marketing literature.

In the 'Getting Started' stage we worked with the following key points from the NSMC planning process: (1) challenge statement; (2) Project Initial Audience Analysis; (3) learning from the competition. These components are listed in the first column of Table 6.1. The second column lists what we did not use from this list, and the third is an overview of what was done, inclusive of selected NSMC components, adaptions and additions, to commence the creation of Lead My Learning.

The Critical Cultural Yarning Sessions

In the early Critical Cultural Yarning Sessions (CCYS), it was recognised that there would be components of the NSMC (2011) process that we either could not use, or could not strictly adhere, and that we would need to reframe 'Getting Started' and use a similar strategy in the remainder of the stages of the NSMC planning process.

Our reviews of the literature at this stage included detailed searches of all programmes on promoting education in the early years (nationally and internationally, the English language). At this early stage we had also conducted searches for conceptual work into the sociological and cultural

Table 6.1 Reframing 'Getting started'

NSMC planning process checklist	Applying a critical cultural assessment of NSMC steps NSMC steps not used or changed	Applying a critical cultural approach to create Lead My Learning (inclusive of NSMC steps used)

• Clarify the issue or challenge
• Make assessment of the available resources, the context you are working in and the key stakeholders
• Potential risks
• Initial plans and timescales
	• NSMC—Internal Audience Analysis
	• Did not use the terms 'Problem Behaviour' and 'Desired Behaviour'
	• *Alternative:* strengths-based approach to parent capacities and knowledges; use critique to identify the construction of 'problem behaviour' and 'desired behaviour' in education; cultural approach to conceptualise construction of identity and subjectivity in the socio-cultural contexts of educational disadvantage
	• Alternative sources consulted
	• Critical literature in sociology of education, strength-based literature on Aboriginal education. These sources used to refine concepts including: campaign purpose; campaign focus; rationale; how social issue understood
	• NSMC—Learning from others research gap analysis
		• Critical Cultural Approaches in Lead My Learning
		• Relationships initiated with services and communities, with the view to maintaining relationships throughout the whole process
		• Preliminary literature reviews
		  – Parents engagement/involvement
		  – Social marketing
		  – Sociology of education
		• Created Critical Cultural Yarning Sessions
		• Included consultation with social marketing experts
		• Aboriginal Protocols guided project management and consultation with key stakeholders. These informed: Relationships; Establishing Respect; Rights to Maintain IP
		• Commenced formative study, with view to having a longer timescale
		• *NSMC steps used* (Project Plan—Start to End; Risk Management Assessment; Contingency Plan; Stakeholder Analysis; SWOT Analysis)

factors that impact on educational participation in higher education for children who live in places impacted by socio-economic disadvantage and have parents who have experienced educational disadvantage. Literature searches also included the socio-cultural context of education, and considerations such as social class, diverse ethnicities, First Nations people, racism and place.

We found parental participation was reported as a critical factor for building educational participation (Berthelsen & Walker, 2008; Hill & Tyson, 2009; Taylor, Clayton, & Rowley, 2004). We also conducted searches on social marketing to look for adaptations, use in education, different conceptual approaches, including sociological and how culture was addressed in social marketing. Other literature reviews at this stage included on survey design for parents of young children and parental involvement.

Through this early process we not only identified what we would not use (which we go on to discuss) as well as what was needed for us to proceed: a clearer articulation for ourselves of how we were being guided by culture. Drawing on our background research and resources, the CCYS (Critical Cultural Yarning Sessions) helped us to clearly articulate how the envisaged campaign would be guided by an emphasis on the cultural. It is important here to emphasise that the CCYS afforded us the opportunity to be open to thinking through how we would engage with the cultural. This led to us clarifying for ourselves and with our partners, how we would be guided by Aboriginal Protocols in a cross-cultural project.

We also used these yarning sessions to discuss the use of a SWOT analysis and risk management analysis. These project planning tools are often used in project management and we gauged that these would be beneficial in this project. We then prepared a contingency plan for the project that was inclusive of our growing sense of the adaptations to the planning process that were to come. This contingency plan was revisited in subsequent sessions as we worked through the adaptations and modifications in our process that lead to the creation of Lead My Learning.

Reframing the Internal Audience Analysis

This component of the NSMC planning process included a focus on identifying the 'problem behaviour and 'desired behaviour'. Our CCYS canvassed the literature and consulted alternative sources to see how others may have approached the conundrum on the emphasis of behaviour.

Guided by our emphasis on critique and on the cultural, we quickly concluded that we could not frame the audience in terms of a problem behaviour, nor could we use the term 'desired behaviour'. As we outlined in Chapter 4, to use terms such as 'problem behaviour' or 'desired behaviour' went against the activity of critique we were engaged in and did not connect with the emphasis on the cultural that we aspired towards.

We resisted using the concept 'desired behaviour' not because there were not behaviours that would be beneficial to promote; but because the parents with whom we were working were people with knowledge about learning, and who were involved in their children's learning (Harwood & Murray, 2019). In our conversations and yarns with those involved, from the parents themselves through to the range of services, groups and communities, we did not want to describe objectives in terms of desired behaviours, or for that matter, problem behaviours. Neither did we wish to conceal this terminology; we were striving to build relationships and consistently share feedback and be influenced by what people shared with us. Consequently, we elected not to incorporate such terminology.

The challenge for us was in firstly appreciating *what was happening* with the parents, which we slowly learned through in-depth fieldwork that included yarning sessions. And secondly, in conceiving how it may be possible to describe what is happening in a manner that not only connected with the parents, but also might have beneficial effects on how they identified as parents involved in their children's learning. The alternative that we created was to focus on discourses that contributed to the constitution of subjectivities about learning and lead learning—and how it is possible to contest the dominant discourse of the *uneducated identity* (Harwood & Murray, 2019).

A Campaign, Not an 'Intervention'

At the outset we decided not to use the term intervention and instead used the term campaign. Our rationale for this decision is important to share not only because this was part of the project planning process, but because it demonstrates how and why we applied a critical and cultural emphasis in practice (see Chapter 1).

Relationships

We recognised that relationships with people, communities and services were vital to the success of the project. We began by identifying project 'stakeholders' in the potential rollout locations, asking ourselves whether engagement might be in their interest, how the project could deliver benefit to them. While we use the term stakeholders here, we do this with the recognition that we are hoping to build partnerships with these potential stakeholders.

In the first stage, contact was made with the key stakeholders initially identified to ascertain their interest in the project. These were not restricted to those directly involved, such as early childhood centres and playgroups. A wider stakeholder audience was sought, which included for instance, Australian federal and state government departments, local councils, libraries, non-governmental organisations (NGOs) and related family services. From this first stage, these contacts both grew and were refined, and we slowly developed partnerships with a number of stakeholders over the period of the project. Whilst doing the stakeholder analysis and engagement processes, we started to consult with potential participating sites. We went to visit and meet with childcare directors and provided each site an overview of the research project and discussed potential involvement.

As our project included a high number of Aboriginal families, it was respectful to also consult with relevant Aboriginal organisations such as the NSW Aboriginal Education Consultative Group (AECG), Land councils and local Elders. We focussed on building relationships with Elders, with Aboriginal services, and Aboriginal childcare services. Learning from Elders and building partnerships occurred as required. We also made sure we attended community meetings (e.g. interagency meetings) and events to have a presence and also to give back to the community. We did not set up a steering committee as suggested in the NSMC Planning Process, but applied a yarning approach with key stakeholders.

Due to the historical and ongoing impacts of colonisation, it has been common that Aboriginal Australian people are far too often treated as 'objects' to be researched (Blair, 2015; Sherwood & Kendall, 2013). The value of Aboriginal cultures and cultural knowledge and practices was/has been overlooked and not recognised for their contributions. We prioritised and paid sustained attention to respect for Ownership, Acknowledgement, Indigenous cultural rights, Consent (informed) and Giving back (reciprocity).

Though our CCYS we decided it was respectful to engage in a more formal partnership where Aboriginal community knowledge might contribute to the design of the campaign. Before we commenced discussion about the design of the campaign promotional products with members of the community-wide campaign in Girral, we created a legally binding contract between the University and the Elders to protect their intellectual property should they decide with us in the yarns to share any of their cultural knowledge in our promotional products (see Chapter 4).

Extending the Formative Study Across Several Stages

As described in Chapter 4, we extended the formative study phase, increasing it to 14 months and using it in several of the planning stages. These stages included 'reframing getting started', 'reorienting scoping' and 'recognising knowledge in development'. The first of our formative sessions were with 39 parents, caregiver and family members across eight sites in regional and remote NSW. These sessions included discussion about education and further education, how and why people engage or did not engage in education and influences or strategies that could encourage people to 'do education'.

The second set of sessions were with 61 parents across six sites. Our participant numbers had increased as a result of both growing interest in our work and the partnerships we were developing with stakeholders in different sites and regions. In these sessions, as well as further discussions about education and learning, we focussed on feedback to three existing social marketing campaigns that represented what we thought were three different styles in broadly the area we were researching. The three existing campaigns used were: (1) a text-based poster with statistical information from the 2012 UNESCO education for all global monitoring report; (2) the Sugar Bites campaign; and (3) a Let's talk about Bedtime campaign. We asked the parents what they liked best and least about these campaigns. We also requested suggestions for: what could be changed; what they thought other parents that they knew might like; what they recommended we use; and where we could use these messages that would likely reach parents in our priority group. What we learned from these sessions we also fed into future sessions in this second cycle, and in this way we were able to build considerable feedback.

In conjunction with these formative sessions, we decided to commence the process of securing a graphic designer to draft logos and concepts. We felt this was important as it provided the opportunity to put the feedback into action, and have this tested. We sourced an appropriate and highly skilled Indigenous business that could deliver designs, based on the design brief we were generating from the formative study. In subsequent feedback sessions, these designs were shared with parents in the formative group. Further sessions were possible because of the rapport we had established with parents and services in our priority group.

In this way we were able to put these design concepts to 'the test' by representatives of our priority group. The parents gave a great deal of feedback, which we gratefully received and which led to numerous modifications and further review by the parents. We went through three version of the design brief. Once the logo, concept and messaging were agreed upon, we created the finalised version of Lead My Learning. A full style guide was provided by the graphic design company. Through this process we ensured that the design of the campaign was parent-led.

Reorienting 'Scoping'

'Scoping', the second planning stage, is "where you consider which interventions to select, based on what is most likely to achieve and sustain the desired outcome, given your resources" (National Social Marketing Centre, 2011, p. 82). Lead My Learning was a small-scale project, with a campaign budget of $AUD76,000 ($AUD60,000 for the campaign and campaign promotional products, and $AUD16,000 for the formative and design research with participants).

By comparison, larger projects have greater financial and other resources. Take for example the 2009–2011 UK government funded *Time to Change* anti-stigma campaign that targeted changing behaviours towards mental illness. This campaign had six 'bursts' (intervention waves) and "campaign expenditure varied significantly, with burst 6 costing the least at £520,000 and burst 5 costing the most at £1.31 million. This resulted in an average campaign burst expenditure of £748,000" (Evans-Lacko, Henderson, Thornicroft, & McCrone, 2013, p. 97). Resourcing in larger projects not only involves direct financial contribution; it also includes leveraging potential, such as via connections with government departments and initiatives and stakeholders. While *Time to Change* is not necessarily the 'largest' social marketing campaign in terms of funding, this example does illustrate the difference in the funds available for this campaign, compared with the Lead My Learning Campaign.

The various activities that are 'typically involved' in this scoping stage are listed in column one of Table 6.2.

As with the 'first stage', in this stage the CCYS enabled us to identify what parts of the 'typical' scoping stage to adopt, what to revise and change, what to not use, as well as where we needed to introduce new ideas.

After creating the basis of our research project plan we started to engage more frequently with our potential participating sites such as childcare centres, playgroup and relevant community organisations. Our communication with the potential sites was not a one-way process; we adopted a two-way communication process that allowed us to learn and work more collaboratively with each individual site.

This meant that as we worked on our appraisal of the scoping stage of the planning process, we had access to the growing insights from our

Table 6.2 Reorienting 'Scoping'

NSMC planning process checklist	Applying a critical cultural assessment of NSMC steps NSMC steps not used or changed	Applying a critical cultural approach to create Lead My Learning (inclusive of NSMC steps used)
• Bringing people together who might be important for the intervention • Forming a steering group and reviewing expectations and resources • Investigating what has already been done • Analysing factors that may affect the issue and what you can do about them • Primary and secondary research • Researching the audience (research plans and different methods) • Developing key actionable insights • Segmenting your audience • Clarifying the exchange • Developing smart behavioural objectives	• No steering group used • Alternatives to bring people together • Situated ourselves in communities, went to numerous sites to consult • Learnt where people are located and who to meet • Identified key stakeholders in government, services, community organisations • Did not adhere to behaviour emphasis or SMART behavioural goals • Alternatives to understanding the audience • Used sociology of education insights into educational disadvantage • Did not do Scoping Report • Alternatives to understanding the complexity of the problem • Continued consultation with stakeholders and continued building partnerships	• Continued formative study • Engaged external graphic designer early for iterative process to create logo based on ongoing relationships in formative studies • Not a health campaign—Made an educational futures campaign • Reframing the exchange—value shaping approach rather than behaviour change • Identifying costs and barriers: – Fear of deviating from social norms – Fear about talking about learning/education – The way they think they need to parent (according to dominant discourses of education) – Need to move out of their comfort zone

formative research and our relationships with the range of people who were our 'stakeholders'. Commenced in Stage One, the formative research continued to provide feedback and, at times, surprises. We found ourselves often challenged, which we learned to deeply appreciate as this continually improved the work, shifting it to a more parent-led process. We came to realise that our early assumptions about the project needed to be changed.

To summarise, extending into the scoping stage, the formative research informed:

Understanding the audience
Identifying Segments
Identifying Insight
Clarifying the exchange
Revisiting the Challenge Statement

Relationships with the diverse range of people, services and communities enabled us to consult with and 'check-in'. And as with the previous stage, we again found our assumptions challenged.

Combined these activities were ongoing and forming an integral component of our critical cultural process. Examples of these changes include: (1) improving the campaign site design from our initial plan of only long day childcare to a focus on connecting with where the parents are, such as in playgroups and community-wide settings; and (2) using novel ways to transmit our message, such as large playmats that were freely provided to the range of services that participated in the campaign.

An Overview of the Ongoing Formative Work—From Reframing Getting Started to Recognising Knowledge in Development

As we have stated, the formative research was increased in our project, extending across several of the stages. Here we provide an overview of this formative research, which although in this section is about 'reorientating scoping', actually connects across three of the stages. Given the way that this process impacted the creation of the Lead My Learning campaign, we have elected not to distribute into the different stages, but rather include a complete description here in order to convey a sense of the process that occurred.

The formative study in the scoping stage included a design discussion with nine parents across two sites. This design discussion was based on a design created from the formative study findings. In this third set of discussions we shared with these representatives of the priority group the design: 'Get the habit' (as parents explained that they wanted to get the habit of leading learning); with a slogan 'Talk up learning' (as parents advised more parents need to talk about it more); and the message that leading learning does fit in with their everyday activities (e.g. family, food, washing, shopping, running around and while they were relaxing). We asked questions regarding what they liked or disliked, which were similar questions to those used when we discussed the three existing social marketing campaigns (second level discussion). These ideas were literally 'picked apart': the constructive criticism meant that these concepts were altered significantly. It was at this point we created a design brief for the external graphic designer who provided multiple logos and concepts including slogans.

A fourth set of sessions took place with 12 parents across two sites. The parents were again asked the same questions (likes and dislikes) to discuss the different creative designs and images developed by the research team, in collaboration with the graphic designers. The purpose was to share the design concepts and get participant feedback. We obtained informative feedback that again led to more refinements. From this point a second design brief was created to hone the design and messaging. The design was revisited and redeveloped based on this feedback from the parents representing the priority group. In the fifth session the Lead My Learning campaign logo was agreed upon (the feet concept), and the visual imaging and colour palette were discussed.

A sixth session took place with 11 parents across two sites that were not in the campaign rollout locations. These sessions looked at the redeveloped posters, message, images and palette colours. In addition, this session also discussed the wording/message 'everyday activities are opportunities', an idea that had been developing in the previous sessions with the parents.

As the parents discussed in this and in the previous session (as well as building on earlier feedback sessions), we based the idea of everyday activities on various locations where parents nominated that they do the learning activities with their children (e.g. barbeque, kitchen, clothesline, loungeroom). However, the group informed us that it would be suitable to have the opportunity to lead learning identified by the activity, for example, cooking and shopping.

Furthermore, in addition to talking with parents, caregivers and family members, throughout the formative study we also met with 38 childcare educators across nine sites to ask them their thoughts about education and how they think families engage in education. It was also important to ask key stakeholders from different communities and who had a range of community roles, about their thoughts on the slogan the parents were indicating for the campaign. Although it was a parent-led design, it was important to also consult and collaborate with an early childhood educator and with Aboriginal community leaders.

Not Using the NSMC Idea of a Steering Group

We identified that due to the needs of the project, we needed more 'input' and direction that could connect with the range of people, groups and services involved, and that could be inclusive of their interest and capacity to be involved. For this reason, we didn't create a steering group and devised other ways to 'bring people together'. As an alternative, we worked with strategies we could use to connect respectfully with existing activities in the communities that were already 'bringing people together'. The latter, for example, included attending and contributing to existing meetings where diverse groups came together. These meetings included: community services provision meetings, community-led meetings, such as on education or community events and meetings held by specific services attended by professionals involved with parents and young children.

We also took more of a yarning approach in community and with services. This involved being 'out in the field' and meeting and keeping in contact with all the project stakeholders on an individual basis. By 'out in the field' we are referring to going to the different communities, places and sites of the formative study and later, of the roll out of the campaign. To identify these various opportunities, we situated ourselves in communities and went to numerous sites to consult with services and with community groups. Through this approach we:

- Learnt where people are located and who to meet
- Identified key stakeholders in government, services, community organisations

Consultation with stakeholders also continued on a one-on-one basis and we worked to build the necessary partnerships. Yarning improved engagement and participation and was a culturally appropriate methodology to learn from stories (Geia, Hayes, & Usher, 2013; Walker, Fredericks, Mills, & Anderson, 2013). As such, yarning was used to consult and adapt the campaign promotional products in all of the sites, and this was done by us as a team of Aboriginal and non-Aboriginal researchers with both Aboriginal and with non-Aboriginal people. As we have explained (Harwood & Murray, 2019), in the Lead My Learning campaign and campaign processes, we prioritised an Aboriginal guided approach and were inclusive of Aboriginal and non-Aboriginal people.

Not Adhering to the Behaviour Emphasis

As discussed, we deviated from a behavioural emphasis. Following our emphasis on prioritising Aboriginal approaches, it was culturally appropriate to have face to face yarns with key stakeholders and consult in an open two-way process. This emphasis was respectful to the Aboriginal Elders and Aboriginal people influencing the campaign, and to our prioritising of Aboriginal approaches. A written report in this instance is not a suitable communication tool. Other alternatives to understanding the audience including drawing on insights from the sociology of education in order to conceptualise educational disadvantage and the impact of social class. We also looked at social norms and how social norms are connected to the dominant discourse.

Not Doing a Scoping Report

We decided that our comprehensive yarning sessions, which we documented provided us with the details that were required, and in a form that worked for our approach and the project. Our alternatives to understanding the complexity of the problem involved continued consultation with stakeholders and the continued building of partnerships throughout our formative research. The ongoing nature of both of these activities meant that over time we got to know people and services, and importantly, they got to know us. This assisted in and created a relationship where detailed feedback and insights were shared.

We took a broad view to understanding 'the problem'. We also listened to what people had to say and what they suggested for who we might speak to. As such we didn't restrict our focus to services that were 'education focussed', such as childcare, playgroups or schools. By connecting with the range of services involved with parents and their young children we were better positioned to appreciate the complexity of problem discourses that (1) parents not being engaged in education; and (2) the impacts that these discourses have on parents and how they perceive the legitimacy of the learning or educational nature of their activities with their children.

Segmentation

As described in Chapters 3 and 4, segmentation is a key feature of social marketing (French, 2017) and a technique drawn from marketing. The basis for segmentation in our project came from the outcomes of our formative work (see Chapter 5). The segment selected, 'Happiness versus Education', was protective and caring of their children; they did want to support their children's educational futures; but with children who are aged 0–6 years it could be considered as 'pushing' if parents are seen to be involving their children in education. As we have previously described, while one segment was selected, we were aware that some of the features of the other segments were likely to be present, but for this segment the prioritisation of 'happiness' was the strongest feature. For this segment, happy time was seen as when the children were not doing learning activities or not doing education activities such as homework. This segment was concerned that they weren't 'pushing education on their children', because this would impact on their young children's happiness. The segment was also concerned with how others, particularly their peers, viewed them. Yet, as we have maintained, these parents were involved in educational activities with their children. The problem is, that not only had learning become known through the dominant discourses of institutional education (such as schooling), the parents' learning practices are rendered unrecognisable by processes of institutional 'education'.

Social Norms, Deficit Discourses and a Different Kind of Change State

We also realised that social norms were influential, and needed to be taken into account. We were faced with a paradox: parents doing learning and education was seen as pushing, and was an activity to be avoided because of the scrutiny and questions that might arise; yet parents were involved in learning. The problem was that this learning just wasn't the 'legitimate' form. The difficulty with this set of issues is that, as we explained in Chapters 1 and 2, parent involvement in their child's learning is a crucial contributor to success in schooling (Harris & Goodall, 2008; Waters, 2016) and, consequently, in the longer term to have the possibility of experiencing higher education.

Since we took the stand that the parents do already lead their children's learning, we were not pursuing 'social change' to get parents to lead. The issue was in the lack of recognition of the legitimacy of their cultural forms of leading learning. Following our extensive formative sessions, we came to realise that what we needed to aim for was a campaign where discourses of parents involved in leading their children's learning take preference over discourses that portray the parents as not involved in their learning.

We used the notion of 'change state' (Duane, Domegan, McHugh, & Devaney, 2016) as a way of conceptualising the exchange concept. The *change state* that we sought to create was one where the discourses of parent involvement in learning of our campaign are taken up over and above any discourses that portray the parents as not involved in their learning. The question of why parents might want to engage in such a change state needs to be differently conceptualised than the conventional interpretation of a marketing 'exchange' (as commercial transaction).

In thinking through the importance of this shift in discourses (or rather, one discourse having more prominence because it was represented, for instance, as legitimate), we drew on the more conventional ideas of value exchange. This assisted us to think through the costs and barriers. Doing so helped us to articulate what the tangible benefits would be, such as happiness for their children with the costs (price), such as time it takes to be involved in learning. The costs and barriers we identified were:

- Fear of deviating from social norms
- Fear about talking about learning/education
- Needing to move out of their comfort zone

We set out to minimise these 'costs', as we explain in Chapter 5.

Recognising Knowledge in 'Development'

The development stage, "is where the interventions selected as a result of scoping are taken forward" (2011, p. 84). Using the term campaign, rather than interventions, this is the stage where we commenced a focus to move the concepts that had now been created into the 'development stage' (Table 6.3).

For this development stage, the CCYS drew on our work from the previous two stages, using these in conjunction with our ongoing relationships to *develop* the Lead My Learning campaign. As the title of this stage suggests, we foregrounded recognition of the knowledge of stakeholders (our partnerships) in the development. Given the significant extent to which their contributions had changed and shaped the work up to this point, it was critical that we continued to prioritise recognising their knowledge as we moved into this stage.

The Total Process Planning Model, on which the NSMC planning process is based, states:

Table 6.3 Recognising knowledge in 'Development'

NSMC planning process checklist	Applying a critical cultural assessment of NSMC steps — NSMC steps not used or changed	Applying a critical cultural approach to create Lead My Learning (inclusive of NSMC steps used)
• Developing a specific intervention based on your understanding of your audience and their behaviours • Deciding combination of methods • Planning your communications • Pre-testing your intervention • Developing an evaluation plan	• *Adapted NSMC stakeholder communication.* Development of campaign closely aligned with community strategies used in community • *Reframed NSMC behavioural goals for target audience* to emphasise strength-based descriptions of parent relationships to their children's learning. Strength based recognise what parents do, their strengths and the impacts of dominant deficit discourses that impact parents • Reframed NSMC concept of intervention to name it a campaign • Continued consultation with stakeholders and continued building partnerships • Adapted NSMC main intervention mix	• Continued formative study • Engaged Aboriginal graphic designer to create the Lead My Learning logo • Emphasised cultural knowledges involved in learning. For example, from extensive formative research; from literature such as Learning by Observing and Pitching In (LOPI) (Correa-Chávez, Mejia-Arauz, & Rogoff, 2015; Rogoff, 2014) • Consulted stakeholders regarding clear message and how they feel the message fitted with community and other programmes in the area • Tested logo, poster design and messages. Pilot products had 5 iterations • Tested survey with community members representative of the audience, including a think aloud test

NSMC planning process checklist	Applying a critical cultural assessment of NSMC steps NSMC steps not used or changed	Applying a critical cultural approach to create Lead My Learning (inclusive of NSMC steps used)
	• *Extended NSMC 4Ps* to include Partnerships (Stakeholder involvement), critique (Position of discourse), and protocols (Philosophical and practical ways)	
	• Permission—(attention to placement but explicit permission to value add social marketing to the community	
	• Adapted evaluation planning to include yarning methodologies, ethnographic approaches to fieldwork, including community members and research assistants	

- Where the behavioural goals and audience insights gained during scoping are developed into a programme, campaign, or intervention.
- Includes specific pre-testing of ideas with the audience(s).
- Checking that the evidence, insights, and assumptions being made are relevant and actionable (Ong & Blair-Stevens, 2009, p. 156).

While emphasising 'behavioural goals' (which is changed in our campaign approach), this description puts forward the core idea of this stage is to develop, and this needs to be accomplished prior to the campaign being implemented (or rolled out). As such we continued our commitment to continued relationships with stakeholders and positioning ourselves so that our work could be subject to scrutiny by our range of partners. In this way, we strove to recognise the knowledge held in communities, by parents and by services and worked for this to continue to inform the development of Lead My Learning. We continued to liaise with stakeholders, which was especially important for aligning the campaign to community strategies.

In this manner the CCYS supported the development of the creative design for the Lead My Learning campaign. Along with deciding on conceptual frameworks, such as Learning by Observing and Pitching In (LOPI) and the adapted marketing mix, we worked to develop the brand, the visual design elements and the range of promotional products and strategies that were to be used for conveying the Lead My Learning message.

Developing the Clear Message, Brand and the Support Elements Sharing and Encouraging Learning

As mentioned above, our work in this stage included developing and refining the creative and design elements, as well as the messaging. For example, we consulted stakeholders regarding the 'clear message'. The final version is:

Everyday Activities are opportunities to Share and Encourage Learning

Doing so ensured we received detailed critical feedback from representatives of the priority group, as well as from a number of services and community groups associated with this group. We responded to this feedback by changing the message, and then submitting it for further review. This resulted in numerous changes and feedback/critique cycles. We elected to continue with these cycles until the groups we were listening to, and learning from, told us they were satisfied with the message. This process was important as the clear message need to 'fit' with community and other programmes in the area.

We also set out to create a Lead My Learning brand. Building the brand involved creating a visual identity and ensuring a strong presence for campaign collateral. The use of our logo was structured based on colour, clear spaces, sizing, location and acceptable logo use. In addition, font was defined along with key and support colours. Based on our understanding of our target audience, "caring and protective" our graphic elements should include shapes that are mildly irregular in style, and shapes taken from the logo.

Key to the campaign are the 'Share' and 'Encourage' support elements, as these are the 'call to action' that we learned through these sessions and our research, that we would like parents to undertake. Each of these support elements was allocated a colour and a banner to be used in the campaign. A full guide was provided by the graphic designer to help with correctly implementing the visual identity of the campaign—and which we envisaged could be shared with others who might want to use the Lead My Learning materials.

Pre-testing the Campaign

Pre-testing in the development stage was necessarily a long process as it included several iterations of feedback cycles. More specifically, these feedback cycles involved a process of designing drafts of campaign content and promotional products: meeting with the representatives of the priority group and getting feedback; 'going back to the drawing board' and revising and redesigning; then taking this to the representatives of the priority group for further review and feedback. This process was repeated several times over until we arrived at the campaign content that the priority group representatives, key stakeholders, and ourselves agreed upon. The details of participant involvement in this process is provided above in the section on extending the formative study.

The aim of pre-testing the campaign was to ensure that not only were the designs, as well as the messages contained within these designs, conveying the proposition statement but also that it was acceptable to our priority group. As described in Chapter 5, the proposition statement for Lead My Learning is:

> *It is possible to lead your child's learning.* It only takes a little time and it can fit in with everyday activities. You can encourage your child's learning without having a specific knowledge of a topic and it gives a child the happy experiences of valuing and enjoying learning.

Honing the proposition statement was especially challenging for a number of reasons: the sensitivity of issues associated with education; because we were striving to disrupt deficit discourses, and because we wanted to strategically produce discourses that could contribute to different subjectivities of parent involvement in learning. The only way, in our view, to produce a campaign with messaging that 'got it right' was to have multiple testing. This is because 'getting right' was when it seen by our priority group as respectfully depicting or describing what they do (their learning practices).

This pre-testing process included consultation with Aboriginal Elders and with services. We also visited four different locations in regional and rural New South Wales and different service types (childcare centres, playgroups, women's centres, community centres). This testing included: Lead My Learning logo; poster design; the messages; and piloting the range of actual products (for example, the Lead My Learning playmat, drink coasters). There were in total five iterations of testing in this testing and design process. In these multiple interactions of testing we tested our brand concepts as well as the logo concepts. We also tested the pre-campaign survey with the parents' representative of the priority group. This included a 'think aloud' test.

Regardful Implementation

The implementation stage focuses, as the name implies on the actual implementation of the campaign and associated tasks. We have rephrased this to 'regardful implementation' because one of the changes we made to the NSMC suggestions for this stage was to maintain our focus on our partnerships—the relationships with the range of stakeholders (Table 6.4).

The CCYS helped us to identify a strategy for implementing the campaign that both drew from resources in the social marketing literature as well as from the NSMC (2011) planning process. Our ongoing relationships with stakeholders and community meant that we were aware of events in the communities, and were able to plan our launch and other activities to be complementary. We also sought and received advice from community members for where to place the promotional products. For example, for the community-wide campaign, we were advised where to place the bus shelter advertisements.

Approval was secured from Aboriginal Elders and our partners for the campaign implementation. While such approval may appear obligatory in a service setting where the campaign is being taken into a childcare centre or playgroup, it may not appear as such in the community setting. Because of the emphasis on Aboriginal Protocols, we followed respectful behaviour for the implementation and discussed our ideas prior to setting them in motion.

This meant on occasions that we needed to make some revisions to our planning, which although it may have appeared to us at the time as 'holding us up' in the long run it resulted in a better implementation process that complemented the community activities. Likewise, too, we aligned the campaign with community strategies with the result that government bodies were willing to assist us in rolling out the campaign.

Flexible Approach to Implementation

Rather than using a lock-step method to the stages, we saw development-refinement occurring in the implementation stage. For example, as our campaign became known, we took opportunities to become involved in

Table 6.4 Regardful implementation

NSMC planning process checklist	Applying a critical cultural assessment of NSMC steps NSMC steps not used or changed	Applying a critical cultural approach to create Lead My Learning (inclusive of NSMC steps used)

• Delivery of intervention
• Write a delivery plan
• Planning for launch
• Spotting opportunities and managing problems
	• *Adapted NSMC Prepare campaign for launch* to include extensive collaboration with stakeholders, alignment with community strategies, recruitment of community helpers. Staged in three-part roll out to facilitate this procedure
	• *Extended NSMC opportunities* to build marketing mix to include sponsorship of community programmes, activities and events
	   – Sporting teams (women and youth)
	   – Elders group
	   – Local radio
	   – Hospital bounty bag for new parents
	   – Aboriginal health centre Christmas Party
	• Community 2 -Enhanced cultural content in the *My Name Is* stickers
		• Continued consultation with stakeholders and community. Attended community interagency meetings, visited fieldwork sites
		• Collected ongoing feedback from services and community members
		• Provided feedback and support for services and community as requested. For example, based on our relationships we were contacted by services for support with funding bids (e.g. letters of support); attended community education provision forums
		• Responsiveness to community
		• Flexible approach to implementation
		• Partnerships with community services led to request for additional products. We provided tailored co-branded products that value-added for the services. For example, children's t-shirts in the childcare services

a range of modalities to 'tweak' the marketing mix. This involved increasing the Accessibility (Place) component by doing sponsorship activities in the community campaign. This included community sporting teams (women and youth) with the campaign logo on sporting uniforms. Other sponsorship included an Elders group, hospital bounty bags for parents of babies, and bounty bags used in the Transition to school programme, and a Community Christmas Party. For the community campaign we also created a radio advertisement with the local community radio station that involved an Aboriginal woman and two Aboriginal children.

Partnerships with community services led to request for additional products. We provided tailored co-branded products that value-added for the services. For example, children's t-shirts in the childcare services were co-branded with the Lead My Learning logo. In Kurrawong, the second community that we were working on the community-wide campaign we changed one of our campaign promotional products specifically for that community. The Elders had asked us to do stickers in two of the local languages. Respecting this direction, after consultation, and based on the instructions of the Elders, the My Name Is Lead My Learning stickers (see Chapter 5) were translated from English to the two Aboriginal languages of the area. As described in Chapter 5, other campaign activities and strategies used included: Facebook competitions; website resources; ongoing consultation with and attendance at community service and agency meetings.

This implementation strategy emphasised partnerships and this meant that at times we assisted the services and community with whom we were working. This was a valuable activity, increasing not only what we were able to 'give back', our reciprocity, to the services and community groups that had supported us, but also it aided in building relationships with the community. This activity included, providing feedback and support for services and community as requested, such as assistance with funding bids (e.g. letters of support) and attending community education provision forums.

The Campaign Launch

We adapted the NSMC campaign for a launch to include extensive collaboration with stakeholders, alignment with community strategies and recruitment of community helpers. Given the campaign was rolled out in different sites, the launches were staged in three parts. The main campaign launch (and the largest) was at a large annual community event in Girral. At this launch we provided free high-quality photos for families and their children at a photobooth. This was followed up for four days after the community event, with a local community service hosting the photobooth. Separate smaller campaign launches were tailored to the other sites, with the launches at the playgroups and childcare services, smaller and introduced by facilitators/educators to suit their service.

Respectful Evaluation

While evaluation is fifth in the order of stages, work on envisaging how the campaign might be evaluated started much earlier. This is a principle that is recommended in the social marketing literature (Lefebvre, 2013; Robinson-Maynard, Meaton, & Lowry, 2013). An overview of our considerations and adaptations of the evaluation is provided in Table 6.5.

Evaluation of our project was broadly conceived as an in-process activity, as well as an end-of-campaign activity. To an extent, this is reflective of discussion in the social marketing literature of two types of evaluation: process evaluation and outcome evaluation. The latter is relatively self-evident: it is evaluating any outcomes of the project, using the objectives of the campaign as a guide. The former, process evaluation, is possibly not used as frequently as outcome style evaluations, yet it has benefits that contribute to a better understanding of a social marketing campaign and what it has (or has not) achieved.

The CCYS provided the opportunity to continually engage in a differently formalised process evaluation, across the various stages and activities of the campaign. This had a formative purpose insofar as it enabled us to check on our work in the stages from scoping and development to the implementation. Indeed, we might even add that this approach was also

Table 6.5 Respectful evaluation

National Social Marketing Centre (NSMC) planning process checklist	Applying a critical cultural assessment of NSMC steps NSMC steps not used or changed	Applying a critical cultural approach to create Lead My Learning (inclusive of NSMC steps used)
• Consider evaluation throughout the social marketing planning process • Evaluation plans in action • Monitoring programme • Assessing the impact and outcomes of the intervention	• *Adapted evaluation to be guided by Aboriginal Protocols and by a critical cultural analysis of campaign impacts* • *Adapted NSMC evaluation of key areas to ensure the process evaluation* included ongoing consultation and feedback with community and services • Adapted outcome evaluation to incorporate research data analysis	• Post campaign interviews (yarning and semi-structured) • Post-survey was reviewed and changed • In-depth qualitative data that drew on interviews (yarning and semi-structured) and surveys of services took priority as post-evaluation method • Evaluated adapted concepts such as the use of strength-based descriptions of parent relationships to their children's learning; parent responses towards the impacts of dominant deficit discourses. Indicators of success included thematic comments such as parents stating: 'we have a name for what we do'—which is leading learning. This had previously been *unacknowledged*

helpful in the evaluation stage for thinking through how outcomes were being investigated and described. One way of thinking about our CCYS was how these supported practices similar to process evaluation, process-evaluation data can be used for both formative and summative purposes. Formative uses of process evaluation involve using process evaluation data to fine-tune the programme (e.g., to keep the program on track; Devaney & Rossi, 1997; Helitzer, Soo-Jin, & Wallerstein, 2000; Viadro, Earp, & Altpeter, 1997). Summative uses of process evaluation involve making a judgment about the extent to which the intervention was implemented as planned and reached intended participants (Devaney & Rossi, 1997; Helitzer et al., 2000). (Saunders, Evans, & Joshi, 2005, p. 136)

While we did not base it on a defined approach (Saunders et al., 2005), our practices in CCYS did connect with some of the principles of using process evaluation. This is particularly the case when we reflect on how the CCYS informed both the formative and summative components, assisting how we evaluated what was occurring, what was being produced and the responses from parents, childcare educators, services and community.

Evaluations that were formative in purpose occurred through the ongoing partnerships, where we consistently welcomed feedback and criticism. We were researchers working in communities with Aboriginal people, who have devastating histories of non-Aboriginal research and researchers. Consequently, there needed to be suspicion of us, and we needed to build rapport, trust and possible reciprocity. This included developing understanding of community needs, responding to community requests and aligning the project and campaign with needs. At times this presented difficulties because it meant we had to 'let go' of ideas and plans we had grown attached to. It also meant that as researchers we had to understand how universities and university researchers can be perceived, as this assisted us in managing our own reactions to any suspicion. Indeed, as we have learned in our work in other projects, such suspicion is welcome, and is a point with which to work in sharing ideas and moving towards a research relationship that may be beneficial or useful or wanted with those with whom and for, the research is being suggested.

The evaluation included a range of activities, and there was provision for adjustment of these during the process:

- Formative research, over 14 months, qualitative semi-structured interviews and interviews (yarning and semi-structured), individual and group
- Pre- and Post-Campaign Survey (online and paper-based)
- Post-campaign online questionnaire for services
- Post-campaign qualitative semi-structured interviews and yarning, in individual and group sessions

This mix of approaches to evaluation enabled us to collect a range of data on Lead My Learning, and importantly, provided us with the option to change our focus on the evaluation technique during the campaign. In this regard, during the campaign we elected to move our focus to the interviews (yarning and semi-structured, both individual and group) rather than relying on the post-surveys for the substantive analysis of the campaign. We changed tack as our suspicions regarding the greater benefits of interviews (yarning and semi-structured) were confirmed. Post-surveys were still distributed, but without the intensive recruitment resourcing used in the pre-surveys. Survey returns were fewer, and while this restricted the possible survey analysis, the interviews (yarning and semi-structured) provided important in-depth data.

The rationale for this significant shift was based on our work with participants, their feedback and our prior research experience. The participants reported that they preferred talking with us over the surveys and we had observed just how difficult it was to get surveys completed. Additionally, while our pre-testing of the survey resulted in an approximate 15-minute time period to complete, our experience in the field differed, with the survey varying in time to complete. There were also issues with how the survey was completed, such as responses tending to be towards the high end of the scales. This flagged for us that any positive change in the post would unlikely be picked up (while negative change would be). A similar issue was noted in the evaluation of the 'No Germs on Me Campaign' in remote Aboriginal communities in Australia (McDonald, Cunningham, & Slavin, 2015). It was therefore important to look to other ways to understand what may or may not be occurring as a result of the Lead My Learning campaign.

The Pre- and Post-Survey

The survey was created by us as there were no available surveys that could be used 'as is' for this campaign. As such, the survey was specifically designed, based on our formative insights and comprehensive literature review of parent involvement/engagement in education. The survey was created in collaboration with Kelly Andrews, an experienced social marketer. The survey used items based on social norms scales and from established quantitative questionnaires: the *Family Involvement Questionnaire* (Perry, Fantuzzo, & Munis, 2002); and the *Parent Involvement Project (PIP) Parent and Student Questionnaires: Study 4* (Hoover-Dempsey et al., 2005). Items from the established questionnaires were incorporated with permission.

Questions in the survey were sensitive to social and educational experiences and cultural needs of the participants. Surveys were made available in online and paper-based formats, with free return postage envelopes. The two formats were used to help to ensure surveys would be available for all to complete and not just those with access to the internet. For instance, in some of the sites where we worked access to the internet was severely limited, and in some places this occurred even though the communities were based only ten minutes from the main part of a large regional town.

The pre- and post-survey questions included both scales (Likert scales with 5 point to 10-point scales) and one open ended question. Questions were organised into the following topics, with an additional question about the campaign in the post-survey.

1. Demographics
2. Open-ended question—what you think you can do at home
3. Social norms
4. Self-efficacy
5. Things you/your children/others do with learning
6. Parental aspirations

The pre-survey contained 43 questions and the post-survey contained 36 questions. As the post-survey included these topics and a number of questions about campaign recall, such as images of the Lead My Learning product promotional products and questions about the use of Lead My Learning. The decision was made to reduce the length of the post-survey, and some of the sub-items were removed from the questions used in the pre-survey. Although we recognised that doing this would have implications for comparison between the pre- and post-surveys, it was decided it was in the best interest of the participants to reduce the size of the post-survey and for the post-survey to focus on campaign recall and key elements such as parent confidence in participation in their child's learning.

In the first round of surveying, the pre-campaign roll-out survey, we had employed community research assistants to help potential participants in order to render this as accessible as possible. This included support with reading the survey due to literacy or cultural differences in understanding the questions, as well as in provision of a supportive environment in which to assess whether to decide to engage in this research. The community research assistants played an important role in answering questions about the survey and the purpose and in clarifying involvement, consent and confidentiality.

This important process proved to be a costly and time-consuming exercise, and given the preference for the interviews (yarning and semi-structured) and the rich and in-depth data these provided, focus was shifted to yarning methodology to collect the post-campaign data. This meant that, with less personnel investment in the post-survey, a lesser number of surveys were completed (511 pre-surveys were collected prior to the roll out of the Lead My Learning campaign across all of the sites; 252 post-surveys were collected after the campaign was completed across all of the sites). The matched surveys (both pre and post) totalled 135, but these required breaking down into their requisite groupings (playgroup focus, community-wide focus, community-wide wait list control). Based on these numbers, we concluded that the matched data set was not sufficient for analysis of the impact of the campaign. Rather, we have focussed on the qualitative data, using the post-survey data to augment our interpretations.

Online Service Questionnaire

The online questionnaire for services was designed to reinforce the strength-based approach. In asking the services about the campaign and the parents, we were mindful that the priority audience of parents who had experienced educational disadvantage and lived in places of socio-economic disadvantage were not portrayed in a deficit manner. To accomplish this, we framed questions in a way that highlighted our priority group as already 'doing' Lead My Learning with their young children. This emphasis is important, not only for respectful evaluation; these surveys are part of the discourse that professionals encounter and it was important that 'instruments' such as questionnaires do not contribute to deficit discourses about the parents and their involvement in learning.

Post Campaign Interviews and Interviews (Yarning and Semi-Structured)

In line with our formative research, the post-campaign interviews also used a yarning approach as well as semi-structured interviews. Having these options allowed for everyone to be comfortable to contribute. We observed that these discussions and/or yarns assisted parents, caregivers and family members to learn about concepts of Lead My Learning. This occurred in situations where parents discussed or yarned about how they used Lead My Learning, were influenced by it or described the positive impact of the Lead My Learning campaign.

Data analysis processes included: descriptive statistical analysis for surveys; thematic analysis of qualitative data from surveys, questionnaires, interviews and yarning. The large data-set was managed using NVIVO software and SPSS.

Resourceful Follow-Up

The 'follow up' stage is the last of the six NSMC planning stages:

> [and] is when the results of the evaluation are considered by you are your stakeholders. Implications are digested and forward plans made. This helps to ensure that you, your organisation and stakeholders learn from the experience and the learning is captured for future work. It is also an important opportunity to recognise and thank those involved. (National Social Marketing Centre, 2011, p. 90)

As can be seen in Table 6.6, we adapted follow-up to better incorporate our partnerships.

Table 6.6   Resourceful follow-up

NSMC planning process checklist	Applying a critical cultural assessment of NSMC steps NSMC steps not used or changed	Applying a critical cultural approach to create Lead My Learning (inclusive of NSMC steps used)
• Learning from how the project was managed • Sharing your results	• *Adapted NSMC Stakeholder* focus to both stakeholders and partnerships to allow opportunities for relationships to develop to more substantial collaborations	• Supporting partners with further development with activities connected with Lead My Learning such as research development and contributing to capacity building. Examples include collaboration in attending research-based conference; publication support; funding bids • Dissemination of Lead My Learning content as well as mechanisms where LML content can contribute to partner activity. For example, a community-wide reading project

Having a 'follow-up' stage as part of the formalised planning process is an excellent way to foreground the importance of planning what will happen or occur after the campaign. We have termed this section 'Resourceful Follow-Up' to highlight a resourceful approach to this stage or part of planning the campaign. In the Lead My Learning campaign we needed to be resourceful in planning for and responding to opportunities for follow-up, as well as forward planning for promotional product resources that could be contributed to this stage. It was important that, even after the campaign had 'finished' we found ways to continue to contribute that were sustainable for a research project that had a defined term and relatively low funding.

In their discussion of the Total Process Planning (TTP) framework (on which the NSMC planning process is based), Ong and Blair-Stevens (2009) emphasise the importance of the follow-up stage. Describing a failure to plan for this as a 'bear-trap':

> In practice, it is common for the greatest efforts to focus on the developing and implementing stages, with evaluation 'tacked on' at the end and little proper handling of any follow-up stage to capture and embed the learning. This is a mistake, since all work needs to be seen in its wider context and timeframe. (2009, p. 158)

While these authors drive home this point by citing the challenges of behaviour change and to "maintain this over time" (p. 158), the argument of planning for follow-up connects with the emphasis on partnerships and relationships in our project. This 'bear trap' is, we could argue, especially problematic in smaller projects with limited resources—and in the unique circumstances of university research-based projects such as ours. Being resourceful, was therefore, paramount.

Planning for 'follow up' as part of a campaign process can have significant benefits. While not comparable in terms of the scope, the value of what we might call 'taking care of follow-up' is underscored in the outcomes of the large scale "Water Campaign" in The Netherlands (Blanchette, van de Gaar, Raat, French, & Jansen, 2016). In this social marketing project, the success of the campaign in terms of 'behavioural change' (as evidenced by the evaluation), together with the substantive relationships that had been established, led to wider implementation from, "90 schools throughout the city of Rotterdam…" to "the 'Water Campaign' was disseminated nation-wide, reaching more than 70 cities across The Netherland" (Blanchette et al., 2016, p. 330).

The Lead My Learning Campaign adapted follow-up to prioritise being 'resourceful'. Heeding the arguments about the importance of planning for follow up (NSMC, 2011; Ong & Blair-Stevens, 2009), we maintained a 'view to the question of follow up' as we worked through the campaign process. This meant, in practice, that we maintained an awareness of the need for follow-up in the day to day activities of the campaign, and were resourceful by being 'on the lookout' for opportunities for follow-up activities at the end of the campaign. We also planned the end of our campaign so that there was time left in our project for follow-up activities.

Follow-up then, not only involved the "thanking strategies" for those who participated, and disseminating findings and outcomes (NSMC, 2011; Ong & Blair-Stevens, 2009, p. 157); it involved resourceful ways that outcomes could be shared and where possible, further used, especially in the communities with which we had worked and formed relationships.

One of the ways we worked in this follow-up stage was in supporting partners in activities that could be connected with Lead My Learning. This included collaboration in a community-wide book project to encourage children to read. Dissemination of Lead My Learning content as well as mechanisms where Lead My Learning content can contribute to partner activity. Other examples include collaboration in attending a research-based conference; publication support; and funding bids. We also disseminated our work through conference participation, invited seminars and academic publications.

References

Berthelsen, D., & Walker, S. (2008). Parents' involvement in their children's education. *Family Matters, 79*, 34–41.

Blair, N. (2015). *Privileging Australian Indigenous knowledge: Sweet potatoes, spiders, waterlilys & brick walls.* Champaign, IL: Common Ground Publishing.

Blanchette, L. M. G., van de Gaar, V. M., Raat, H., French, J., & Jansen, W. (2016). The development of the "Water Campaign". *Journal of Social Marketing, 6*(4), 318–334. https://doi.org/10.1108/JSOCM-09-2015-0069.

Correa-Chávez, M., Mejia-Arauz, R., & Rogoff, B. (2015). *Children learn by observing and contributing to family and community endeavours: A cultural paradigm* (Vol. 49). Waltham, MA: Academic Press.

Devaney, B., & Rossi, P. (1997). Thinking through evaluation design options. *Children and Youth Services Review, 19*(7), 587–606.

Duane, S., Domegan, C., McHugh, P., & Devaney, M. (2016). From restricted to complex exchange and beyond: Social marketing's change agenda. *Journal of Marketing Management, 32*(9–10), 856–876. https://doi.org/10.1080/0267257X.2016.1189449.

Evans-Lacko, S., Henderson, C., Thornicroft, G., & McCrone, P. (2013). Economic evaluation of the anti-stigma social marketing campaign in England 2009–2011. *The British Journal of Psychiatry, 202*(Suppl. 55), S95–S101. https://doi.org/10.1192/bjp.bp.112.113746.

French, J. (2017). The importance of segmentation in social marketing strategy. In T. Dietrich, S. Rundle-Thiele, & K. Kubacki (Eds.), *Segmentation in social marketing: Process, methods and application* (pp. 25–40). Singapore: Springer.

Geia, L. K., Hayes, B., & Usher, K. (2013). Yarning/Aboriginal storytelling: Towards an understanding of an Indigenous perspective and its implications for research practice. *Contemporary Nurse, 46*(1), 13–17. https://doi.org/10.5172/conu.2013.46.1.13.

Harris, A., & Goodall, J. (2008). Do parents know they matter? Engaging all parents in learning. *Educational Research, 50*(3), 277–289. https://doi.org/10.1080/00131880802309424.

Helitzer, D., Soo-Jin, Y., & Wallerstein, N. (2000). The role of process evaluation in the training of facilitators for an adolescent health education program. *The Journal of School Health, 70*(4), 141–147. https://doi.org/10.1111/j.1746-1561.2000.tb06460.x.

Hill, N. E., & Tyson, D. F. (2009). Parental involvement in middle school: A meta-analytic assessment of the strategies that promote achievement. *Developmental Psychology, 45*(3), 740–763. https://doi.org/10.1037/a0015362.

Harwood, V., & Murray, N. (2019). Strategic discourse production and parent involvement: Including parent knowledge and practices in the lead my learning campaign. *International Journal of Inclusive Education, 23*(4), 353–368. https://doi.org/10.1080/13603116.2019.1571119.

Hoover-Dempsey, V. K., Walker, T. M. J., Sandler, M. H., Whetsel, D., Green, L. C., Wilkins, S. A., et al. (2005). Why do parents become involved? Research findings and implications. *The Elementary School Journal, 106*(2), 105–130.

Lefebvre, R. C. (2013). *Social marketing and social change: Strategies and tools for improving health, well-being, and the environment.* Chichester: Wiley.

McDonald, E., Cunningham, T., & Slavin, N. (2015). Evaluating a handwashing with soap program in Australian remote Aboriginal communities: A pre and post intervention study design health behavior, health promotion and society. *BMC Public Health, 15*(1). https://doi.org/10.1186/s12889-015-2503-x.

National Social Marketing Centre. (2011). Big Pocket Guide to using social marketing for behaviour change. In National Social Marketing Centre (Ed.). London: NSMC.

Ong, D., & Blair-Stevens, C. (2009). The Total Process Planning (TPP) framework. In J. French, C. Blair-Stevens, M. Dominic, & M. Rowena (Eds.), *Social marketing and public health: Theory and practice.* Oxford: Oxford University Press.

Perry, M., Fantuzzo, J., & Munis, P. (2002). *Manual—Family involvement questionnaire.* Philadelphia, PA: University of Pennsylvania.

Robinson-Maynard, A., Meaton, J., & Lowry, R. (2013). Identifying key criteria as predictors of success in social marketing: Establishing an evaluation template and grid (ETG). In K. Kubacki & S. Rundle-Thiele (Eds.), *Contemporary issues in social marketing* (pp. 41–58). Newcastle upon Tyne: Cambridge Scholars Publishing.

Rogoff, B. (2014). Learning by observing and pitching into family and community endeavours. *Human Development, 57,* 69–81.

Saunders, R. P., Evans, M. H., & Joshi, P. (2005). Developing a process-evaluation plan for assessing health promotion program implementation: A how-to guide. *Health Promotion Practice, 6*(2), 134–147.

Sherwood, J., & Kendall, S. (2013). Reframing spaces by building relationships: Community collaborative participatory action research with Aboriginal mothers in prison. *Contemporary Nurse, 46*(1), 83–94. https://doi.org/10.5172/conu.2013.46.1.83.

Taylor, C. L., Clayton, D. J., & Rowley, J. S. (2004). Academic socialization: Understanding parental influences on children's school-related development in the early years. *Review of General Psychology, 8*(3), 163–178. https://doi.org/10.1037/1089-2680.8.3.163.

Viadro, C., Earp, J. A. L., & Altpeter, M. (1997). Designing a process evaluation for a comprehensive breast cancer screening intervention: Challenges and opportunities. *Evaluation and Program Planning, 20*(3), 237–249.

Walker, M., Fredericks, B., Mills, K., & Anderson, D. (2013). "Yarning" as a method for community-based health research with Indigenous women: The Indigenous women's wellness research program. *Health Care for Women International, 35*(10). https://doi.org/10.1080/07399332.2013.815754.

Waters, B. S. (2016). *We can speak for ourselves parent involvement and ideologies of black mothers in Chicago.* Rotterdam: SensePublishers.

7

Analysing and Reviewing the Critical Cultural Social Marketing Approach Used in Lead My Learning

In this chapter we consider the contribution of Lead My Learning to promoting education and we review the 'lessons learned' from our work in applying a critical cultural social marketing approach. Firstly, we ask, what did the Lead My Learning campaign do, offer or contribute? Asking this we draw from the range of data collected as part of our research processes. This data includes: interviews (yarning and semi-structured) with parents that were held in the formative research, throughout the campaign and in the post campaign; interviews with service providers such as childcare educators; post-campaign survey with service providers; and relevant data from our pre- and post-campaign survey.

Campaign Design, Methodologies and Analysis

As set out in Chapter 1, the design for the Lead My Learning campaign used three different modalities. These were:

© The Author(s) 2019
V. Harwood and N. Murray, *The Promotion of Education*,
https://doi.org/10.1007/978-3-030-25300-4_7

1. A community-wide campaign in Girral, a regional NSW town. A wait-list control site was located in Kurrawong.
2. A multi-playgroup campaign in the Eastside Region that included Aboriginal playgroups, in partnership with a service provider in regional NSW (11 sites).
3. An early childhood centre campaign in four Aboriginal owned and operated services (Madden Island, Broadhurst Child and Family Centre, Bushwick Central Preschool, Upper Eastside Children's Centre) with Aboriginal-led centres that rely on bus transport for children in regional NSW.

Methodologies engaged throughout the project were: formative and post-campaign individual and group interviews (yarning and semi-structured) with services and parents; pre- and post-surveys for parents; fieldwork visits to services, community organisations and communities; and a post-campaign online service provider survey.

A wait-list control design was used for modality (1) the Community-wide campaign. Kurrawong, the wait-list community, was comparable to Girral and received a revised version of the campaign. The campaign was delivered seven months after the completion of the campaign in Girral and after post-survey collection was completed across all of the sites. This timing was required as the pre- and post-surveys conducted in Kurrawong were designed to ascertain whether there were any other influences that might explain a change other than the Lead My Learning Campaign. From the post-surveys and from our informal discussions with Kurrawong services prior to the campaign roll out at this site, we did not detect any influences in Kurrawong. We did, however, note that a small number of participants in the Kurrawong post-surveys reported seeing Lead My Learning promotional products prior to these being introduced to this community. While it is not possible to explain this occurrence, it may be due to those survey participants possibly travelling to Girral and seeing the campaign promotional products in the community.

Post Interviews (Yarning and Semi-Structured)

The post interviews (yarning and semi-structured) were held with 122 parents in 53 interviews (yarning and semi-structured) in the Girral region and in the Eastside Region. As stated above, the campaign in Kurrawong was rolled out after post surveying was completed. Due to time constraints, a smaller number of post interviews were conducted in Kurrawong. Two post individual interviews and three group interviews (yarning and semi-structured) were held, involving 22 parents. This post-campaign data collection occurred in Kurrawong during the follow-up visit to meet with Elders and services about the campaign. The interviews (yarning and semi-structured) were organised into six discussion topics:

1. About parenting/caring relationships with children
2. About recognition of the Lead My Learning campaign
3. Engaging with Lead My Learning
4. Use, influence or impact of the Lead My Learning campaign
5. Sharing and Encouraging Learning
6. Before the Lead My Learning campaign—and Now

Feedback received via the post interviews (yarning and semi-structured) was, as expected, far more detailed than those in the survey. Due to the limits imposed by large distances, post interviews (yarning) weren't held in two of the Childcare Services (which used the bus stickers).

Surveys

As explained in Chapter 6, due to the effectiveness of the interviews (yarning and semi-structured) and the preference of the participants, in the campaign, the decision was made during the campaign to shift from an emphasis on the pre- and post-survey to gather information about the campaign, to a focus on the individual and small groups interviews (yarning and semi-structured). The surveys were based on quantitative items, with one qualitative question in the pre-survey, and 3 qualitative items in the post-survey, with a total of 43 questions in the pre-survey and

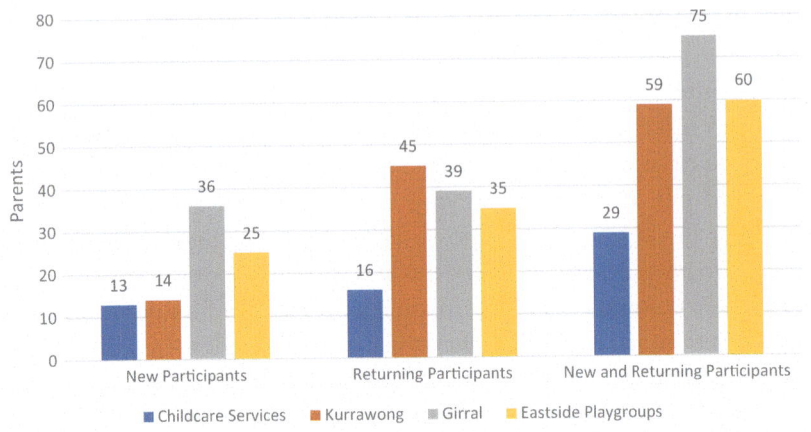

Fig. 7.1 Number of new and returning participants, post-survey

36 questions in the post-survey. The total responses to the pre-survey were 511 (with 482 suitable for analysis) and 233 responses to the post-survey. The responses to the post-survey are summarised in Fig. 7.1.

Using the wait-list control design, we had initially aimed to use pre- and post-matched surveys as a means to measure any change due to the campaign. While the pre-survey delivered 482 responses suitable for analysis, the decision was made to change the focus in the post-campaign data collection methodologies to interviews (yarning and semi-structured), with less resources directed to the survey collection and administration.

The change to the interviews (yarning and semi-structured) as the methodology of choice to collect post-campaign data was due to several reasons. The survey was extremely difficult as a methodology for the participants in this project, requiring considerable time and expense to carry out appropriately and respectfully. Feedback from parents and from services indicated a preference for yarning and for semi-structured interviews. Consequently, post-campaign data collection was changed to these methodologies.

Additionally, review of the pre-survey revealed responses tended to be towards the higher end of the Likert scales, which had implications for the utility of the post-survey in measuring positive change. For example, the pre-survey contained the question '*As a parent, I really encourage my child(ren) to learn*', with responses available, 'Rarely', 'Often', 'Sometimes', 'Always'. For this question, from a total of 469 responses (13 responses were missing to this question), 374 respondents selected 'Always', from a total of 469; a percentage of 79.7%. In terms of demonstrating the involvement in children's learning by the parents from our priority group, this result challenges deficit accounts. However, in terms of attempting to measure any change after the campaign, this left little room for an indication of positive change. Based on our formative work and the survey pre-testing, this response hadn't been anticipated. Responses tending towards the highest end of the scale (representing the most positive) were also found in the evaluation of the 'No Germs on Me Campaign' in remote Aboriginal communities in Australia (McDonald, Cunningham, & Slavin, 2015). As these authors explain:

> In general, for both survey rounds, all participants scored individual questionnaire items (40 items in total) towards the high end of scales if not provided a perfect score. Therefore mean scores for items were high at community, regional and total population levels pre and post intervention and any difference in mean scores for items between survey rounds were small. (McDonald et al., 2015, p. 6)

Reviewing their study, McDonald et al. (2015) suggest that this "is likely to include over reporting as this is generally the case with similar surveys when participants desire to provide the perceived socially correct answer" (2015, p. 9). Following this reasoning, this could possibly also be an issue in the Lead My Learning study. For instance, while the participants differ (our survey included Aboriginal and non-Aboriginal people; it was located in regional and rural settings; the content was education and learning focussed with parents of young children), there may well be the issue of perceived stigmatisation. Given the deficit stereotyping of parents who have experienced educational disadvantage and live in places of socio-economic disadvantage, it may be possible that parents were aware of this issue and responded to the survey items with this in mind. This is a consideration with which to contend with in designing evaluations in future research on the promotion of education with those who have experienced educational disadvantage.

Importantly, there is also too the possibility that the parents are encouraging their children to learn and that a more nuanced approach to question construction may have yielded results that could have better measured any change. These issues were not picked up in the pilot testing that was conducted, suggesting that should surveys be used with this cohort, extensive formative survey design research and pilot testing is needed.

For the discussion in this chapter we draw on data from the post-survey, which had a total of 223 responses that were usable. Of these, 88 responses were by new participants and 135 responses were from returning participants (matched surveys (pre and post) totalled 135 responses). The four sites where the survey was administered were,

- Childcare Services—4 early childhood services in regional and rural NSW;
- Kurrawong Community—Wait-list control site
- Girral—Community-wide campaign
- Eastside Services Playgroups—11 playgroups

Analysis in this chapter draws on both this post-survey data, together with the rich in-depth data from the interviews (yarning and semi-structured). In this discussion we draw on descriptive statistics from the post-survey data, and due to the limited sample size, do not use the pre-and post-matched surveys.

What Did Lead My Learning Do, Offer or Contribute? The Potential of Strategic Discourse Production in the Promotion of Education

I'm sure it has but definitely for me like it's more … I'm more conscious of it now. I haven't noticed other parents talking about it as such but, you know, that doesn't mean they're not talking about it. (Deanne, Girral Kindergarten)

The perhaps unusual paradox of the Lead My Learning campaign was that it wasn't setting out to 'improve' or 'change' but rather, to 'reaffirm' in a respectful manner what parents did do, and to provide a 'talking point' about these practices. In this sense, Lead My Learning was designed with (1) attention to the ways that dominant discourses may delegitimise some parents' involvement in their children's learning and (2) attention to what the parents were doing and how to communicate this to the parents. Deanne's comment in the above quote that she is "more conscious of it now" is a good example of the type of feedback that we received. The Lead My Learning proposition statement (the 'offer' to the priority group) is:

It is possible to lead your child's learning. It only takes a little time and it can fit in with everyday activities. You can encourage your child's learning without having a specific knowledge of a topic and it gives a child the happy experiences of valuing and enjoying learning.

Feedback from the parents and the childcare services indicates that this proposition was successful. When parents did interact with the Lead My Learning campaign via the various promotional products, the proposition that 'It is possible to lead your child's learning' met with acknowledgement. Likewise, the various points that are connected with this proposition, from taking little time and everyday activities through to being able to encourage without specific knowledge and being happy and enjoying learning were also well received, and as Deanne explains, "I'm more conscious of it now".

As we have outlined (Harwood & Murray, 2019) through the use of a critical cultural social marketing approach we were able to engage in what we have termed 'strategic discourse production'. This strategic activity is defined as:

We define strategic discourse production as a process to strategically produce discourses of subjugated knowledges (Foucault, 1980) that interrupt dominant procedures of truth. (Harwood & Murray, 2019, p. 354)

By 'subjugated knowledges', Foucault was referring to "those blocs of historical knowledge which were present but disguised within the body of functionalist and systematising theory and which criticism – which obviously draws upon scholarship – has been able to reveal" (1980, p. 82). This statement not only helps us to appreciate how subjugated knowledges occur and are 'disguised', but significantly also, the role of 'criticism' in revealing these. As we have outlined, in this project, "subjugated knowledges are the learning practices of parents, while the procedures of truth we are seeking to interrupt are the truths that 'educationally disadvantaged parents are not involved in children's learning'" (Harwood & Murray, 2019, p. 355). The idea of strategic discourse production is to engage in *both* revealing and listening to subjugated knowledges (and here an appreciation of the cultural is paramount) and the truths that subjugate—and based on collaborative processes, develop ways to create different truths that may connect with practices of subjectivation.

Foucault's later work emphasised the activeness of subjectivation (Foucault, 2011, 2014a, 2014b, 2016, 2017). In this view, there is a relationship with the self in the production of subjects—that is, subjects are not simply produced through processes that exclude the self. This is not, however, to imply that selves can 'magically' free themselves from the 'chains that bind'. Such an assumption misses the point because it fails to fully appreciate the powerful effects of discourses and practices associated with these, as well as the material, the social, the affective and the cultural. The case in point discussed in this book is the tyranny of effects wrought by being known as uneducated—known that is by the powerful legitimating systems of society, by others and, significantly, by the self.

We might ask, then, if discourses are implicated in those processes that are external to the subject, but that influence the production of subjects, what of the discourses that might be produced by the self, or taken up by the self—how might these be involved?

Foucault encourages attention to how practices of subjectivation are tied to how the subject tells what is true (such as via confession or through techniques of the self). Returning to our discussion of education and parent involvement in learning, we can argue that the modes of veridiction used by institutional education are very likely to be influential in relation to a parent's techniques of subjectivation. From this angle, it becomes clear that parents who have experienced educational disadvantages such as an 'incomplete education' can become obligated to tell truths of an 'uneducated status', and this influences their practices of subjectivation. (Harwood & Murray, 2019, p. 356)

By 'modes of veridiction' we are referring to Foucault's (2014b) pluralistic description (Barker, 2018) of what we could loosely term 'modes of truth-telling'. We say loosely, because "veridiction is a neologism coined by Foucault" (Barker, 2018) in his 1983–1984 Collège de France lectures, published as *The Courage of the Truth (The Government of Self and Others II)* (Foucault, 2011). The translation from the French is explained by the translator of this text, "we have decided to maintain the same neologism in English in order to maintain the two essential parts: the Latin root 'ver' for truth, and 'diction' for speaking, pronouncing, or telling" (Sawyer, translator, in Foucault, 2011, p. 19).

The plurality of the modes of veridiction causes us to think of the myriad and intersecting ways in which truth is produced and with what consequences. There is thus a need for a critical approach—or what Foucault terms, "a critical philosophy of veridictions":

In the case of a critical philosophy of veridictions, the problem is not that of knowing how a subject in general may understand an object in general. The problem is that of knowing how subjects are effectively tied within and by the forms of veridiction in which they engage … In a word, in this critical philosophy it is not a question of a general economy of the true, but rather of a historico politics, or a political history of veridictions. (Foucault, 2014b, p. 20)

Taking up this challenge and paraphrasing, how are these parents effectively tied within and by the forms of veridiction of education in which they engage? A critical philosophy of the modes of veridiction of education would turn the gaze not to the 'general economy of the true', but rather to the "political history of veridictions".

When we also consider that subjectivation is influenced by these modes of veridiction, the relationship between these becomes clearer. So too do the opportunities for a critical practice that might intervene somehow in modes of veridiction that prompt avowals from parents such as 'I am uneducated' or 'I am not involved in my children's learning' (see Harwood & Murray, 2019 for an extended discussion of avowal).

The point here is the challenge of grasping an appreciation of knowledges that are subjugated and how these knowledges become obligated to certain truths. This challenge likewise involves recognising how to respectfully produce discourses that might go against the grain of such truths. It is a challenge to listen for and appreciate knowledges that are subjugated. This is because such knowledges are so often delegitimated and obscured by the dominant that these are difficult to ascertain not only for those who experience such subjugation, but also for those who might want to think though how to create strategic discourse production. Through the use of a critical cultural social marketing approach, it was possible to accomplish strategic discourse production, which in our example, was to promote the involvement of parents in their children's learning.

> we maintain different possibilities can occur when subjugated discourses are 'promoted' (in both senses of the word). Such promotion, we propose, respectfully engages with the otherness of the parents, and can be met by avowals and practices of subjectivation about involvement in learning. Strategic discourse production in Lead My Learning sought to differ from dominating demands that expect an avowal such as 'I am uneducated and can't (properly) help my child learn'. (Harwood & Murray, 2019, p. 364)

To our mind, a strategic discourse about parent involvement in learning is very much part of the project to promote education—and to us one of the key findings from our research. We now turn to discuss different facets of the Lead My Learning campaign.

Campaign Recall and Recognition: Campaign Messages and Promotional Products

To gauge campaign recall and recognition after the campaign had finished, two methodologies were used with the parents, the post-surveys and the post-interviews (yarning and semi-structured). While fewer participants were recruited to complete the post-survey, results from the questions about the campaign do provide some insight into the campaign. Questions about recall and recognition covered the Lead My Learning campaign messages, as well as items about campaign promotional products.

As we described in Chapter 5, the clear message of Lead My Learning is: *Everyday Activities are opportunities to Share and Encourage Learning.* The associated messages are:

> Lead my Learning is all about turning everyday activities into opportunities to lead a child's learning. Children love to learn and they'll love the moments when you lead their learning.

> You can start now. Sharing and encouraging learning creates a fun learning relationship to build a child's future. Any time is a good time to start!

> It only takes a minute to create a learning moment. Learning moments happen in our everyday life. Share and Encourage – It's that simple! (Murray & Harwood, 2018)

The post-survey asked about the Lead My Learning Message using closed questions and one open ended question (written response) (Fig. 7.2). The closed questions were:

> Do you recall any of the messages? You can select more than one.
> 1. Lead My Learning.
> 2. Lead My Learning is all about turning everyday activities into opportunities to lead a child's learning.
> 3. Everyday activities are opportunities to Share and Encourage learning.
> 4. Start now for my future.
> 5. You can share learning with me when you're doing your everyday activities; Cooking, Washing, Shopping, Out and About.
> 6. Everyone's an expert at encouraging learning. You can encourage learning with me by giving me; High fives, fist pumps, thumbs up, or even a big smile.
> 7. None of the above. (Lead My Learning post-survey)

Of the different messages, the first three in the list above were the most popular. These three messages were included on a number of the promotional products, including posters, corflutes, the Lead My Learning

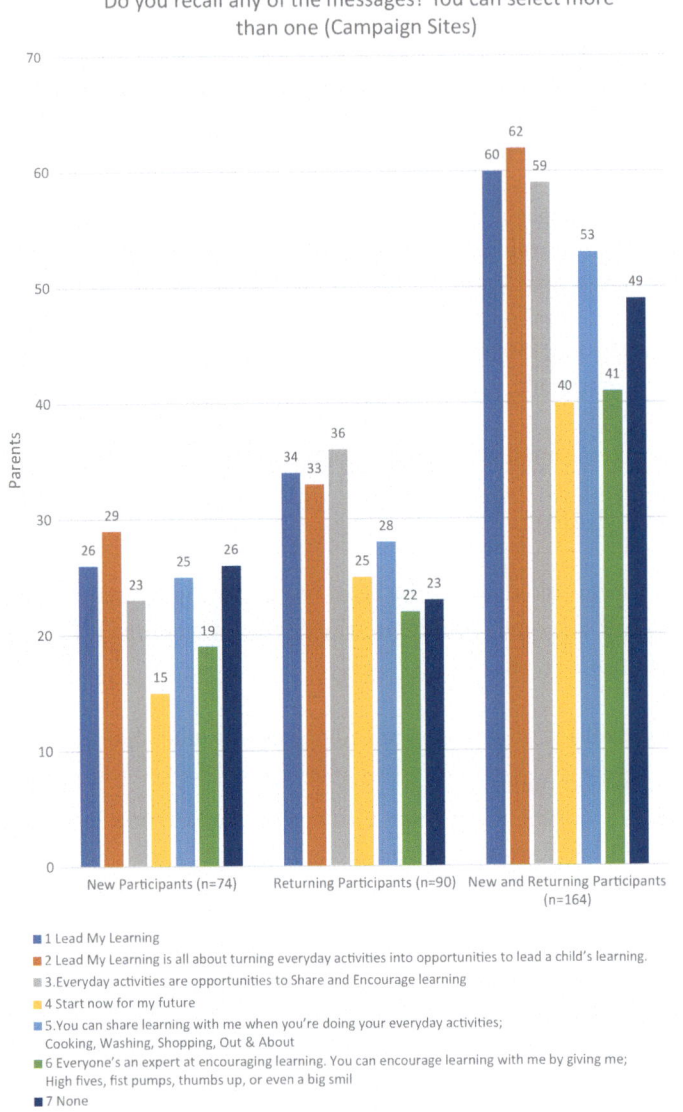

Fig. 7.2 Lead My Learning messages, campaign sites only

website, the Lead My Learning information pamphlet and coasters (see Figs. 5.3 and 5.4, promotional products). Information about the Lead

My Learning messages was also collected in the post-surveys using the open-ended question:

Thinking about the things you have seen, read or heard, <u>what is the main message you remember?</u>

The responses below are from the multi-playgroup campaign in the Eastside Region (11 sites),

That you can use everyday events to extend children's learning. (Sara, Eastside Playgroup)

That the parent is an important part of a child's learning journey. (Megan, Eastside Playgroup)

Parents can lead children's learning. (Nicole, Eastside Playgroup)

Parents have a primary role in leading their child's learning. Learning happens in daily activities such as playing, cooking, shopping, reading, singing – all things parents can use to teach their children lots of things. (Elizabeth, Lower Eastside Playgroup)

These written comments indicate usage of the Lead My Learning messages, and how these parents consider these may be integrated.

The post-survey question, 'We are interested to know if you have seen any of the Lead My Learning marketing material' gave respondents the opportunity to select 11 different promotional products (with images supplied in the survey to assist with the responses).

1. Posters (Sharing)
2. Posters (Encouraging)
3. Message poster
4. Advertisement on taxi
5. Advertisement on local bus shelter
6. Large corflute sign
7. Drink coaster
8. Playmat

Fig. 7.3 Lead My Learning promotional products, campaign sites only

9. Children's preschool t-shirt
10. Information booklet (z fold flyer)
11. Bus window stickers
12. I have not seen any of these materials

The most seen campaign promotional products for all of the campaign participants (childcare services, Girral community-wide, and Eastside Services playgroups) were the three posters that had the messages: Everyday Activities are opportunities to Share and Encourage Learning; Sharing Learning; and Encouraging Learning. Figure 7.3 provides data on responses to this question for all (1) of the post-survey responses, including Kurrawong; and (2) aggregated data for the campaign participation sites only (Childcare Services, Girral and Eastside Services playgroups). For the Childcare modality, the bus window stickers had a marginally lower response than the Sharing Posters. For the playgroup, the posters, followed by the playmats were the most seen promotional products.

Everyday Opportunities to Share and Encourage Learning

The post-survey asked questions about three of the Lead My Learning activities: *Sharing learning, Encouraging learning,* and *Lead My Learning and Everyday Activities.* The question is summarised below:

Could you tell us if the things you've seen, read or heard about Lead My Learning have been used to:

1. Share Learning
2. Encourage Learning
3. Lead A Child's Learning while doing everyday activities

These questions gave four possible responses: I thought about it; I tried it; I use it; and Not applicable. Figure 7.4 depicts responses to these questions, with (1) an overview of the data from all of the post-survey responses, that is, inclusive of Kurrawong, the wait-list control site; and (2) an overview of the aggregated responses to interaction with these activities (I thought about it + I tried it + I used it). The overview of data from the post-survey responses provides an indication of the different levels of interaction with Lead My Learning from this sample.

The aggregated responses indicate that for this small post-survey sample, there was more interaction with the campaign, than no interaction, and that this was the case in each of the three campaign modalities. However, given the small sample size, it is not possible to 'generalise' these results

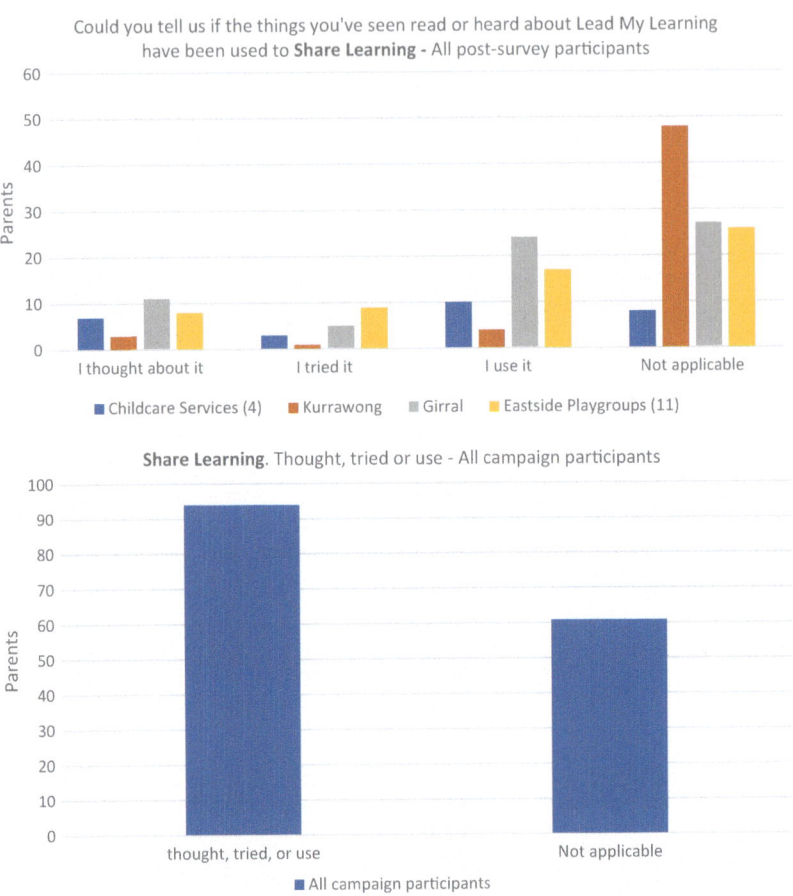

Fig. 7.4 Thought, tried or use it—share learning, encourage learning, lead a child's learning while doing everyday activities

to each of the modalities where the campaign was conducted. Rather, we use these as helpful signposts in our analysis and to assist in the analysis of post-interviews (yarning and semi-structured). For instance, this data shows that in this small sample, there is a lower frequency for the response 'I use it' in the Lead My Learning campaign. The surveys revealed a mixed response for the Eastside playgroups—suggesting parents in these playgroups differently interacted with the Lead My Learning campaign.

The post-surveys provided data on all of the possible playgroups that were involved in the campaign, for instance, facilitated playgroups and the voluntarily facilitated playgroups in Girral, and the post-yarning sessions and semi-structured interviews helped to unpack how Lead My Learning was 'taken up and used' in these different playgroups. When used, there was a greater influence for some of the parents who participated in playgroups. It also seems that when Lead My Learning was incorporated by the facilitators in the playgroups in Girral (voluntary or service facilitated) that the parents reported high levels of interaction with the Lead My Learning (such as talking about it, using it).

A Language for Leading Learning—A Discourse of Parent Involvement

Two common findings emerged from the post interviews (yarning and semi-structured). Firstly, the parents had difficulty saying what Lead My Learning *is*. Secondly, the parents didn't have a language to hand for this involvement in learning. We observed that the parents would resort to using 'Lead My Learning' as a term to describe this type of parent and child learning activity that involved everyday opportunities to share and encourage learning. One way of thinking through this finding is that what the parents are involved in is not usually or commonly how *education* is labelled. This issue is noted in Waters' (2016) study with Black mothers in Chicago. In this work it is argued that the school's construal of 'involvement' failed to connect with those parents. As Waters explains:

> When the mothers talked specifically about parent involvement, it was most often in the context of the school. Whereas this appears to be the traditional way we conceptualize parent involvement as a schooling process, this is not in fact how the mothers' families functioned ... their involvement is better highlighted when the mothers talk about how they engage and prepare their children for the world outside of their homes. ... These women talk about involvement in ways that are not always charted in expensive curricula or statistical spreadsheets, but in specific ways that build an awareness of race, character development, leadership, and responsibility into daily activities. (2016, p. 82)

While this study was concerned with an elementary school and not the early years of education, and with a specific cohort, it does share some similarities in terms of experiences of having parent knowledge disqualified. For instance, the parents in our study experienced a similar emphasis of how 'involvement' is construed. What the parents who we interviewed were doing was involvement; yet it was not labelled as such nor was it something that might be noticed in "expensive curricula or statistical worksheets" (Waters, 2016, p. 82). Practices by the parents, in both our study and in Waters (2016) are significant practices of involvement in children's learning. We suggest that the Lead My Learning campaign went some way to making contributions not only to describing some of these, but also to offering a way that parents could speak of them.

Members of the Girral Mother's Group, a community playgroup run by volunteers, noted how Lead My Learning integrates into what parents are doing. In the excerpt below, Natalie and Evie talk about using Lead My Learning, with the conversation starting with Natalie answering in the affirmative about her use of Lead My Learning:

Natalie: Yeah for sure.

Evie: I think I see it as not so hard in involving the kids in everyday activities, you make it fun.

Natalie: Yeah just, I don't know, it seems easier to look at something as 'Oh, what's this?'… and I'll be like 'Okay we can do something now' and get … you know, here's a bit of energy out of the way and then I can go back to focusing on a task easier, rather than me saying 'I'm gonna do this first' and then go away but, you know, it's just easier to get him involved and then when as soon as he loses interest then I can just go about doing whatever. (Natalie and Evie, Girral Mother's Group)

An example of this contribution by the Lead My Learning campaign is described by us in Harwood and Murray (2019) and which we include again here. In this important example, Kacey, a grandmother, who was parenting two 'grannies' aged three and nine, comments on Lead My Learning, stating, "I think it's good" (Eastside Services Aboriginal-C, 2017). Kacey also kindly described how she shares and encourages learning.

Sharing Learning

Counting strawberries in the bowl and count the grapes in the bowl. We'll count in the fridge ... we'll just count different things, how many we have on the plate, how many this, I just want the little one to get an idea ... and the older one, she still counts how many people. She's always been a counter. (Kacey, Eastside Services playgroups)

Encouraging Learning

And encourage anything, encourage because I know they can. And I always complement them on how well they've done, you know, what they know, how clever they are, things like that because I don't believe you have to be super-smart to go to university. (Kacey, Eastside Services playgroups)

As we observed (Harwood & Murray, 2019, pp. 362–363), "Kacey's descriptions resonate with the content of Lead My Learning, or rather, as Kacey signalled with a nod to our posters, *they* connected with *her* approach." This example is important for two reasons. Firstly, it is a contribution to us from an Elder in the community that not only appraises Lead My Learning, but significantly, is a moment where if we listen carefully we are being educated about sharing and encouraging learning. Secondly, the example demonstrates how Lead My Learning connected with what was occurring, rather than presuming to know more and taking a position that told people what to do.

Describing a Learning Practice That Is 'Subjugated' by 'Official' Education Discourses

That the parents had knowledge about learning with their children was evident in the data we collected prior to the campaign. What Lead My Learning did or contributed, was to offer ways to describe this involvement in learning with children. In the following discussion from a community-run playgroup in Kurrawong, following a comment by Sabrina and a question from the interviewer, Caroline expands on her realisation that this form of involvement in learning "*it's a thing you know*"

Sabrina: Yeah. Oh, I think it's wonderful ... Unless it's spoken about, you know, people don't really realise how important or easy it is.

I: So would you say the campaign has helped start conversations with other parents?

Caroline: Yeah … I remember when the survey came out and reading through it and actually thinking 'Oh, ***it's a thing, you know?***' Like it actually … you know, when just being a mum and you're just doing everyday things you don't realise. So yeah just talking about how when doing everyday things you can involve your kids and like interact with them – like it's part of it, definitely. And seeing the mat as well, you know, cos it … they say 'What a cool mat' and then you can say it's Lead My Learning, and the mat comes out every day. (Sabrina and Caroline, Kurrawong North Playgroup, emphasis added)

Kurrawong was the second of our community placement sites and was the waitlist control for Girral. As we detailed in Chapter 5, this site received similar promotional products as did the first site (Girral), but did not have the same launch events. Caroline's comment picks up on a theme that emerged in the research—that parents didn't have a language for what they were doing, and many parents didn't put it into the 'education' basket. Importantly too, in this excerpt Caroline comments on the impact participating in the survey had in her recognition that 'it's a thing too' [parents leading learning by doing everyday activities]. While we hadn't anticipated this type of response to the survey, this interaction perhaps suggests the survey might be viewed as a legitimate document and that this can work too as a form of strategic discourse production. In this instance, this was possibly prompted by seeing the range of Lead My Learning items or the questions about 'everyday activities' in the recall section of the survey.

Playgroups and Parent Take up of a Strategic Discourse

As we have suggested, Lead My Learning created an opportunity for the take up and use of a strategic discourse about parent involvement in their children's learning. We have also noted that the post-survey sample, while small, suggests that this strategic discourse was differently interacted with, and some parents responded that they hadn't interacted with Lead My

Learning (see Fig. 7.4 for example). Those that did report interacting with Lead My Learning in the post-interviews (yarning and semi-structured), offered a number of comments about their involvement in their children's learning. The following question was asked in both the pre- and post-surveys:

> We are interested in what YOU think you can do at home to help YOUR child learn: Please write 1 or 2 sentences.

A sense of the contribution by the Lead My Learning campaign can be grasped by considering the pre- and post-survey responses to this question by the Eastside playgroups.

Pre-survey responses from the Eastside Playgroup, where the campaign was rolled out across 11 playgroup sites were dominated by comments about reading, homework and books, for example:

- Read every night. Explain everything.
- Assist with homework. Listening to readings. Help brainstorm with older children. Play educational games.
- Bed time story.
- Read, shapes, colours, books, picture, puzzles.
- Reading to them every day, help with homework, teaching the right way to work things out for themselves. Playing games and imagination play. Help them develop motor skills.
- DVD born to read, flashcards, songs, reading.
- Learn to read and write. Books, flash cards. (Eastside Playgroups, pre-survey)

Some responses included reading and mentioned other activities:

- Spend time with them. Read, talk, count with them in play.
- Sing songs and read books.
- Engage in play with them. Model appropriate behaviour interactions.
- We read to our children before bed every night as well we read sometimes in afternoon school. We do craft and art, listen to music, dancing, watch documentarys [sic] on TV.

- Reading, playing games, puzzles, messy play, outdoor activities.
- Read books. Let them help with things. Give them freedom to play.
- Reading stories. Playing with them.
- Reading, asking questions, open responses, transparency. Responsibility, democratic approach to some decisions, exploratory learning approach, Art activities.
- Read, sing, colour, shape cards, number games. Be inventive, caring, patient, loving. I do these things at home.
- Read books, play with them, interact with them, sing, dance, lots of fun, messy things, play outside, tell them that you love them every day. (Eastside Playgroups, pre-survey)

Some of the responses describe activities that mention or allude to activities described in the Lead My Learning campaign:

- Craft games, bike riding, taking them outside rather than stay indoors on the TV. Using their imagination to create new things.
- To help your child learn at home you can read to your child, ask them about things on each page. You can use, for example, a ball pit to teach colours, painting out what colour the ball is that the child picks up.
- Lots of free play, reading stories, limited screen time.
- Play, explain ideas, look.
- Life skills, cooking, cleaning, language skills, talking with them and modelling; numeracy: talking about numbers and patterns; literacy: reading, writing, talking about letters and sounds; creativity, social skills, manners, etiquette. (Eastside Playgroups, pre-survey)

Four of the 79 responses included the word 'encourage'. Three of these responses are provided below:

- Play, encourage learning and praise.
- Be a role model, read a lot to encourage learning.
- Encourage reading, play games, and puzzles with colour/shares and patterns recognition games that involve strategy and choice. Watch programmes and activities together and highlight learning in a fun and supporting way. (Eastside Playgroups, pre-survey)

Overwhelmingly the comments from the pre-survey seemed to connect with activities that were traditionally school directed, such as 'reading'.

While of course this is useful and to be welcomed, we noticed something different in comments written in the post-surveys: there was greater variety in the descriptions of learning, and this variety was inclusive of the range of ways parents are involved in learning.

The post survey repeated the open-ended question:

> We are interested in what YOU think you can do at home to help YOUR child learn.
> Please write 1 or 2 sentences.

The responses in the post survey from the Eastside playgroup included references to reading:

- More reading time and less computer games.
- Continue reading, writing and talking with my children.

Significantly, these comments also mentioned learning that occurs in everyday activities, such as, "Offer support and teach my child through playing and everyday activities" (Eastside playgroup post-survey). More examples of these responses are provided below:

> Let them help in the kitchen, measuring and getting ingredients. Helping with handling and folding washing to sort colours. (Brittany, Eastside Playgroup)

> Spotting shapes, counting objects, cooking, measurements, I-spy, sorting pegs. (Lauren, Eastside Playgroup)

> Involvement in everyday activities – reading the junk mail, cooking, chores. Jobs can contain conversations and learning that isn't formal. (Nicole, Lower Eastside Playgroup)

> Offer support and teach my child through playing and everyday activities. (Megan, Eastside Playgroup)

Play with my child, encourage my child to be curious about the world and question everything. (Tiffany, Eastside Playgroup)

We walk and spot numbers on mail boxes, letters on street signs. We dry dishes/cutlery and count them, name them and name a normal use and a silly use. We play eye spy shapes, or circle table, rectangle door. (Amber, Eastside Playgroup)

One of the comments drew together the Lead My Learning message that children 'love to learn', with reading and the word encourage:

Most important is a love of learning, to help and encourage them to ask questions and think about possible answers. Teach by example – ask questions, show value of reading and maths, listen and value my children. (Crystal, Eastside Playgroup)

In addition to conveying the variety of parent involvement, the above comments contain examples of usage of the language and messaging from the Lead My Learning campaign. For instance, 'everyday opportunities', 'share and encourage' and learning moments such as in the kitchen or the washing. Compared with the pre-survey, these responses have more variety and describe everyday activities.

In the post-survey we also asked a question to gauge if parents were talking about Lead My Learning—and if so, what they talked about. This question was asked in the post-survey because during the campaign we learned from parents, as well as from service providers that they had observed parents discussing Lead My Learning. The following quotes are again from the multi-playgroup campaign in the Eastside Region.

Remembering conversations about Lead My Learning. We are interested in what you talked about.
Please write 1 or 2 sentences

Responses from the parents in the Eastside playgroups included:

Everyday learning such as cooking or watching TV could be a learning activity. (Jessica, Eastside Playgroup)

About how everyday activities can be just as important in learning. (Megan, Eastside Playgroup)

I was home schooled, I spoke to my mum about the way we were raised and how lead my learning style is so similar, so normal, that's it's great to see it being shown to the rest of the world, to people who didn't know, to parents who stress about the little things. Just how much of an amazing programme it is. (Amber, Eastside Playgroup)

Angela, a service provider, gave an overview of the responses from the different coordinators of the 11 playgroups in this service, "I spoke with the coordinators of playgroup. Importance of involving children in all activities" (Angela, service provider, Eastside Playgroup). The feedback, 'involving children in all activities' connects with both the ethos of the playgroups and with the phrases used in Lead My Learning. Overall, this feedback from the playgroup participants suggests that the campaign was well received.

Mixed Results in the Eastside Playgroups: Not Always Used, but When Used Lead My Learning Was Helpful

Not everyone in the Eastside playgroups reported using Lead My Learning, but those that did, reported enjoying it and found it beneficial. Despite the important influence that the campaign in the multi-playgroup in the Eastside Region appeared to have, not all parents in the post-survey from the playgroup cohort reported using the campaign. The results indicate that for the playgroup campaign placement approximately half of the parents report interacting with it, with around one third indicating that 'I used it'. As discussed above, there were mixed responses to the post-survey question that asked:

Could you tell us if the things you've seen, read or heard about Lead My Learning have been used to: share learning; encourage learning; lead a child's learning while doing everyday activities?

This does raise questions about whether more could have been done to improve take up of the campaign. Yet we do note that over half of those parents surveyed from the playgroup campaign placement modality did interact with the campaign, with 37% using it, does indicate that the presence of the campaign in the playgroups did have some beneficial impact. However, in the interviews (yarning and semi-structured) the benefits of Lead My Learning to those who engaged with it, become apparent.

Below we discuss some of the responses from the Eastside Services multi-playgroup cohort to four of the questions asked during the post-campaign yarns. One of these questions asked: *Could you describe any examples of using any ideas from Lead My Learning?*

> I think we do it like my son (2yrs old) helps hang out the washing we tell him to like count the pegs and sort them into colours and things. (Isabella, Eastside Playgroup)

> Yeah like I get her (4yrs old) to help me scan the things in Woolworths … like weigh the bananas. (Maci, Eastside, Playgroup)

Similar to the survey, the interviews (yarning and semi-structured) included recall questions, such as: In the past few weeks can you think of a time when you have Shared or Encourage learning activities?

> Yeah like when I bake, I like bake muffins and stuff I just think 'Oh I just wanna get it done' and she goes 'Oh can I help?' cos I know there's just gonna be so much more mess and it's gonna take a hundred times longer but you just try some … sometimes I have to just get it done quickly … and sometimes I go okay I'll just get her to help me. And I guess they can learn like one cup … doing measurements … yeah and pouring. (Isabella, Eastside Playgroup)

> I try and umm to do different things with him… But yeah, he's at that age where he just goes active, I can't get him to sit for more than five minutes so it's very hard, so when I get him I sort of count to five and sort of, you know … and in the bath he counts 3, 2, 1 and stands in the bath sort of thing. So it's pretty much in the everyday stuff whether it's playing or bath time or anything like that. (Lauren, Eastside Playgroup)

A third question was asked about the possible usefulness of the Lead My Learning message:

> Do you think Lead My Learning message can be useful/helpful for parents to utilise in their everyday activities (for instance, that it doesn't impose/take extra time)?

Responses to this question from the Eastside Services multi playgroup included:

> Yes. They need all the help they can get today. (Yvette, Eastside Playgroup)

> I think definitely for ones that don't realise how simple it could be. (Vivien, Eastside Playgroup)

> Definitely cos they learn from us. (Sabrina, Eastside Playgroup)

The fourth question sought to understand whether there was any change in their involvement in learning activities with their children:

> Have you been doing this more? Thinking of people you know or have seen – do you think they are talking about or using Lead My Learning content, ideas and/or resources?

Again, from the Eastside Services multi playgroup, responses included:

> Well it was something that I probably always did but never really thought of it sort of ... I guess when you see as an opportunity you find you do it a little more and more aware of it. (Colin, Eastside Playgroup)

> I have been doing before but I have learnt more from the material. (Bianca, Eastside Playgroup)

The recurring theme, to quote Colin, one of 'something I probably always did but never really thought of' or Bianca, 'I have been doing it before but I have learnt more from the material'. These comments, together with the earlier remarks, demonstrate that the parents have been involved in learning, and at the same time, hadn't always realised that they what they were doing was being involved in learning.

Contributions of Lead My Learning in the Community-Wide Campaign

As well as the playgroup campaign placement modality, parents at other sites also discussed talking about Lead My Learning. In the excerpt below, three parents in a community-run playgroup in Girral, from the community-wide campaign, describe how it is used with their playgroup, but not 'so much' outside of the playgroup:

> *Makayla:* Probably within this group.
> *Fiona:* Yeah within this group.
> *Paige:* It's changed in the conversation and the way we talk about.
> *Fiona:* Yeah.
> *Paige:* Different things and involve our kids more I think.
> *Makayla:* Definitely.
> *Paige:* But maybe not so much my friends that are outside of playgroup.
> *Makayla:* Yeah.
> *Fiona:* Yeah, I agree. (Makayla, Fiona and Paige, Girral Play Centre)

In Girral, the community-wide modality, we spoke with parents in a range of settings that included a range of services and playgroups that were either voluntary community-run playgroups or playgroups facilitated by specific services.

Helen and Wayne, from the playgroup at the Girral Aboriginal Learning Centre commented about parents talking about Lead My Learning.

> *Helen:* I think they talk about it more.
> *Wayne:* Yeah they do. They talk about it more. (Girral Aboriginal Learning Centre 2017)

While Helen and Wayne note that parents do 'talk about it more", they didn't specify whether they were referring to parents in playgroups only, or to parents who they know more broadly.

The key difference between the campaign in Girral and in Eastside, are that Girral received a wide array of messaging beyond the playgroup setting, while Eastside had campaign promotional products only in the playgroups. So, for example, although playgroups in Girral and Eastside both had Lead My Learning playmats and other products, such as the z-fold brochures that described Lead My Learning, in Girral there was also messaging in the wider community such as on the bus shelter in the town centre, the community radio advert, and the various team and community sponsorships. Despite this wider reach of the campaign, this conversation from the Girral playgroup reports that use of Lead My Learning is 'not so much' with 'friends outside the playgroup'. When considered alongside the feedback from the parents in the Eastside area who only had access in playgroups, this observation reinforces our point that playgroups are a particularly generative way to deliver the messages of an education promotion campaign such as Lead My Learning.

The Balancing Act of a Strategic Discourse

While Lead My Learning managed to achieve this nuanced contribution, it did also receive comments that signalled possibly more conventional marketing impact. For instance, Lisa from Girral Kidz Corner, one of the children's centres in the community-wide campaign, commented:

> Yes and I always was aware of that but it may be stuck in front of my head a bit more and made me go okay I need to make more of an effort to do it. (Lisa, Girral Kidz Corner)

As Lisa states, it wasn't something new that Lead My Learning offered as she was aware; but it caused her to 'make more of an effort to do it'. While this 'more of an effort' signals use of Lead My Learning and may well be of benefit, there is an important cautionary note. Namely, that however well-intentioned, carefully crafted and actively critical, strategic discourses can connect with discursive forms of governmentality (Wright & Harwood, 2009). In the above quote the narrative of 'make more of an effort' sways dangerously close to compunction of improvement and possibly the sense of something 'lacking'. This is suggestive of the need to be attentive to such effects, as well as to build planning to respond to this in the design of education promotion campaigns. For instance, a critical stance on the idea of effort could be useful here; especially one that recognised the effort of parents that is already occurring.

Responses from Services

As well as showing that the campaign was having a positive impression on parents, the responses to Lead My Learning indicted that in some cases, there was benefit for early childhood educators. For example, Lara from Girral Kindergarten explained:

> I guess it has changed a bit cos you can use your flyers and that type of thing as an example to show them that other people are doing this sort of stuff to encourage growth and that type of thing in learning. So yeah I believe yes it would. (Lara, Girral Kindergarten)

In Kurrawong, the second community-wide setting, feedback from the Kurrawong Aboriginal Nursery Centre indicated the influence of Lead My Learning in that setting, and in contrast to feedback in Girral, did not comment favourably on the messaging design. This child and family service operated playgroups for Aboriginal families, and also worked closely with families. Feedback, submitted via the online post-campaign services survey, noted that the service has seen and used Lead My Learning campaign promotional products, such as mats, pens and the Lead My Learning song button. This service reported that they

> Have noticed changes in parents and involvement. Families getting more engaged with their children and getting involved with their play. (Kurrawong Aboriginal Nursery Centre)

While the respondent stated that they think [Lead My Learning] is useful, the following comment is made:

I think the messages are important, however I don't think they are particularly portrayed in a useful or engaging way. (Kurrawong Aboriginal Nursery Centre)

Unfortunately, this feedback wasn't further expanded upon. There are two key points here: (1) Lead My Learning messages are important. The campaign has picked up on important concepts about the involvement of parents in learning that rarely gets talked about. (2) This feedback suggests it may be useful to further test the campaign messaging delivery and design *for this site*. That is, perhaps it needed to be further piloted for the cohort in this community—or even for this particular service.

Feedback from the Eastside service, the site of the playgroup campaign placement included a number of points including:

- Lead my Learning messages are simple/accessible.
- Activities are cost effective and can be spontaneous and 'anywhere'.
- Parents better understood the value of sharing their knowledge using conversations and demonstrating to children. Language reinforced learning.
- Parents learned that simple encouragement, such as 'thumbs up' gave children valuable feedback.
- Developed resources were used as visual cues and reminders.

The last reference, to the 'developed resources' refers to the range of promotional products produced for the campaign, such as the large Lead My Learning playmat. For instance, the service described how the playmat was used regularly in playgroup sessions, with playgroup facilitators integrating conversation about the mat into the playgroup sessions with the parents and their children. We note here too that services groups in other locations also mentioned how the playmat was quickly and easily integrated into their settings.

The Different Modalities: Playgroups, Community-Wide and Childcare Services Using a Bus

The design incorporated three different modalities: childcare services (four services) which used a bus to transport children to and from home; the community-wide campaign in Girral; and the playgroup focussed modality at Eastside Services (11 playgroups). Of the three, the use of the bus for messaging parents was the least successful in communicating with parents about Lead My Learning for a number of reasons. One was that while the buses had large highly visible window stickers with the Lead My Learning messages, these messages needed support in other formats to engage the parents. The parents we were seeking to access for the campaign were challenging to reach as they did not attend childcare centres regularly. These parents were also difficult to recruit for the research on the project, with for example the post-survey numbers for childcare totalling 20 responses (from an estimated of between 100 and 150 parents, depending on the enrolment of the centres). In terms of delivery of the campaign, the bus stickers proved to be unwieldly and required specialised fitting. This is an issue in sites in regional or rural settings which do not have such services, and thus increases the cost of the campaign. There is a need for education promotion in such sites; the challenge is how education promotion could be created and delivered. One improvement might be if the stickers on the bus were part of integrated campaign activities tailored specifically to those parents. This would need to be the subject of further research.

In comparison with the 'childcare services using a bus for child transport' setting, the community-wide and playgroup settings were more successful. And out of the two, our findings point to playgroups as key sites for education promotion campaigns for parents with young children. Both of these modalities included playgroups, with playgroup modality using these exclusively, while the community-wide campaign included playgroups. The community-wide campaign used a number of methods, taking a 'multiple channel' approach, based on feedback from community participants (parents, services, Elders, community organisations). In terms of an effective education promotion campaign that parents engage with and enjoy, playgroups are especially useful and were a cost-effective modality for the campaign, as well as suitable and accessible for researching its potential contribution.

Lessons Learned from the Lead My Learning Campaign

When we set out to produce what became Lead My Learning our vision was to create an early childhood consumer-researched campaign designed to promote educational futures. Through the process described in the previous chapters, we created an educational futures campaign with the aims to firstly show parents that they are involved in their children's learning and secondly, to assist parents to recognise the ways in which they are involved. The campaign was infused with the message that learning was enjoyable—and this was done not because parents didn't enjoy learning with their children, but because of the barrier between education and children being happy. We wanted the campaign to overtly connect learning and enjoyment since, based on our formative research, we recognised that the parents we were working with prioritised their children's happiness, and, while valuing education, they considered education as unconnected with happiness. What follows is a practical analysis of lessons learned from the Lead My Learning campaign. In Chapter 8 we refer specifically to critical cultural social marketing.

Listening and Appreciating the Knowledge and Skills of the Parents

We found that leading learning was a practice that parents already practice, and do so in diverse ways that go largely unrecognised due the dominance of tropes of education that depict parent involvement in their child's learning as only being 'scholarly' activities such as reading. While we are in no way suggesting reading is not important, what we are pointing out is that in the rush to focus on a narrow range of practices, many others are overlooked. One poignant example is the variety of ways 'reading' can occur in the daily activities of parents. When reading is only understood by parents as a 'sit down and read a book activity' a considerable number and variety of reading activities in which parents can or may be involved in with their children are not recognised.

Lack of recognition about parent involvement in their children's learning not only impacts what parents think they are doing (or not doing) and how they feel about their place in being involved in institutional education practices; it also affects how they might make connections with institutional education itself. To have one's practices and involvement in learning go unrecognised has significant implications for how some parents may or may not connect with the dominant cultural forms of involvement in education (such as practices that occur in schooling). The parents in our priority group are involved in myriad ways; the problem is that for some, due to the dominant discourses and the notions of deficit (such as 'uneducated') they may not 'know' what they are doing is 'involvement'. The parents do have knowledge about learning with their children and there is a significant challenge for education to be promoted in this space. Our task as researchers, then, is to find ways to describe this parent involvement that is acceptable to the parents, that reaffirms their involvement.

It was therefore imperative that we demonstrated to our priority audience that we acknowledge their culture, their knowledge, skills and practices. We are showing that as researchers we are not assuming that something is 'wrong' and needs to be intervened in. In setting out to speak of this 'unrecognised' practice, we took account of what parents perceived as the barriers to involvement in their children's learning. In the main these were: the pressures of day to day life (energy and time) and past educational trauma. Listening to the parents, the Lead My Learning campaign was designed to take account of the barrier of time—and by situating everyday activities as opportunities, as well as acknowledging these as 'learning moments', it also took account of how parents can be involved in their children's learning while they continue their daily lives.

One of the contributions made by the Lead My Learning campaign was to address the problem that while the parents undertook involvement in learning with their children, they just did not have a name for such a practice. We noticed from our post-surveys and our fieldwork that parents were, at times, using terms 'lead my learning' and referring to the range of activities described in the promotional products such as everyday activities, and share and encourage learning, to describe what it is that they are doing in their involvement in learning with their children.

Moving Away from the Emphasis on Behaviour

By engaging in a critique of 'problem behaviour' in education, we were in a position to develop a nuanced cultural approach to reframing the social marketing concept of 'behaviour change.' To achieve this we began by drawing on a number of contributions that support the need to shift social marketing away from isolated behavioural change to ongoing social change (Hastings, 2007), from immediate to distal factors of social problems (Andreasen, 2006) and to find a better balance between upstream and downstream strategies (Kamin & Anker, 2014, p. 106). It was likewise important to draw on literature from beyond the social marketing discipline, to literature in the sociology of education that casts a critical gaze on practices of education (Youdell, 2011) and to decolonising methodologies (Smith, 2012) that critically think through how research is conducted with First Nations people.

We took a strengths based (Rogoff et al., 2017) approach to thinking through this core concept in terms of the socio-cultural contexts of educational disadvantage. In practice this emphasised recognising both that there are many cultural practices that occur in learning between parents and their children and, secondly, that these are all too frequently overlooked or are unrecognisable in dominant discourses. This demanded taking the stance that these practices of parents are not an issue to fix— but rather the problem is the uncontested dominant discourse which produces what we might term the *dominant discourse effect*. In its essence, this dominant discourse effect produces both 'unrecognisability' of learning practices that differ, as well as their delegitimation.

The strength-based emphasis aided in ensuring that a non-deficit approach was crafted. Attention to critique meant we remained vigilant not only to deficit accounts, but also to building our understanding of the processes that impacted educational disadvantage. On the occasions when actions (or what might be termed 'behaviour') was considered, it was done so in terms of parents being able to describe or to say what they are doing in the midst of the negative/deficit dominant discourses that 'defined' learning and parent participation in learning. It was not in terms of a problem behaviour. As such we focused our efforts as not having an issue to solve—but rather a challenge to speak of something that has become, to cite Foucault, subjugated. This demanded both comprehending that a practice had been delegitimised and rendered unrecognisable—and imagining how it might be made more recognisable.

Careful Attention to Discourses

Leading My Learning pays careful attention to discourses from numerous angles. This means, for instance, not only an attentiveness to subjugated discourses of learning but also to dominant discourses of 'education'. Through this attentiveness we not only were able to notice the different discourses of learning, but also to appreciate how these were impacted by dominant discourses. One way that dominant discourses create impacts is through what we could say is a directly perceivable action, such as a negative experience with the school where a parent may feel inadequate as an educator. Another was a discourse that education was not associated with happiness. This impacted parents' prioritisation of their children's happiness *over* education. This is important to dwell on, because by education they meant schooling/institutional forms of education—and not learning. Yet they were involved in learning. And their children appeared to be happy doing this learning with their parents. Lead My Learning sought to explicitly connect learning with happiness, and in so doing, to recognise not only the learning that parents were involved in, but also that happiness is occurring. In making this explicit connection different discourses about learning and happiness are hopefully produced.

There were, too, many other discourses, and these are not always direct, but rather circulate and re-circulate in 'micro' ways. These effects were made clear to us in the group yarning sessions held in the formative stage of the project. In this excerpt, Karyn shares with the group her experience of engaging with the school:

Karyn: I'm really like as I said before really Nazi *[sic]* about it. Like with Jye, every night we read his home reader, like we practice it and he'll sit there and go 'I don't wanna read it' and I'll go 'Well the TV's going off until you read it' and then we read it and he reads it perfectly the first time and I'm like 'See? Be proud of yourself, now you can put it away'. But I'm one of those parents that's like 'Excuse me. Where's the newsletter? Can I just grab a copy of that? Thank you'. Like I'm – *I'm one of them parents* – I really am one of them parents.

I: Why do you call it Nazi? *[sic]*

Karyn: I don't know. Because I probably feel like other parents are looking at me going 'Look at this bitch. Who cares about a newsletter. Like seriously?' Yeah but I'm like – [about home readers] I don't think he enjoys it but yeah I don't know I just – yeah I guess I just don't know if other parents are as over-the-top as I am about it. (Karyn, Broadhurst Child and Family Centre)

Acknowledging the problematic use of the term 'Nazi' (which we later yarned about), Karyn was communicating to us the profound way in which engagement with the dominant discourses of education clashed with the discourses of what it means for her to bring up happy children. There is a tension here between the discourse of institutional education and the discourses shared by other parents who do value education and who also value the happiness of their children. For Karyn to be pursuing school newsletters or to follow the edicts of the school and home readers required, as she saw it, to go against prevailing parent and community discourses that seek to prioritise the children's happiness. From this angle, for a parent to do what Karyn is doing is to *push education* and this is problematic because it doesn't prioritise the happiness of the child.

This is a difficult thing to do and filled with tension for Karyn because it is seen to be at odds with what it means to care for her child's happiness. This unresolved tension left Karyn describing herself as 'one of those parents'. This was later discussed at length in this group yarning sessions, with other parents and child educators saying to Karyn that what she did was 'great', to which Karyn appeared both surprised and relieved.

Karyn's comments show the complexity of discourses about institutional education for parents, and the issues that can arise. While Lead My Learning was not able to address this type of conundrum that parents experience, we suggest that this issue is certainly worth further research and could likely benefit from an education promotion style campaign that was appreciative of these complexities of engaging in the education system.

Appreciating Difference/Disrupting Researcher Dominant Views

These two points could be discussed separately, however, we are considering these together because disrupting researcher dominant views is integral to creating a research context where difference can be appreciated. For instance, by disrupting dominant views regarding what constituted learning we were able to better listen to what the parents shared with us in the formative research. Due to listening in this way, we slowly came to appreciate the depths of difference in learning practices between the parents involved in our project and the legitimated learning of institutional education. This enabled us to connect with the literature on Learning by Observing and Pitching In (LOPI) (Rogoff, 2014). As we have outlined in Chapters 2 and 4, we drew on this work to base our resources for parents to engage in conversation with their children.

Embracing the Demands of Cross-Cultural Research

Lead My Learning can be described as a cross-cultural project. We worked cross culturally as a team. Nyssa is a Dunghutti Woman, and Valerie is a non-Aboriginal woman, born on Kaurna Country (Adelaide) to parents with English, Scottish, Welsh and German heritage. Our participants were Aboriginal people from a number of different Countries, and non-Aboriginal people, with the latter including diverse ethnicities. The similarities that participants had in common was the experience of educational disadvantage, having young children for whom they were in parenting roles and living in places where there were high levels of socio-economic disadvantage.

To undertake such work was challenging, and central to our achievement was being clear about how we appreciated the cultural and being able to articulate how we engaged with cultural practices. We were guided here by Aboriginal Protocols, which we found were important for everyone, Aboriginal and non-Aboriginal. Aboriginal protocols were followed for the entirety of the project, including in the project management and consultation with key stakeholders.

At times we were challenged by ideas and concepts from the parents. One example of this occurred during the design phase when we were working on the colour elements. During one of the feedback sessions two of the non-Aboriginal parents stated that 'blue is Aboriginal'. At this point the logo was in several blue tones, and these two parents viewed these colours as signifying it was for Aboriginal people only. We were seeking to create as inclusive a campaign as possible for our priority group of Aboriginal and non-Aboriginal parents. We wanted to listen to the participants yet we were challenged by how to respond to these comments. As we have previously stated, and we requote here, Lead My Learning has been designed to be:

> Available to Aboriginal parents and non-Aboriginal parents, we were guided by Aboriginal people. This approach to promoting education flips 'mainstream' strategies. Aboriginal people consulted in our research were pleased that non-Aboriginal people were welcome to participate in the campaign. Thus, while our approach did incorporate consultation with non-Aboriginal people, we ensured this was in keeping with the Aboriginal guided approaches. (Harwood & Murray, 2019, p. 354)

So when faced with this feedback we returned to the protocols and maintained our commitment to being guided by these. In this case, we did adjust the design slightly, but were only willing to do so if it did not change what had been expressed as important by the Aboriginal parents.

Respecting this emphasis meant insisting that we strive to be guided by Aboriginal approaches. In striving to do this, we sought to pay attention to the problem of what Watson terms the "colonialist indifference to Indigenous philosophy" (Watson, 2014, pp. 517–518). Our commitment to being guided by Aboriginal approaches helped us to work against such indifference, and to undertake our research in ways aimed for a "centring of Indigenous knowledges" (Watson, 2014, p. 519).

Relationships Are Everything

Relationships with the participants and stakeholders were integral to every stage of the Lead My Learning project. These relationships were immensely productive, guiding our thinking and the development of the project. For example, through our relationships with child educators (in childcare and playgroups), the issue of how parental engagement is perceived was brought to our attention. The relationships guided us to modify our initial research design; decisions on who should participate were refined, and in some cases, changed. This was because after engaging in discussions with some of these sites we soon realised that our project design needed to be reviewed. For example, we discovered that some of the childcare centres we had initially identified were already engaged in the demands of research projects, and consequently, were time limited. It was decided it was not appropriate to conduct research in these sites, and alternative locations were preferable.

We also found that the families and children that were the focus of research were not regularly using childcare. We therefore elected to broaden the research design to different modalities for reaching parents. The decision was made to include playgroups, and as some children were not attending childcare or playgroup the design was altered to include a whole-community approach. Through the relationships we gained approvals from potential participating sites for the formative study and also commenced discussion for the potential campaign rollout.

Adhering to the Aboriginal Protocols meant that in having a relationship we had a responsibility to that relationship. And this responsibility continued through the project. Building relationships involved establishing who should be consulted and requesting permission from the appropriate Elders and community leaders. For example, several meetings took place to learn from the local Aboriginal people before discussing the research project. Sharing the project design, benefits and outcomes helped create 'buy in' and build connections so that the project could be discussed, reviewed and refined. These relationships also assisted us in our conduct in fieldwork settings and how the campaign could be designed to possibly value-add and have the least impact on the delivery of services by the participating organisations. These connections also increased the participation needed for disseminating the social marketing campaign in the community. Building a strong relationship further created the opportunity to establish respect in a *two-way* process.

Through our efforts to build relationships, we were able to interact with stakeholders in a way that could be assessed and ascertain whether we acted in a way that was in accordance with respect for protocols. It was crucial that as researchers we earned the respect of Aboriginal and non-Aboriginal stakeholders. Respect has supported us to connect with a wider network than we had anticipated, and this has greatly improved the design and dissemination of the Lead My Learning campaign.

Evaluation Needs to Be Appropriate to the Priority Group

Evaluating the campaign—or finding out what it may have or may not have achieved was a crucial part of the Lead My Learning project, and our planning for this commenced in the early stages of our work. We used a mixed-method design that involved using primarily interviews (yarning and semi-structured) for the qualitative component and a pre- and post-campaign survey that comprised mainly quantitative questions, with some open-ended written responses. We augmented this design with service provider online surveys (using Survey Monkey) as well as informal yarns for feedback. In addition, we also spent time in the 'field', conducting our fieldwork in the various sites in the project.

While we elected to use the survey component as this is commonly used in social marketing, we were patently aware that we may well encounter considerable challenges in using the quantitative survey format with our priority group. One of the key issues was distrust for surveys and the need for rapport with participants in order to have meaningful information shared. For this reason, the yarning approach is more appropriate. Nevertheless, we attempted to develop a survey approach that may be differently engaged with by firstly designing and pre-testing the survey specifically for our project.

The specialised recruitment strategy for the survey involved in-person contact by community members employed as research assistants and was important for the conduct of the survey. These community research assistants were able to explain the survey in person, and answer any questions as participants completed the survey (see also Chapter 6 for details). For instance, the community research assistants assisted the recruitment for surveys in local shopping centres. Randomised selection wasn't viable, nor preferable, given the cohort in our research.

Interviews (yarning and semi-structured) were the best approach for working with the participants. Yarning methodology provided a culturally safe space and was perceived as more trustworthy by the participants. The survey data was used—but in a different way to what we had initially envisaged. For instance, the pre-survey results are being used to explore the notion of self-efficacy and parent involvement, which will be the subject of a forthcoming paper. In this book, the post-survey data has offered a useful perspective on the campaign and the insights from the post interviews (yarning and semi-structured).

This responsiveness in evaluation enabled us to recognise the opportunity of gaining feedback from services using online surveys. Originally, this hadn't been in our evaluation plan, but as the relationships grew with the services, we realised that this would be an important method for ascertaining feedback, with the added benefit of not imposing in terms of time required to complete and ease of access online.

Being Open to Formative Contributing to More Than the Early Stage

One of the many things that we learned in creating Lead My Learning was the crucial importance that formative research had in enabling us to engage in the process of using a critical cultural social marketing approach. Without this formative research, which we not only extended, but also continued to draw on in different stages of the campaign process, we would not have been able to create Lead My Learning. As we described in Chapters 3 and 4, formative research is integral to social marketing. In this project we built on this keystone element, integrating it into different stages and activities. These formative activities clearly demonstrate the extent of the involvement of our partnerships and how these impacted the project and guided the research team over time.

The term formative is usually used to describe the initial research required to understand the issues at hand. Referring to the way in which social marketing draws on the use of formative research in marketing, Evans and Nicols (2016) explain:

> The overall purpose of formative research in support of social marketing is to understand how best to benefit the audiences rather than the marketers. The research processes are often the same – exploration of target audiences' wants and needs and their social environment. (2016, p. 3)

Kubacki and Rundle-Thiele (2016) also point out the information gathering purpose of formative research, however, they underscore the necessity for a more nuanced approach that addresses the 'complexity of social issues':

> Formative research is the process used by social marketers to gain insights and understanding about the very issue(s) they are seeking to influence and change, and as most social issues are complex problems, a single-perspective and one-method approach will rarely provide us with a sufficient understanding. (Kubacki & Rundle-Thiele, 2016, p. 3)

Our decision to extend our formative study phases was based on the need for sustained relationship building and in-depth research to 'explore' much, much more than the 'target audiences' wants and needs'. Indeed, perhaps the words 'insights and understandings' and 'social issues are complex problems' better conveys the challenge we had to create an appropriate education promotion campaign.

What we needed to understand included: the complexities of the production of educational disadvantages; the contexts of the parents, the communities, as well as education and education related services; and we needed to learn about the cultural knowledges and practices of learning by parents who experience educational disadvantage. Extending the formative study enabled us to increase the number of interviews (yarning and semi-structured), the range of people who could inform us, to visit sites on a number of occasions and over time, and to build an approach that emphasises us as 'participant-observers', contributing ideas where invited (such as at education forums) or sharing conversations and ideas as we conducted fieldwork in playgroups. We also used this extended time to create a number of feedback cycles where we could subject our work to scrutiny and check our interpretations. Below we provide a brief outline of some of these sessions.

In summary, there were 'four types' of formative sessions that occurred: three types of sessions were centred on the design process; the other type of session is best described as the initial building knowledge about parents and learning with their children. However, while characterising these sessions in this way, cultural information about the parents and their involvement in learning was continually being shared with us, or put another way, we as researchers were always learning more about the cultural practices of learning the parents implemented, realising how these were delegitimated, and building our knowledge of the impacts of deficit discourses and educational disadvantage as these impacted the parents in our priority group.

This approach with these types of formative sessions was not a set template. The planning process unfolded to an extent because we were being responsive to the parent feedback. The four levels of formative study discussions (including the extensive design feedback) occurred to ensure that the campaign, the visual design and messaging, would be appropriate for the parents in the priority group.

Fieldwork Complexities

Creating Lead My Learning required engaging in fieldwork in a range of settings. In the earlier stages of the process, a greater number of sites were visited that required air and road travel to regional and remote locations in NSW identified as matching the criteria for our potential priority groups. That is, places of distinctive educational disadvantage and socio-economic disadvantage. The former, educational disadvantage, included significant under-representation in participation in higher education. During these visits we stayed in the area and conducted interviews (semi-structured and yarning) and informal discussions with various service providers and community organisations who worked with parents who have young children. These initial visits helped us to hone the sites for the eventual roll out of the Lead My Learning campaign. Decisions for where and to whom the roll out was provided was challenging. This was because while there may have been a distinct need in a certain location, other requirements for the roll out were not available, such as participation with service providers or interest from playgroups.

Fieldwork complexities occurred for a number of reasons, and not only due to the distances to be travelled; even at services that were significantly closer there were delays and changes that impacted the progress of the project. One of the important lessons that we learned was the importance of time spent in the field in communities, getting to know people and services, understanding how to contribute and building relationships. These processes were undertaken in an in-depth manner in the community-wide site (Girral) and in the playgroup campaign setting (Eastside). Due to our research capacity, we undertook this to a lesser extent at the wait-list control site (Kurrawong). To make up for this decreased depth of time, we instead decided to tailor the products in the roll out to this community based on consultations with community Elders and with services.

The key lesson for this type of research is to be prepared for fieldwork complexities, for things to shift and for the time needed to establish and build relationships in fieldwork. Another take home point is that it was via this sustained commitment to fieldwork that we perhaps had some of the most beneficial insights for the campaign, such as promotional products. Examples include our learning of the important place that photographs of children had in the homes of the parents. These images were beautifully framed and proudly placed in prominent positions on the walls in family homes (such as the loungeroom where the photographs could be seen by residents and visitors). Learning this gave us the insight to create the free commercially produced photos of parents and children 'leading learning' that were suitable for framing (see Chapter 5).

Another example are the bus stickers, designed for the buses that transport young children to and from the Aboriginal early childhood centres in the regional locations. The idea for this modality was generated by our fieldwork visits to regional and remote New South Wales and the numerous times we observed these buses—which everyday travelled throughout the communities, meeting with the parents. The early childhood centres and staff, on the other hand, were unable to go into the communities and meet with the parents frequently. Ideas for two other products also originated from our visits to fieldwork settings and our conversations with service staff in these settings. These are the popular Lead My Learning playmats and the preschool t-shirts that were co-sponsored by us and the Aboriginal early childhood centres in Girral.

Flexibility

As the foregoing discussion makes evident, flexibility was key to the work undertaken to produce Lead My Learning. Indeed, while we had assumed that we were flexible, we soon came to realise that we needed to adjust our assumptions and re-evaluate our own expectations and become more flexible. This included adjusting time-frames to better accommodate the needs of participants, as well as changing the formative work so that it continued to exert a palpable influence over us as we engaged in the multiple stages of the design process.

Interestingly, in addition to the various activities described so far, social media was also a method that supported flexibility. Through the Lead My Learning Facebook page we were able to be responsive to parent feedback and, combined with the ongoing relationships maintained throughout the campaign roll out, we quickly realised that we could connect with parents in creative ways through the Lead My Learning Facebook page. This included running competitions associated with involvement in learning for the parents. Prizes included products such as the Lead My Learning playmat and 'back to school packs' for children, timed near the commencement of the school year.

Flexibility was also applied to the promotional materials. Here we thought creatively about their use beyond initial plan—and again, this was influenced by feedback from participants, services and communities. One example is the change that was made to the Lead My Learning Name Is sticker. In the first community-wide campaign (Girral), these stickers were in English. For the campaign in the wait-list community (Kurrawong) these were translated into two of the Aboriginal Languages, and were popular with both Aboriginal and non-Aboriginal participants. (The languages are not specified here in order to respect confidentiality.) Examples of the flexible use of promotional products also include the use of Lead My Learning branding and messaging to co-produce bags to be given to parents of babies at the local hospital. In this example, the Lead My Learning concepts were brought together with a health promotion initiative for new parents.

References

Andreasen, A. R. (2006). *Social marketing in the 21st century*. London: Sage.

Barker, C. (2018). How to tell the political truth: Foucault on new combinations of the basic modes of veridiction. *Contemporary Political Theory*. https://doi.org/10.1057/s41296-018-0253-0.

Evans, D. W., & Nicols, C. (2016). Formative research. In D. W. Evans (Ed.), *Social marketing research for global public health* (pp. 1–47). Oxford: Oxford University Press.

Foucault, M. (1980). Two lectures. In C. Gordon (Ed.), *Power/knowledge: Selected interviews and other writings 1972–1977* (pp. 78–108). Sussex: Harvester Press Ltd.

Foucault, M. (2011). *The courage of the truth (the government of self and others II): Lectures at the Collège de France, 1983–1984*. New York and Houndmills, Basingstoke, Hampshire, UK: Palgrave Macmillan.

Foucault, M. (2014a). *On the government of the living: Lectures at the Collaege de France, 1979–1980* (G. Burchell, Trans.). Basingstoke, UK: Palgrave Macmillan.

Foucault, M. (2014b). *Wrong-doing, truth-telling: The function of avowal in justice* (F. Brion, B. E. Harcourt, & S. W. Sawyer, Eds.). London, Chicago, and Louvain-la-Neuve;: University of Chicago Press.

Foucault, M. (2016). *About the beginning of the hermeneutics of the self: Lectures at Dartmouth College, 1980* (H.-P. Fruchaud, D. Lorenzini, L. Cremonesi, A. I. Davidson, O. Irrera, & M. Tazzioli, Eds.). London and Chicago: The University of Chicago Press.

Foucault, M. (2017). *Subjectivity and truth: Lectures at the Collège de France, 1980–1981* (F. Gros, F. Ewald, & A. Fontana, Eds.). London: Palgrave Macmillan.

Harwood, V., & Murray, N. (2019). Strategic discourse production and parent involvement: Including parent knowledge and practices in the Lead My Learning campaign. *International Journal of Inclusive Education, 23*(4), 353–368. https://doi.org/10.1080/13603116.2019.1571119.

Hastings, G. (2007). *Social marketing: Why should the devil have all the best tunes?* Amsterdam: Elsevier Science.

Kamin, T., & Anker, T. (2014). Cultural capital and strategic social marketing orientations. *Journal of Social Marketing, 4*(2), 94–110. https://doi.org/10.1108/JSOCM-08-2013-0057.

Kubacki, K., & Rundle-Thiele, S. (2016). *Formative research in social marketing: Innovative methods to gain consumer insights.* Singapore: Springer.

McDonald, E., Cunningham, T., & Slavin, N. (2015). Evaluating a handwashing with soap program in Australian remote Aboriginal communities: A pre and post intervention study design health behavior, health promotion and society. *BMC Public Health, 15*(1). https://doi.org/10.1186/s12889-015-2503-x.

Murray, N., & Harwood, V. (2018). *Lead My Learning.* Retrieved from lead-mylearning.com.au.

Rogoff, B. (2014). Learning by observing and pitching into family and community endeavours. *Human Development, 57,* 69–81.

Rogoff, B., Coppens, A. D., Alcalá, L., Aceves-Azuara, I., Ruvalcaba, O., López, A., & Dayton, A. (2017). Noticing learners' strengths through cultural research. *Perspectives on Psychological Science, 12*(5), 876–888. https://doi.org/10.1177/1745691617718355.

Smith, L. T. (2012). *Decolonizing methodologies: Research and indigenous peoples* (2nd ed.). London: Zed Books.

Waters, B. S. (2016). *We can speak for ourselves parent involvement and ideologies of Black mothers in Chicago.* Rotterdam: Sense Publishers.

Watson, I. (2014). Re-centring first nations knowledge and places in a terra nullius space. *AlterNative: An International Journal of Indigenous Peoples, 10*(5), 508–520. https://doi.org/10.1177/117718011401000506.

Wright, J., & Harwood, V. (Eds.). (2009). *Biopolitics and the 'obesity epidemic': Governing bodies.* New York: Routledge.

Youdell, D. (2011). *School trouble: Identity, power and politics in education.* Abingdon, Oxon: Routledge.

8

A Critical Cultural Social Marketing Approach

In this final chapter we discuss how, based on our experiences, a critical social marketing approach might be 'conceptualised' and applied. We are mindful that we are not proposing a 'template' but rather are signalling how attention to a critical and cultural approach can be used to engage with concepts and methods from social marketing in education. That is, that a critical and cultural emphasis can be utilised for thinking through how social marketing ideas and techniques might be drawn upon for the promotion of education. Our work on Lead My Learning, described in this book, is shared as an example of a critical cultural social marketing approach.

In writing this book we have been patently aware that in many places we have not adhered to certain conventions of social marketing. And in so doing, there is always the risk of the objection that what we are describing does not meet the criteria of social marketing. We acknowledge and accept that such objections may occur, and argue that given the beneficial ways in which the techniques developed in social marketing can be used, it is worthwhile to investigate ways in which adaptations can be made. From this perspective then, our work might be a stimulus for creating other

© The Author(s) 2019
V. Harwood and N. Murray, *The Promotion of Education*,
https://doi.org/10.1007/978-3-030-25300-4_8

campaigns in education that can respond to the twofold needs of practices of critique and attention to the cultural.

As such, the objective of this book has been to share an example of the application of a critical cultural social marketing approach to the promotion of education. That a template is not possible is evident when we think through the sheer importance of the approach being guided by the people and/or communities with whom we are working. The ideas, insights, understandings and revisions were all possible because of the ongoing in-depth interactions with participants. And these interactions were always guided by our approach to partnerships, and specifically in our project, by Aboriginal Protocols. It was not simply an 'academic' claim to understanding, but a commitment to listen and to learn from participants and a commitment and determined willingness to recognise assumptions at all stages of the process.

We commence by returning to the discussion of critique and the cultural and why it is worthwhile to bring these together when we think about promoting education. Then in the sections that follow, we summarise some of the aspects of critical cultural social marketing that we recommend, which are crucial to engage with and to carefully consider.

Practising Critique

Throughout this book we have made the case for the use of the critique. Understood in an active sense, critique affords us the opportunity to look differently at what we *know* and to reconsider what is treated as *truth*. Cited in Chapter 1, we again use this quote from Foucault to remind us of the potential contribution that an engagement in critique may offer,

> critique will be the art of voluntary insubordination, that of reflected intractability. Critique would essentially insure the desubjugation of the subject in the context of what we could call, in a word, the politics of truth. (1997, p. 32)

Critique then, has a useful contribution to make to efforts that set out to make education more inclusive. In this book we have discussed at length how the legitimised forms of education produce legitimised knowledges, such as of learning. This knowledge, and the associated educational practices informed by it, effectively subjugate certain people, rendering their practices 'unknowable'. Critique is crucial here because it enables this knowledge, and the associated practices and forms of power, to be differently examined. It is possible to employ critique to 'get at' and expose the politics of educational truths. Via this very process that desubjugation can occur.

Appreciating the Social and Cultural Contexts

An appreciation of social and cultural contexts enables, as we have maintained, a fuller understanding of education, and its processes of educating some and not others. And significantly, it supports awareness of the forms of learning and education that are not within the compass of the large, albeit limited, institutionalised formats of education. But this is not to imagine that we, as researchers, can 'know' and define another's culture—or draw on the appraisals of someone else who is claiming to do this. This issue of how culture is imagined was closely interrogated in Chapter 2. Abu-Lughod's comments below, while referring to the problematic use of the term in anthropology, have prescience here:

> Yet it could also be argued that culture is important to anthropology because the anthropological distinction between self and other rests on it. Culture is the essential tool for making other. (2014, p. 390)

It is imperative that in a critical cultural social marketing approach such formulaic othering is not repeated. To undertake critique requires a critical awareness of this history of the use of the term, particularly in the Western colonial imagination that wrongly thought it could study and describe the 'other', when what actually occurred was that via this study it *produced its other.*

As we have described in the previous chapters, one of the ways in which we worked to prioritise the cultural in Lead My Learning was to be guided by Aboriginal Protocols and to form respectful ways for collaborating cross-culturally with Aboriginal people and non-Aboriginal people. We elevated the importance of thinking critically about 'the cultural' in learning and this enabled us to be mindful of approaches such as Learning by Observing and Pitching In (LOPI) (Correa-Chavez, Mejia-Arauz, & Rogoff, 2015; Rogoff, 2014) and other learning practices of the parents.

Engaging with the social and cultural to adapt social marketing for use in education makes sense, even if it might pose a problem in terms of transposing what might work in one discipline, such as health, to considerations of education inclusion. Here we are suggesting that in appreciating the social and cultural contexts, we might do well to be mindful of simply importing an emphasis on behaviour change. Our reasoning here is that when we look to the social and cultural contexts of people's lives—and their experiences with institutional education, a wider view is helpful. Perhaps this might connect with an emphasis on the cultural, rather than on behaviour, or at the very least, disturbing (or making strange) the familiarity of 'behaviour change' as the default position. Tapp and Spotswood (2013) comment that "culture change may sit uncomfortably within existing definitions of social marketing, which emphasises influencing people and requires a voluntary shift in behaviour based on a cognitive assessment of the marketing offer made" (p. 286). We are not advocating that 'culture change' is inserted in the space once occupied by 'behaviour change'; but rather, to pointing to the challenges involved in thinking differently about how social marketing techniques might be drawn upon and how a critical cultural approach might differently engage with understandings of the social and the cultural.

Bringing Together Practices of Critique and Attention to the Cultural

This next point is the logical consequence of our case for employing critique and emphasising the cultural—and has been a premise for the approach described in this book. It is, to risk repeating ourselves, vital to bring critique into this conversation because it is imperative to throw the spotlight onto the practices that subjugate—as opposed to reverting to a fall-back position of 'studying' the subjugated. The excerpt below by Povinelli points precisely to the problem of how culture is 'seen':

> If culture is a lens through which the local group mediates the practices and policies of the larger system (Ortner, 1989, p. 93), then what of the lens of the larger system and its practices of knowing? Is a lens sufficient to explain the manner in which culture and power articulate'? (1995, p. 506)

Ortner's work calls our attention to looking at the 'larger system' from the vantage point of the local group. And this is, in her words, "because it is these cultural frames and structural contradictions that mediate both the meaning and the impact of the larger political and economic forces in question" (Ortner, 1989, p. 83). Yet Povinelli's point leaves us with more questions—is a 'lens' that we need to use to achieve this profoundly important task? One way forward is to, as we have maintained, continually be absorbed by need for the activity of critique. This is to say, not that critique is placed on the researcher's 'list' of things to do, but rather critique is a type of becoming (Hickey-Moody, 2005) in which one continually participates.

The Research Team

Who is undertaking the research is a pivotal consideration when setting out to use a critical cultural approach to social marketing. The team needs to be comprised of people with background experience in the social and cultural contexts that are the focus of the envisaged project. The team will also need to bring together an understanding of the educational context that supports an active form of critique that can, to paraphrase Povenilli, "explain the manner in which culture and power articulate" (1995, p. 506).

Reflecting on the work undertaken for Lead My Learning, as a team we brought expertise in the sociology and anthropology of education, relationships with Aboriginal communities and knowledge and experience in collaborative community projects. Through this teamwork we were able to engage in the critical cultural yarning sessions (CCYS), and collaboratively build the cross-cultural project to include comprehensive feedback via the partnerships and participants. Our work was informed by these relationships together with the comprehensive literature reviews undertaken throughout the project. For instance, the earlier reviews picked up on the problem of deficit discourses in education, as well as a sociological and cultural understanding of how educational disadvantage is produced, and these strengthened the interpretations that were made as we worked together on the formative data and feedback from services.

While there were two main team members who worked on the project over a period of four years, at different points in the process we employed research assistants with specialised skill sets to undertake certain tasks. These tasks included a range of data collection duties including: formative work; longitudinal interviews; post-campaign interviews (yarning and semi-structured); and researchers in the community-wide settings to assist with the survey recruitment. This work also involved a review of early childhood education concepts by a qualified early childhood educator; and research assistants working on the qualitative and quantitative data preparation and analysis.

The capacity to adapt in this project is, in large part, an outcome of this teamwork. This teamwork, through the range of partnerships and participants, enabled us to draw on a wider sphere of influence and this continually improved how the concepts and campaign were developed and refined.

The Challenges of Understanding and Reporting What Is Achieved

Taking cues from the emphasis on evaluation in social marketing, understanding what a campaign may or may not have achieved is likewise integral to the process of a critical cultural social marketing approach. Yet evaluation, or understanding and describing what has or has not been accomplished, is not something that can be implemented like a recipe, but rather needs to be designed for the specific campaign under consideration. Added to this, we suggest that this process also needs to plan for contingencies and be open to the possibility of flexibility should new insights occur.

In the Lead My Learning example, because we had started out with what could be described as a methodological framework that included several methodologies, we were in the position to be able to choose to focus more on the interviews (yarning and semi-structured) for our post-campaign data collection. This meant we did not have to rely on the surveys (and especially the matched pre- and post-surveys) as the only means to understand the possible contributions of the campaign. We were also able to develop, trial and get Human Research Ethics approval for a new method, the online service survey.

We now briefly turn to discuss a different evaluation technique that sets out a systematic approach through the use of a set of questions. Saunders, Evans, and Joshi (2005), working from a health promotion orientation, list a set of possible process evaluation questions that can be used as a guide. Their guide is structured on a process-evaluation plan that is adapted from Steckler and Linnan (2000) and from Baranowski and Stables (2000), which covers six areas. These areas and a selection of the example questions are:

Fidelity: to what extent was the intervention implemented consistently with the underlying theory and philosophy?;

Dose delivered: to what extent were all of the intended units or components of the intervention or program provided to program participants?;

Dose received: how did participants react to specific aspects of the intervention;

Reach: what proportion of the priority target audience participated in (attended) each program session?;

Recruitment: what planned and actual recruitment procedures were used to attract individuals, groups and/or organizations? What were the barriers to recruiting individuals, groups and organizations?;

Context: what factors in the organization, community, social/political context, or other situational issues could potentially affect either intervention implementation or intervention outcome? (Saunders et al., 2005, p. 140)

Although the above six terms convey a health promotion focus (particularly the concept of 'dose'), we note that such questions might be useful, and include them here for this reason. For instance, these types of questions might be touched on and considered in the ongoing discussions when using a critical cultural social marketing approach. The evaluation and research discussions in the CCYS, while not using these six concepts, were organised to craft our appraisal of the National Social Marketing Centre (NSMC, 2011), and these sessions were documented in order to guide, and assist us in reflecting on our process.

Actively Engaging with Social Marketing: Adapting New Ways and Explaining Why

A critical cultural social marketing approach actively engages with social marketing. Doing so involves adapting social marketing concepts, techniques and practices, at times creating new ways that are supportive of the critical and cultural emphasis and setting out to explain this active engagement. To an extent, the objective of Chapter 6 was to offer an account that explained the active engagement with social marketing that produced Lead My Learning.

Lead My Learning was created by using a critical and cultural emphasis to respond to the NSMC planning process, bringing the broader social marketing literature into this conversation. It was not a straightforward process, and several activities overlapped into our reconfiguration of the NSMC planning stages. Following the principle of critique and attention to the cultural, these planning processes were judiciously considered, and where required, adapted and reframed so as to create an approach that best suited the needs of our communities and the problem of educational injustice that they faced.

While we used the NSMC (2011) social marketing planning process as a way to structure our engagement with social marketing and to be steered by a critical and cultural priority, others approaches are, of course, possible. For instance, the engagement could be explicitly structured by a critical and cultural analysis of the benchmarks as these may or may not apply with a given social marketing project. Such an approach could involve working closely with the more recent discussions of the benchmark criteria, and draw on, for example French and Russell-Bennet's (2015) 'Hierarchical Model of Social Marketing'. This model could also be used as a touchstone for creating a social marketing project that has a critical and cultural priority. French and Russell-Bennett's (2015) model organises social marketing into 'three proposed categories of criteria … (1) principle, (2) concepts and (3) techniques" (2015, pp. 148–149), this model situates these criteria in a 'hierarchical relationship'.

> The core principle … is social value creation through marketplace exchange. This core principle, which is a unique feature of social marketing, is supported by four essential social marketing concepts … (1) social behavioural influence, (2) citizen/customer/civic society-orientation focus, (3) social offerings and (4) relationship building … The third category of criteria are techniques, these are a wide array of methods, models and tactics that are often used in social marketing but are not exclusive to it … Five core techniques are: (1) integrated intervention mix, (2) competition analysis and action, (3) systematic planning and evaluation, (4) insight driven segmentation, (5) co-creation through social markets. (French & Russell-Bennett, 2015, pp. 149–151)

Considering our own work with Lead My Learning one inroad to critically and culturally appraising this model is to look not only at the list of content, but how this content is put together. To take this further, a useful point of entry to such an analysis could be the statement, "What makes social marketing unique is the interplay between this core marketing principle and its four supportive, marketing-derived concepts" (French & Russell-Bennett, 2015, p. 149). Here, rather than concentrating on the different content elements to ask how these may or may not support creating a social marketing campaign for the parents we are working with, we can also think through the inter-connections—or what the authors term "the interplay" (French & Russell-Bennett, 2015, p. 149) between them. We could then ask, how does the interplay between core principle of social value creation and the concept of social behavioural influence work under the demands of the critique we are imposing and the respectful attention to cultural contexts that are required. What if behavioural influence is an imposition precisely because it misses the nuances of cultural learning practices and the impacts of deficit discourses in education? From this stance, by ensuring the critical and cultural 'steer' the way, we would need to reassess not only the concept of social behavioural influence, but also the interplay between this concept and the core principle. Navigating these, and having an informed and explainable understanding of the decisions made, makes for a strong argument for why these choices are made in critical cultural social marketing—and why it is vital that these are informed by a critically and culturally informed approach. Had we used a different social marketing planning process, we would have also needed to assess and possibly reframe and adapt various components. This is, in our view, part and parcel of the critical cultural approach: it actively works with concepts and techniques from social marketing to devise a campaign to promote education.

There is then a key problematic at the heart of this critical cultural approach, namely, how will a particular project actively respond to social marketing concepts and techniques. In our example we found that it was helpful for this response to be structured on a well-articulated planning process—which for us was the NSMC Six Stage Planning Process (2011). It is important to emphasise that a different campaign would have different needs and a different critical cultural social marketing approach with different planning processes may be drawn on, together with different style of reframing social marketing processes, planning, benchmarks, criteria, techniques. The salient point is that using critical cultural social marketing is on a case by case basis and that always prioritises culture, sociocultural context, and sets out to be actively engaged in the practice of critique.

The Beauty of Formative Research, Collaboration and Critical Feedback

Formative research is, to us, an especially beneficial techniques highlighted in the social marketing discipline. Our tactic was to increase the scope of this formative work, and we found support to pursue this idea in the social marketing literature. Brought together with the angle that we took to be attentive to the cultural, the attention to the formative component resulted in significant insights and many improvements for the Lead My Learning campaign. We learned how to be corrected, how to let go of our vision for a campaign design and we built a deep appreciation for a design process that sincerely aspired to listen to and act on the feedback from participants in the priority group. Without the attention to the formative research, this would not have been possible.

Critical Methodologies

There is certainly a requirement for critical methodologies in an approach such as critical cultural social marketing. By critical methodologies, we refer to the various methodologies that share a commitment to a critical interrogation of the production of knowledge. This also necessarily involves researcher reflexivity (Mao, Mian Akram, Chovanec, & Underwood, 2016). Critical research methodologies "attempt to reveal the sociohistorical specificity of knowledge and to shed light on how particular knowledges reproduce structural relations of inequality and oppression" (Muncie, 2006, p. 100). In our work, it was crucial to draw on decolonising approaches to research (Smith, 2012) and to connect with research methodologies that emphasised a strength-based approach, and Indigenous methodologies such as yarning.

The effort to engage critical methodologies extends to how research is reported. Reflecting on anthropological writing, Rosaldo observes that, "no mode of composition is a neutral medium, and none should be granted exclusive rights to scientifically legitimate social description" (1993, p. 49). This means that the texts that we produce as researchers are far from neutral and every effort needs to be made to consider how research is represented. Using methodologies from different disciplines has been a topic of discussion in some of the social marketing literature. Whitford, for instance, discusses the usefulness of anthropology:

> Many times the information that is needed is not readily available and as such social marketers design and conduct primary research to understand the key motivators that drive people to change. For this reason, anthropology is a natural fit with social marketing, as it honors people's values and respects the goals they set for their own lives. (Whiteford, 2015, p. 286)

Others have discussed the use of an ethnographic approach in social marketing (Gordon, Russell-Bennett, & Lefebvre, 2016; Hill, 2011). Based on our experience in Lead My Learning, approaches such as critical ethnography could certainly be beneficial given the explicit commitment, as Dutta (2014) states to "disrupting the status quo". As Dutta goes on to explain:

> Committed to the construction of knowledge that privileges the perspectives of those who have been subjugated, critical ethnographic approaches simultaneously examine axes of race, class, culture, gender, and history … the goal of critical ethnography is to offset colonial models of ethnographic research, striving towards greater civic engagement, advocacy, activism, and collaboration. (Dutta, 2014, p. 92)

This attentiveness to the "construction of knowledge that privileges … [the] subjugated" is suggestive of what critical methodologies such as this can offer. It also points to the possibilities that a critical cultural social marketing approach offers to the project of such knowledge construction.

Concluding Thoughts

When adapting and changing an approach such as social marketing, the question needs to be asked, just how much is too much? How much can be adapted and at the same time, a claim made that it is social marketing? Perhaps here the response is to pose a different kind of question, that rather than claim critical cultural social marketing *is* social marketing, we might be wiser to suggest that a critical cultural social marketing approach is just that: an approach to the use of social marketing that is led by the critical and the cultural. In a sense, our work in this book connects with and hopefully contributes to efforts to differently work with social marketing concepts and ideas. Take for instance the observation that:

> As early as 1995, Goldberg called for 'radical approaches in social marketing' (Goldberg, 1995, p. 347) envisioning a discipline that moved beyond promoting behavioural change to an individual towards activities which deconstruct the negative social structures constraining our behaviours. (Duane, Domegan, McHugh, & Devaney, 2016, p. 856)

Duane et al.'s (2016) comments connect with the critical approach that we are advocating, one that analyses negative social structures—which education can unfortunately be for many people—and the complexities of its discursive repertoires.

One of the objectives of this book was to explain and justify how a critical and cultural social marketing approach guided decisions to adopt, change, adapt or reject social marketing techniques and concepts in order to create an education promotion campaign for a specific audience (priority group). In concluding this book, it is important to emphasise that there are likely many opportunities to apply a critical cultural social marketing approach to the promotion of education. Just as social and cultural contexts differ, so too do educational institutions and their associated practices. Accordingly, then, critical cultural social marketing approaches need to be responsive to these differences. In this way then, what we have hoped to demonstrate is an approach that, while certainly not a template, might be useful for consideration of how social marketing might be put to use in the promotion of education.

When we began this book we pointed out that there is a misconception about the involvement of parents who have experienced educational disadvantage, in the learning activities of their children. There is too a misconception that parents with difficult educational experiences do not value education. We pause here to again reiterate that a quite different perspective came into view in our formative research, and this view is important to stress because accessing this view meant the development of a respectful and accurate critical campaign to promote parent involvement in their children's learning.

In Chapter 4 we reported that the parents valued education. This is a significant point to reflect on, given the deficit discourses that abound about parents who have experienced educational disadvantage and who live in places of substantial socio-economic disadvantage. Our early formative research showed us that one hundred per cent of the parents said that they valued education. The parents strongly valued the role of schools and education. At the same time, these parents describe having problematic feelings towards education and educational futures. This clearly is not the same as not valuing education. Connie, one of the parents who participated in this research, told us, when asked of her thoughts about education:

> It's the start of the future I suppose. (Connie, Redville West Public School Preschool)

That Connie connects education with the start of her child's future reveals her valuing of education. As we have discussed, parents can value education and also view education as a threat to the happiness of their children. Parents can experience social and cultural pressures, and expectations cast recognised forms of involvement (understood in the dominant sense as connected to education) as poor parenting.

The question might be raised, is Lead My Learning promoting education? Well, possibly not in the traditional or commonly known sense; it is different because it is critical and cultural and as such, is not necessarily adhering to a mainstream and arguably, top down hegemonised method. Indeed, in employing critique it has sought to work against discourses that, for instance, mark out who is and isn't educated and who can and cannot lead their child's learning. The term 'educational futures' refers to the idea that an individual's future must be inclusive of education in all its myriad forms. This is to include not just the institutional and officially sanctioned sites of education, but also to take in the compass of education sites that exist in numerous ways. Though it might seem far from the caps and gowns of the university, widening participation very much needs to be concerned with entrenched problems where certain learning practices are rendered unrecognisable.

Strategic discourse production (Harwood & Murray, 2019) can be created through a critical cultural social marketing approach, and this can contribute to desubjugation. There are difficulties in this approach, and these include grasping the mechanisms of social and cultural structures such as education, and at the same time, appreciating the different impacts that these can have on people and communities. This last point prompts us to again comment on the shift in focus that we are advocating. Povinelli's description of her own work, is thought provoking in this regard, since as she writes, it was not a matter "of producing ethnographic texts that explain their culture and society to others but of helping to analyze how late liberal power appears when encountered from their lives" (2016, pp. 22–23). In this spirit, we suggest a focussing of the energy away from the notion of 'describing the other' and onto an interrogation of the production of knowledge *about* the other. Doing so opens out opportunities for strategic discourse production that, in our project, were able to tell of the learning involvement that parents do with their children and that as our interviews (yarning and semi-structured) showed, provided a language for this important activity.

A critical cultural social marketing approach helped us to devise a bespoke process that could better connect both with the cultural emphasis we required and the critique that we demanded of the deficit accounts that are influential in education discourses. As we hope this book has shown, just as there is a need for sustained attention to the forces that construct educational deficits and the mechanisms through which parents come to understand themselves and their relationships to learning with their children, and to education, so too there is a need for strategic discourses that can promote education and learning.

References

Abu-Lughod, L. (2014). Writing against culture. In H. L. Moore & T. Sanders (Eds.), *Anthropology in theory: Issues in epistemology* (pp. 386–399). Chichester, West Sussex: Wiley.

Baranowski, T., & Stables, G. (2000). Process evaluations of the 5-a-day projects. *Health Education & Behavior, 27*(2), 157–166. https://doi.org/10.1177/109019810002700202.

Correa-Chavez, M., Mejia-Arauz, R., & Rogoff, B. (Eds.). (2015). *Children learn by observing and contributing to family and community endeavors: A cultural paradigm.* (1st ed.). Amsterdam, Netherlands: Academic Press.

Duane, S., Domegan, C., McHugh, P., & Devaney, M. (2016). From restricted to complex exchange and beyond: Social marketing's change agenda. *Journal of Marketing Management, 32*(9–10), 856–876. https://doi.org/10.1080/0267257X.2016.1189449.

Dutta, U. (2014). Critical ethnography. In J. Mills & M. Birks (Eds.), *Qualitative methodology: A practical guide* (pp. 89–106). London: Sage.

Foucault, M. (1997). What is critique? In S. Lotringer & L. Hochroth (Eds.), *The politics of truth: Michel Foucault* (pp. 23–82). New York: Semiotext(e).

French, J., & Russell-Bennett, R. (2015). A hierarchical model of social marketing. *Journal of Social Marketing, 5*(2), 139–159. https://doi.org/10.1108/jsocm-06-2014-0042.

Goldberg, M. E. (1995). Social marketing: Are we fiddling while Rome burns? *Journal of Consumer Psychology, 4*(4), 347–370. https://doi.org/10.1207/s15327663jcp0404_03.

Gordon, R., Russell-Bennett, R., & Lefebvre, R. C. (2016). Social marketing: The state of play and brokering the way forward. *Journal of Marketing Management, 32*(11–12), 1059–1082. https://doi.org/10.1080/0267257X.2016.1199156.

Harwood, V., & Murray, N. (2019). Strategic discourse production and parent involvement: Including parent knowledge and practices in the Lead My Learning campaign. *International Journal of Inclusive Education, 23*(4), 353–368. https://doi.org/10.1080/13603116.2019.1571119.

Hickey-Moody, A. (2005). *Unimaginable bodies: Intellectual disability, performance and becomings.* Adelaide: University of South Australia.

Hill, P. (2011). Impoverished consumers and social marketing. In G. Hastings, K. Angus, & C. A. Bryant (Eds.), *The SAGE handbook of social marketing* (pp. 319–329). London: Sage.

Mao, L., Mian Akram, A., Chovanec, D., & Underwood, M. L. (2016). Embracing the spiral: Researcher reflexivity in diverse critical methodologies. *International Journal of Qualitative Methods, 15*(1). https://doi.org/10.1177/1609406916681005.

Muncie, J. (2006). Critical research. In J. Muncie & E. McLaughlin (Eds.), *The Sage dictionary of criminology* (2nd ed., pp. 100–102). London: Sage.

National Social Marketing Centre (Ed.). (2011). *Big pocket guide to using social marketing for behaviour change.* London: NSMC.

Ortner, S. B. (1989). *High religion: A cultural and political history of Sherpa Buddhism.* Princeton, NJ: Princeton University Press.

Povinelli, E. A. (1995). Do rocks listen—The cultural polities of apprehending Australian Aboriginal labor. *American Anthropologist, 97*(3), 505–518.

Povinelli, E. A. (2016). *Geontologies: A requiem to late liberalism.* Durham: Duke University Press.

Rogoff, B. (2014). Learning by observing and pitching in to family and community endeavours. *Human Development, 57*(2–3), 69–81.

Rosaldo, R. (1993). *Culture and truth: The remaking of social analysis*. Boston: Beacon Press.

Saunders, R. P., Evans, M. H., & Joshi, P. (2005). Developing a process-evaluation plan for assessing health promotion program implementation: A how-to guide. *Health Promotion Practice, 6*(2), 134–147.

Smith, L. T. (2012). *Decolonizing methodologies: Research and Indigenous peoples* (2nd ed.). London: Zed Books.

Steckler, A., & Linnan, L. (2000). Process evaluation for public health interventions and research. In A. Steckler & L. Linnan (Eds.), *Process evaluation for public health interventions and research* (pp. 1–23). San Francisco: Jossey-Bass.

Tapp, A., & Spotswood, F. (2013). Beyond persuasion: A cultural perspective of behaviour. *Journal of Social Marketing, 3*(3), 275–294. https://doi.org/10.1108/JSOCM-01-2013-0006.

Whiteford, L. (2015). Global health, medical anthropology, and social marketing: Steps to the ecology of collaboration. *Collegium Antropologicum, 39*(2), 285.

References

Abu-Lughod, L. (1993). *Writing women's worlds: Bedouin stories.* Berkeley: University of California Press.

Abu-Lughod, L. (2014). Writing against culture. In H. L. Moore & T. Sanders (Eds.), *Anthropology in theory: Issues in epistemology* (pp. 386–399). Chichester, West Sussex: Wiley.

ACER. (2010). *Australasian Survey of Student Engagement—Australasian Student Engagement Report: Doing more for learning: Enhancing engagement and outcomes.* Camberwell, VIC.

Ajzen, I. (1991). The theory of planned behavior. *Organizational Behavior and Human Decision Processes, 50*(2), 179–211. https://doi.org/10.1016/0749-5978(91)90020-T.

Alim, H. S. (2011). Hip hop and the politics of ill-literacy. In *A companion to the anthropology of education.* Malden: Wiley-Blackwell.

Allan, J., & Harwood, V. (2013). Medicus interruptus in the behaviour of children in disadvantaged contexts in Scotland. *British Journal of Sociology of Education, 35*, 413–431. Published online 27 April.

Almosa, Y., Parkinson, J., & Rundle-Thiele, S. (2017). Littering reduction: A systematic review of research 1995–2015. *Social Marketing Quarterly, 23*(3), 203–222. https://doi.org/10.1177/1524500417697654.

Andreasen, A. R. (2006). *Social marketing in the 21st century.* London: Sage.

Andersen, C., Bunda, T., & Walter, M. (2008). Indigenous higher education: The role of universities in releasing the potential. *Australian Journal of Indigenous Education, 37*(1), 1–8. https://doi.org/10.1017/S1326011100016033.

Andreasen, A. R. (1984). A power potential approach to middlemen strategies in social marketing. *European Journal of Marketing, 18*(4), 56. https://doi.org/10.1108/EUM0000000004786.

Andreasen, A. R. (1994). Social marketing: Its definition and domain. *Journal of Public Policy and Marketing, 13*(1), 108. https://doi.org/10.1177/074391569401300109.

Andreasen, A. R. (1995). *Marketing social change: Changing behaviour to promote health, social development and the environment.* San Francisco: Josey-Bass.

Andreasen, A. R. (2002). Marketing social marketing in the social change marketplace. *Journal of Public Policy and Marketing, 21*(1), 3–13.

Andreasen, A. R., & Mirabella, R. (2006). *Social marketing in the 21st century* (Vol. 17, pp. 235–237). Thousand Oaks: Sage.

Andrew, Y. (2016). The unavoidable salience of gender: Notes from Australian childcare work. *Gender, Place & Culture, 23*(12), 1738–1749. https://doi.org/10.1080/0966369X.2016.1249353.

Appadurai, A. (1996). *Modernity at large cultural dimensions of globalization.* Minneapolis: University of Minnesota Press.

Appadurai, A. (2004). The capacity to aspire: Culture and terms of recognition. In R. Vijayendra & M. Walton (Eds.), *Culture and public action* (pp. 59–84). Stanford: Stanford University Press.

Apple, M. (1996). *Cultural politics and education.* New York: Teachers College Press.

Apple, M. (2014). Immigration, social realities, and the complex politics of education. *Race ethnicity and education, 17*(2), 291–298. https://doi.org/10.1080/13613324.2013.873571.

Arendt, H. (2003). Thinking and moral considerations. In J. Kohn (Ed.), *Responsibility and judgment* (1st ed., pp. 159–189). New York: Schocken Books.

Association, Australian Indigenous Doctors. (2010). *Health impact assessment of the Northern Territory Emergency Response.* Canberra: Australian Indigenous Doctors' Association.

Australian Institute for Aboriginal and Torres Strait Islander Studies. (2012). *Guidelines for ethical research in Australian Indigenous studies.*

Australian Institute of Aboriginal and Torres Strait Islander Studies. (2019 [1996] 4, October). *Aboriginal Australia Map*. Available https://aiatsis.gov.au/explore/articles/aiatsis-map-indigenous-australia.

Ball, S. J., Davies, J., David, M., & Reay, D. (2002). 'Classification' and 'judgement': Social class and the 'cognitive structures' of choice in Higher Education. *British journal of sociology of education, 23*(1), 51–72.

Bandura, A. (1986). *Social foundations of thought and action: A social cognitive theory*. Englewood Cliffs, NJ: Prentice-Hall.

Bandura, A. (2001). Social cognitive theory: An agentic perspective. *Annual Review of Psychology, 52*(1): 1–26.

Baranowski, T., & Stables, G. (2000). Process evaluations of the 5-a-day projects. *Health Education & Behavior, 27*(2), 157–166. https://doi.org/10.1177/109019810002700202.

Barker, C. (2018). How to tell the political truth: Foucault on new combinations of the basic modes of veridiction. *Contemporary Political Theory*. https://doi.org/10.1057/s41296-018-0253-0.

Barnes, M., Chanfreau, J., & Tomaszewski, W. (2010). *Growing up in Scotland: The circumstances of persistently poor children*. Edinburgh.

Baskin, C. (2005). Storytelling circles: Reflections of Aboriginal protocols in research. *Canadian Social Work Review/Revue canadienne de service social, 22*(2), 171–187.

Battiste, M. (2002). *Indigenous knowledge and pedagogy in first nations education: A literature review with recommendations*. Ottawa: Indian and Northern Affairs Canada.

Behrendt, L. (Writer). (2017). *After the apology* (M. Purske, Producer). Waverley, NSW: Pursekey Productions.

Behrendt, L. (2018). *After the apology*. Retrieved from http://aftertheapology.com/.

Bellew, W., Bauman, A., Freeman, B., & Kite, J. (2017). Social countermarketing: Brave new world, brave new map. *Journal of Social Marketing, 7*(2), 205–222. https://doi.org/10.1108/JSOCM-09-2016-0052.

Bertely-Busquets, M. (2016). *Análisis y propuestas para el fortalecimiento del programa de educación inicial no escolarizada de CONAFE* [Analysis and proposals for strengthening the informal early education program of CONAFE]. Mexico City.

Berthelsen, D., & Walker, S. (2008). Parents' involvement in their children's education. *Family Matters, 79*, 34–41.

Bessarab, D., & Ng'Andu, B. (2010). Yarning about yarning as a legitimate method in Indigenous research. *International Journal of Critical Indigenous Studies, 3*(1), 37–50.

Bhabha, H. K. (2004). *The location of culture.* London: Routledge.

Blair, N. (2015). *Privileging Australian Indigenous knowledge: Sweet potatoes, spiders, waterlilys & brick walls.* Champaign, IL: Common Ground Publishing.

Blanchette, L. M. G., van de Gaar, V. M., Raat, H., French, J., & Jansen, W. (2016). The development of the "Water Campaign". *Journal of Social Marketing, 6*(4), 318–334. https://doi.org/10.1108/JSOCM-09-2015-0069.

Boas, F. (1940). *Race, language and culture.* New York: Macmillan.

Bourdieu, P. (1986). The forms of capital. In J. Westport (Ed.), *Handbook of theory and research for the sociology of education* (pp. 214–258). New York: Greenwood.

Bourdieu, P. (1990). *Reproduction in education, society, and culture* (1990 ed., Preface by Pierre Bourdieu, Ed.). London: Sage in association with Theory, Culture & Society, Department of Administrative and Social Studies, Teesside Polytechnic.

Bourdieu, P., & Passeron, J. C. (1990). *Reproduction in education, society, and culture* (1990 ed., Preface by Pierre Bourdieu, Ed.). London: Sage in association with Theory, Culture & Society, Department of Administrative and Social Studies, Teesside Polytechnic.

Bower, H. A., & Griffin, D. (2011). Can the Epstein model of parental involvement work in a high-minority, high-poverty elementary school? A case study. *Professional School Counseling, 15*(2), 77–87.

Bowler, J. M., Price, D. M., Sherwood, J. E., & Carey, S. P. (2019). The Moyjil site, south-west Victoria, Australia: Fire and environment in a 120,000-year coastal midden—Nature or people? *Proceedings of the Royal Society of Victoria, 130,* 71–93.

Bradley, D., Noonan, P., Nugent, H., & Scales, B. (2008). *Review of Australian higher education, final report.* Canberra.

Brennan, L., & Binney, W. (2008). Concepts in conflict: Social marketing and sustainability. *Journal of Nonprofit & Public Sector Marketing, 20*(2), 261–281. https://doi.org/10.1080/10495140802224951.

Brennan, L., Fry, M.-L., & Previte, J. (2015). Strengthening social marketing research: Harnessing "insight" through ethnography. *Australasian Marketing Journal (AMJ), 23*(4), 286–293. https://doi.org/10.1016/j.ausmj.2015.10.003.

Brennan, L., Previte, J., & Fry, M.-L. (2016). Social marketing's consumer myopia. *Journal of Social Marketing, 6*(3), 219–239. https://doi.org/10.1108/JSOCM-12-2015-0079.

Bryant-Stephens, T., Garcia-Espana, J., & Winston, F. (2013). Boosting restraint norms: A community-delivered campaign to promote booster seat use. *Traffic Injury Prevention, 14*(6), 578–583. https://doi.org/10.1080/15389588.2012.733840.

Burarrwanga, L., Ganambarr, R., Ganambarr-Stubbs, M., Ganambarr, B., Maymuru, D., Wright, S., Suchet-Pearson, S., & Lloyd, K. (2013). *Welcome to my country.* Melbourne: Allen & Unwin.

Burrow, S., & Thomson, N. (2006). Yarning places: Using web resources and electronic yarning to promote Indigenous health. *Aboriginal and Islander Health Worker Journal, 30*(4), 17.

Butler, J. (1990). *Gender trouble: Feminism and the subversion of identity.* New York: Routledge.

Butler, J. (1997). *Excitable speech: A politics of the performative.* New York: Routledge.

Butler, J. (2001a). Giving an account of oneself. *Diacritics, 31*(4), 22–40. https://doi.org/10.1353/dia.2004.0002.

Butler, J. (2001b). *What is critique? An essay on Foucault's virtue.* Retrieved from http://eipcp.net/transversal/0806/butler/en.html.

Butler, J. (2010). Performative agency. *Journal of Cultural Economy, 3*(2), 147–161. https://doi.org/10.1080/17530350.2010.494117.

Buyucek, N., Kubacki, K., Rundle-Thiele, S., & Pang, B. (2016). A systematic review of stakeholder involvement in social marketing interventions. *Australasian Marketing Journal (AMJ), 24*(1), 8–19. https://doi.org/10.1016/j.ausmj.2015.11.001.

Clarkson, C., Jacobs, Z., Marwick, B., Fullagar, R., Wallis, L., Smith, M., … Pardoe, C. (2017). Human occupation of northern Australia by 65,000 years ago. *Nature, 547*, 306. https://doi.org/10.1038/nature22968, https://www.nature.com/articles/nature22968#supplementary-information.

Collins, K., Tapp, A., & Pressley, A. (2010). Social marketing and social influences: Using social ecology as a theoretical framework. *Journal of Marketing Management, 26*(13/14), 1181. https://doi.org/10.1080/0267257X.2010.522529.

Comaroff, J. (2010). The end of anthropology, again: On the future of an in/discipline. *American Anthropologist, 112*(4), 524–538. https://doi.org/10.1111/j.1548-1433.2010.01273.x.

Correa-Chávez, M., Mejia-Arauz, R., & Rogoff, B. (2015). *Children learn by observing and contributing to family and community endeavours: A cultural paradigm* (Vol. 49). Waltham, MA: Academic Press.

Correa-Chavez, M., Mejia-Arauz, R., & Rogoff, B. (Eds.). (2015). *Children learn by observing and contributing to family and community endeavors: A cultural paradigm.* (1st ed.). Amsterdam, Netherlands: Academic Press.

Crawshaw, P. (2012). Governing at a distance: Social marketing and the (bio) politics of responsibility. *Social Science and Medicine, 75*(1), 200–207. https://doi.org/10.1016/j.socscimed.2012.02.040.

Crawshaw, P., & Newlove, C. (2011). Men's understandings of social marketing and health: Neo-liberalism and health governance. *International Journal of Men's Health, 10*(2), 136. https://doi.org/10.3149/jmh.1002.136.

Cullen, E. T., Matthews, L. N. H., & Teske, T. D. (2008). Use of occupational ethnography and social marketing strategies to develop a safety awareness campaign for coal miners. *Social Marketing Quarterly, 14*(4), 2–21. https://doi.org/10.1080/15245000802546187.

Cummings, C., Laing, K., Law, J., McLaughlin, J., Papps, I., Todd, L., & Woolner, P. (2012). *Can changing aspirations and attitudes impact educational attainment: A review of interventions.* London.

Currie, J. (2009). Healthy, wealthy, and wise: Socioeconomic status, poor health in childhood, and human capital development. *Journal of Economic Literature, 47*(1), 87–122.

Curtis, D., & McMillan, J. (2008). *School non-completers: Profiles and initial destinations* (Longitudinal Surveys of Australian Youth, Research Report 54). Camberwell, VIC.

Daniel, K. L., Prue, C., Taylor, M. K., Thomas, J., & Scales, M. (2009). 'Learn the signs. Act early': A campaign to help every child reach his or her full potential. *Public Health, 123*(1), e11–e16.

Dei, G. J. S., Mazzuca, J., & McIsaac, E. (2016). *Reconstructing 'dropout': A critical ethnography of the dynamics of Black students' disengagement from school.* Toronto: University of Toronto Press.

Devaney, B., & Rossi, P. (1997). Thinking through evaluation design options. *Children and Youth Services Review, 19*(7), 587–606.

Dibb, S., & Carrigan, M. (2013). Social marketing transformed: Kotler, Polonsky and hastings reflect on social marketing in a period of social change. *European Journal of Marketing, 47*(9). https://doi.org/10.1108/EJM-05-2013-0248.

Dietrich, T., Rundle-Thiele, S., & Kubacki, K. (2017). *Segmentation in social marketing: Process, methods and application.* Singapore: Springer.

Domegan, C., McHugh, P., Devaney, M., Duane, S., Hogan, M., Broome, B. J., … Piwowarczyk, J. (2016). Systems-thinking social marketing: Conceptual extensions and empirical investigations. *Journal of Marketing Management, 32*(11–12), 1123–1144. https://doi.org/10.1080/0267257X.2016.1183697.

Donovan, R. J., & Henley, N. (2010). *Principles and practice of social marketing: An international perspective.* Cambridge: Cambridge University Press.

Duane, S., Domegan, C., McHugh, P., & Devaney, M. (2016). From restricted to complex exchange and beyond: Social marketing's change agenda. *Journal of Marketing Management, 32*(9–10), 856–876. https://doi.org/10.1080/0267257X.2016.1189449.

Dudley-Marling, C., & Lucas, K. (2009). Pathologizing the language and culture of poor children. *Language Arts, 86*(5), 362–370.

Dutta, U. (2014). Critical ethnography. In J. Mills & M. Birks (Eds.), *Qualitative methodology: A practical guide* (pp. 89–106). London: Sage.

Edgar, T., Huhman, M., & Miller, G. (2015). Understanding "place" in social marketing: A systematic review. *Social Marketing Quarterly, 21*(4), 230.

Epstein, J. (Ed.). (2009). *School, family, and community partnerships: Your handbook for action* (3rd ed.). Thousand Oaks, CA: Corwin Press.

Evans, C., & Carr, K. (2011). *Have your say on Indigenous higher education* [Media Release]. Retrieved from https://ministers.employment.gov.au/evans/have-yoursayindigenous-higher-education.

Evans, D. W., & Nicols, C. (2016). Formative research. In D. W. Evans (Ed.), *Social marketing research for global public health* (pp. 1–47). Oxford: Oxford University Press.

Evans-Lacko, S., Henderson, C., Thornicroft, G., & McCrone, P. (2013). Economic evaluation of the anti-stigma social marketing campaign in England 2009–2011. *The British Journal of Psychiatry, 202*(Suppl. 55), S95–S101. https://doi.org/10.1192/bjp.bp.112.113746.

Firestone, R., Rowe, C. J., Modi, S. N., & Sievers, D. (2017). The effectiveness of social marketing in global health: A systematic review. *Health Policy and Planning, 32*(1), 110–124. https://doi.org/10.1093/heapol/czw088.

Fluckiger, B., Diamond, P., & Jones, W. (2012). Yarning space: Leading literacy learning through family-school partnerships. *Australasian Journal of Early Childhood, 37*(3), 53–59.

Foucault, M. (1980). Two lectures. In C. Gordon (Ed.), *Power/knowledge: Selected interviews and other writings 1972–1977* (pp. 78–108). Sussex: Harvester Press Ltd.

Foucault, M. (1983). The subject and power. In H. L. Dreyfus & P. Rabinow (Eds.), *Michel Foucault: Beyond structuralism and hermeneutics* (2nd ed., pp. 208–226). Chicago: University of Chicago press.

Foucault, M. (1991). Politics and the study of discourse. In G. Burchell, C. Gordon, & P. Miller (Eds.), *The Foucault effect: Studies in governmentality* (pp. 53–72). London: Harvester Wheatsheaf.

Foucault, M. (1997). What is critique? In S. Lotringer & L. Hochroth (Eds.), *The politics of truth: Michel Foucault* (pp. 23–82). New York: Semiotext(e).

Foucault, M. (2000). Governmentality. In J. D. Faubion (Ed.), *Power, the essential works of Michel Foucault* (Vol. III, pp. 201–222). New York: The New Press.

Foucault, M. (2011). *The courage of the truth (the government of self and others II): Lectures at the Collège de France, 1983–1984.* New York and Houndmills, Basingstoke, Hampshire, UK: Palgrave Macmillan.

Foucault, M. (2014a). *On the government of the living: Lectures at the Collaege de France, 1979–1980* (G. Burchell, Trans.). Basingstoke, UK: Palgrave Macmillan.

Foucault, M. (2014b). *Wrong-doing, truth-telling: The function of avowal in justice* (F. Brion, B. E. Harcourt, & S. W. Sawyer, Eds.). London, Chicago, and Louvain-la-Neuve: University of Chicago Press.

Foucault, M. (2016). *About the beginning of the hermeneutics of the self: Lectures at Dartmouth College, 1980* (H.-P. Fruchaud, D. Lorenzini, L. Cremonesi, A. I. Davidson, O. Irrera, & M. Tazzioli, Eds.). London and Chicago: University of Chicago Press.

Foucault, M. (2017). *Subjectivity and truth: Lectures at the Collège de France, 1980–1981* (F. Gros, F. Ewald, & A. Fontana, Eds.). London, UK: Palgrave Macmillan.

Fredericks, B. (2013). 'We don't leave our identities at the city limits': Aboriginal and Torres Strait Islander people living in urban localities. *Australian Aboriginal Studies* (1), 4–16.

Fredericks, B., Adams, K., Finlay, S., Fletcher, G., Andy, S., Briggs, L., Briggs, L., & Hall, R. (2011). Engaging the practice of Indigenous yarning in action research. *ALAR: Action Learning and Action Research Journal, 17*(2), 12–24.

French, J. (2010). Social marketing on a shoestring budget. In J. French, C. Blair-Stevens, D. McVey, & R. Merritt (Eds.), *Social marketing and public health: Theory and practice* (pp. 248–262). Oxford: Oxford University Press.

French, J. (2011). Why nudging is not enough. *Journal of Social Marketing, 1*(2), 154–162. https://doi.org/10.1108/20426761111141896.

French, J. (2017a). Key principle, concepts, and techniques of social marketing. In *Social marketing and public health: Theory and practice.* Oxford: Oxford University Press.

French, J. (2017b). *Social marketing and public health* (2nd ed.). Oxford: Oxford University Press.

French, J. (2017c). Social marketing planning. In J. French (Ed.), *Social marketing and public health: Theory and practice* (2nd ed.). Oxford: Oxford University Press.

French, J. (2017d). The importance of segmentation in social marketing strategy. In T. Dietrich, S. Rundle-Thiele, & K. Kubacki (Eds.), *Segmentation in social marketing: Process, methods and application* (pp. 25–40). Singapore: Springer.

French, J., & Blair-Stevens, C. (2006). *The big pocket guide to social marketing.* London: National Consumer Council, National Social Marketing Centre.

French, J., & Blair-Stevens, C. (2008). *The total process planning framework for social marketing.* London: National Social Marketing Centre.

French, J., & Gordon, R. (2015). *Strategic social marketing.* Los Angeles: Sage.

French, J., & Russell-Bennett, R. (2015). A hierarchical model of social marketing. *Journal of Social Marketing, 5*(2), 139–159. https://doi.org/10.1108/jsocm-06-2014-0042.

Fry, M.-L., Previte, J., & Brennan, L. (2017). Social change design: Disrupting the benchmark template. *Journal of Social Marketing, 7*(2), 119–134. https://doi.org/10.1108/jsocm-10-2016-0064.

Gale, T., Sellar, S., Parker, S., Hattam, R., Comber, B., Tranter, D., & Bills, D. (2010). *Interventions early in school as a means to improve higher education outcomes for disadvantaged (particularly low SES) students.* Underdale, Australia: National Centre Student Equity in Higher Education. Retrieved from http://dro.deakin.edu.au/view/DU:30040776.

Geia, L. K., Hayes, B., & Usher, K. (2013). Yarning/Aboriginal storytelling: Towards an understanding of an Indigenous perspective and its implications for research practice. *Contemporary Nurse, 46*(1), 13–17. https://doi.org/10.5172/conu.2013.46.1.13.

Gibson, P. (2017, June 21). *10 impacts of the NT intervention.* Retrieved from https://www.sbs.com.au/nitv/article/2017/06/21/10-impacts-nt-intervention.

Gillard, J. (2009). *Funding boost helps low-SES higher education places.* Canberra: Commonwealth of Australia.

Gillard, J. (2010). *Keynote address: Australia's productivity challenge: A key role for education.* John Curtin Institute of Public Policy. Canberra: Commonwealth of Australia.

Ginsburg, H. P. (2006). Mathematical play and playful mathematics: A guide for early education. In *Play = learning: How play motivates and enhances children's cognitive and social-emotional growth*. New York: Oxford University Press.

Goldberg, M. E. (1995). Social marketing: Are we fiddling while Rome burns? *Journal of Consumer Psychology, 4*(4), 347–370. https://doi.org/10.1207/s15327663jcp0404_03.

Gonzalez, N. (1999). What will we do when culture does not exist anymore? *Anthropology & Education Quarterly, 30*(4), 431–435.

González, N., Moll, L. C., & Amanti, C. (Eds.). (2005). *Funds of knowledge: Theorizing practices in households, communities and classrooms*. Mahwah, NJ: Lawrence Erlbaum Associates.

Goodman, A., Gregg, P., & Washbrook, E. (2011). Children's educational attainment and the aspirations, attitudes and behaviours of parents and children through childhood in the UK. *Longitudinal and Life Course Studies, 2*(1), 1–18.

Gordon, R. (2011). Critical social marketing: Definition, application and domain. *Journal of Social Marketing, 1*(2), 82–99. https://doi.org/10.1108/20426761111141850.

Gordon, R., Russell-Bennett, R., & Lefebvre, R. C. (2016). Social marketing: The state of play and brokering the way forward. *Journal of Marketing Management, 32*(11–12), 1059–1082. https://doi.org/10.1080/0267257X.2016.1199156.

Gould, S., & Semaan, R. W. (2014). Avoiding throwing out the baby with the bathwater: Critically deconstructing contested positions on social and macromarketing in the health domain. *Journal of Macromarketing, 34*(4), 520–531. https://doi.org/10.1177/0276146714530165.

Green, C. L., Walker, J. M. T., Hoover-Dempsey, K. V., & Sandler, H. M. (2007). Parents' motivations for involvement in children's education: An empirical test of a theoretical model of parental involvement. *Journal of Educational Psychology, 99*(3), 532–544. https://doi.org/10.1037/0022-0663.99.3.532.

Grier, S., & Bryant, C. A. (2005). Social marketing in public health. *Annual Review of Public Health, 26*(1), 319–339. https://doi.org/10.1146/annurev.publhealth.26.021304.144610.

Gurrieri, L., Previte, J., & Brace-Govan, J. (2013). Women's bodies as sites of control: Inadvertent stigma and exclusion in social marketing. *Journal of Macromarketing, 33*(2), 128. https://doi.org/10.1177/0276146712469971.

Harrell, P. E., & Forney, W. S. (2003). Ready or not, here we come: Retaining hispanic and first-generation students in postsecondary education. *Community College Journal of Research and Practice, 27*(2), 147–156. https://doi.org/10.1080/713838112.

Harris, A., & Goodall, J. (2008). Do parents know they matter? Engaging all parents in learning. *Educational Research, 50*(3), 277–289. https://doi.org/10.1080/00131880802309424.

Harwood, V. (2006). *Diagnosing 'disorderly' children: A critique of behaviour disorder discourses*. Oxford: Routledge.

Harwood, V. (2010). The new outsiders: ADHD and disadvantage. In L. J. Graham (Ed.), *(De)constructing ADHD: Critical guidance for teachers and teacher educators* (pp. 119–142). New York: Peter Lang.

Harwood, V., & Allan, J. (2014). *Psychopathology at school: Theorising mental disorders in education*. Oxford: Routledge.

Harwood, V., Hickey-Moody, A., McMahon, S., & O'Shea, S. (2017). *The politics of widening participation and university access for young people: Making educational futures*. London: Routledge.

Harwood, V., McMahon, S., O'Shea, S., Bodkin-Andrews, G., & Priestly, A. (2015). Recognising aspiration: The AIME program's effectiveness in inspiring Indigenous young people's participation in schooling and opportunities for further education and employment. *Australian Educational Researcher, 42*(2), 217. https://doi.org/10.1007/s13384-015-0174-3.

Harwood, V., & Murray, N. (2019). Strategic discourse production and parent involvement: Including parent knowledge and practices in the Lead My Learning campaign. *International Journal of Inclusive Education, 23*(4), 353–368.. https://doi.org/10.1080/13603116.2019.1571119.

Harwood, V., & Rasmussen, M. L. (2004). Studying schools with an ethic of discomfort. In B. Baker & K. Heyning (Eds.), *Dangerous coagulations? The uses of Foucault in the study of education* (pp. 305–321). New York: Peter Lang.

Harwood, V., & Rasmussen, M. L. (2013). Practising critique, attending to truth: The pedagogy of discriminatory speech. *Educational Philosophy and Theory, 45*(8), 874–884. https://doi.org/10.1111/j.1469-5812.2011.00834.x.

Hastings, G. (2007). *Social marketing: Why should the devil have all the best tunes?* Oxford: Elsevier.

Hastings, G. B. (2009). Critical social marketing. In J. French, C. Blair-Stevens, D. McVey, & R. Merritt (Eds.), *Social marketing and public health: Theory and practice* (pp. 263–280). Oxford: Oxford University Press.

Hastings, G. B., & Elliot, B. (1993). Social marketing practice in traffic safety. In *Marketing of traffic safety, chapter III* (pp. 33–53). Paris: OECD.

Helitzer, D., Soo-Jin, Y., & Wallerstein, N. (2000). The role of process evaluation in the training of facilitators for an adolescent health education program. *The Journal of School Health, 70*(4), 141–147. https://doi.org/10.1111/j.1746-1561.2000.tb06460.x.

Hickey-Moody, A. (2005). *Unimaginable bodies: Intellectual disability, performance and becomings.* Adelaide: University of South Australia.

Hill, N. E., & Tyson, D. F. (2009). Parental involvement in middle school: A meta-analytic assessment of the strategies that promote achievement. *Developmental Psychology, 45*(3), 740–763. https://doi.org/10.1037/a0015362.

Hill, P. (2011). Impoverished consumers and social marketing. In G. Hastings, K. Angus, & C. A. Bryant (Eds.), *The SAGE handbook of social marketing* (pp. 319–329). London: Sage.

HM Treasury, & DEFES. (2007). *Policy review of children and young people: A discussion paper.* Norwich.

Holloway, S. L., & Pimlott-Wilson, H. (2011). The politics of aspiration: Neo-liberal education policy, 'low' parental aspirations, and primary school extended services in disadvantaged communities. *Children's Geographies, 9*(1), 79–94.

Hoover-Dempsey, V. K., Walker, T. M. J., Sandler, M. H., Whetsel, D., Green, L. C., Wilkins, S. A., & Closson, K. (2005). Why do parents become involved? Research findings and implications. *The Elementary School Journal, 106*(2), 105–130.

Hossain, D., Gorman, D., Willams-Mozley, J., & Garvey, D. (2008). Bridging the gap: Identifying needs and aspirations of indigenous students to facilitate their entry into university. *Australian Journal of Indigenous Education, 37*(1), 9–17.

Hue, D. T., Brennan, L., Parker, L., & Florian, M. (2015). But I am normal: Safe? driving in Vietnam. *Journal of Social Marketing, 5*(2), 105–124. https://doi.org/10.1108/JSOCM-07-2013-0048.

Huhman, M., Kelly, R. P., & Edgar, T. (2017). Social marketing as a framework for youth physical activity initiatives: A 10-year retrospective on the legacy of CDC's VERB campaign. *Current Obesity Reports, 6*(2), 101. https://doi.org/10.1007/s13679-017-0252-0.

Human Rights and Equal Opportunity Commission. (1997). *Bringing them home: Report of the National Inquiry into the separation of Aboriginal and Torres Strait Islander children from their families.* Sydney: Human Rights and Equal Opportunity Commission.

Ingold, T. (2017). *Anthropology and/as education: Anthropology, art, architecture and design.* Abingdon, Oxon and New York, NY: Routledge.

International Social Marketing Association. (2013). *Social marketing definition.* Retrieved from https://www.i-socialmarketing.org/social-marketing-definition#.XD1nqHozbu4.

Johnson, K. M., Jones, S. C., & Iverson, D. (2009). Guidelines for the development of social marketing programmes for sun protection among adolescents and young adults (Report). *Public Health, 123,* e6–e10.

Jones, R., Pykett, J., & Whitehead, M. (2011). Governing temptation: Changing behaviour in an age of libertarian paternalism. *Progress in Human Geography, 35*(4), 483–501. https://doi.org/10.1177/0309132510385741.

Jones, S., Andrews, K., & Francis, K. (2017). Combining social norms and social marketing to address underage drinking: Development and process evaluation of a whole-of-community intervention. *PLoS One, 12*(1), e0169872. https://doi.org/10.1371/journal.pone.0169872.

Kamin, T., & Anker, T. (2014). Cultural capital and strategic social marketing orientations. *Journal of Social Marketing, 4*(2), 94–110. https://doi.org/10.1108/JSOCM-08-2013-0057.

Kemp, G., Eagle, L., & Verne, J. (2011). Mass media barriers to social marketing interventions: The example of sun protection in the UK. *Health Promotion International, 26*(1), 37–45. https://doi.org/10.1093/heapro/daq048.

Kennedy, A.-M. (2017). Macro-social marketing research: Philosophy, methodology and methods. *Journal of Macromarketing, 37*(4), 347–355. https://doi.org/10.1177/0276146717735467.

Kenway, J. (2013). Challenging inequality in Australian schools: Gonski and beyond. *Discourse: Studies in the Cultural Politics of Education, 34*(2), 1–23. https://doi.org/10.1080/01596306.2013.770254.

Kenway, J., & Hickey-Moody, A. (2011). Life chances, lifestyle and everyday aspirational strategies and tactics. *Critical Studies in Education, 52*(2), 151–163.

Kirka, D. (2017, August 17). Malala Yousafzai, shot for promoting education in Pakistan, earns admission to Oxford. *India-West.* Retrieved from http://www.indiawest.com/news/global_indian/malala-yousafzai-shot-for-promoting-education-in-pakistan-earns-admission/article_75d65d5e-83a9-11e7-9b24-03304e5280be.html.

Kleykamp, M. (2006). College, jobs, or the military? Enlistment during a time of war*. *Social Science Quarterly, 87*(2), 272–290. https://doi.org/10.1111/j.1540-6237.2006.00380.x.

Kotler, P. (2009). *Up and out of poverty the social marketing solution.* Upper Saddle River, NJ: Pearson.

Kotler, P., & Lee, N. (2009). *Up and out of poverty: The social marketing solution.* Upper Saddle River, NJ: Wharton School Publishing.

Kotler, P., & Lee, N. (2015). *Up and out of poverty: The social marketing solution.* Upper Saddle River, NJ: Pearson Education.

Kotler, P., & Levy, S. (1969). Broadening the Concept of Marketing. *Journal of Marketing (pre-1986), 33*(1), 10.

Kotler, P., & Zaltman, G. (1971). Social marketing: An approach to planned social change. *Journal of Marketing, 35*(3), 3. https://doi.org/10.2307/1249783.

Kotlowitz, A. (1991). *There are no children here: The story of two boys growing up in the other America* (1st ed.). New York: Doubleday.

Kristeva, J. (1982). *Powers of horror: An essay in abjection*. New York: Columbia University Press.

Kubacki, K., & Rundle-Thiele, S. (2016). *Formative research in social marketing: Innovative methods to gain consumer insights*. Singapore: Springer.

Kubacki, K., & Szablewska, N. (2017). Social marketing targeting Indigenous peoples: A systematic review. *Health Promotion International, 34*, 133–143. https://doi.org/10.1093/heapro/dax060.

Ladero, M. M. G., & Alves, H. M. (Eds.). (2019). *Case studies on social marketing: A global perspective*. Cham: Springer.

Ladson-Billings, G. (2006). It's not the culture of poverty, it's the poverty of culture: The problem with teacher education. *Anthropology & Education Quarterly, 37*(2), 104–109. https://doi.org/10.1525/aeq.2006.37.2.104.

Lee, N., & Kotler, P. (2011). *Social marketing: Influencing behaviors for good* (4th ed.). Thousand Oaks, CA: Sage.

Lee, N. R., & Kotler, P. (2015). Social marketing influencing behaviours for good: Quick reference guide. In *Social marketing services* (5th ed.). Mercer Island, WA: Social Marketing Services.

Lee, N. R., & Kotler, P. (2016). *Social marketing: Changing behaviours for good*. New York: Free Press.

Lee, N. R., & Kotler, P. (2019). *Social marketing: Behavior change for social good* (6th ed.). Thousand Oaks, CA: Sage.

Leeson, S., Smith, C., & Rynne, J. (2016). Yarning and appreciative inquiry: The use of culturally appropriate and respectful research methods when working with Aboriginal and Torres Strait Islander women in Australian prisons. *Methodological Innovations Online, 9*(1), 1.

Lefebvre, R. C. (2013). *Social marketing and social change: Strategies and tools for improving health, well-being, and the environment*. Chichester: Wiley.

Lefebvre, R. C., & Flora, J. (1988, Fall). Social marketing and public health intervention. *Health Education Quarterly, 15*(88), 298–315.

Lehmann, W. (2009). Becoming middle class: How working-class university students draw and transgress moral class boundaries. *Sociology, 43*(4), 631–647.

Levinson, B., A., Foley, D., E, & Holland, D., C (Eds.). (1996). *The cultural production of the educated person: Critical ethnographies of schooling and local practice.* Albany, NY: State University of New York Press.

Lin, I., Green, C., & Bessarab, D. (2016). 'Yarn with me': Applying clinical yarning to improve clinician–patient communication in Aboriginal health care. *Australian Journal of Primary Health, 22*(5), 377–382. https://doi.org/10.1071/PY16051.

Lowe, B., Lynch, D., & Lowe, J. (2015). Reducing household water consumption: A social marketing approach. *Journal of Marketing Management, 31*(3–4), 378–408. https://doi.org/10.1080/0267257X.2014.971044.

Luca, N. R., Hibbert, S., & McDonald, R. (2016). Towards a service-dominant approach to social marketing. *Marketing Theory, 16*(2), 194–218. https://doi.org/10.1177/1470593115607941.

Luca, N. R, & Suggs, L. (2013). Theory and model use in social marketing health interventions. *Journal of Health Communication, 18*(1), 20. https://doi.org/10.1080/10810730.2012.688243.

Luecking, C. T., Hennink-Kaminski, H., Ihekweazu, C., Vaughn, A., Mazzucca, S., & Ward, D. S. (2017). Social marketing approaches to nutrition and physical activity interventions in early care and education centres: A systematic review. *Obesity Reviews, 18*(12), 1425–1438.

Madill, J., Wallace, L., Goneau-Lessard, K., Stuart MacDonald, R., & Dion, C. (2014). Best practices in social marketing among Aboriginal people. *Journal of Social Marketing, 4*(2), 155–175. https://doi.org/10.1108/JSOCM-08-2013-0056.

Magnuson, K., Sexton, H., Davis-Kean, P. F., & Huston, A. (2009). The effects of increases in maternal education on young children's language skills. *Merill Palmer Quarterly, 55,* 319–350.

Mamdani, M. (2002). Good Muslim, bad Muslim: A political perspective on culture and terrorism. *American Anthropologist, 104*(3), 766–775. https://doi.org/10.1525/aa.2002.104.3.766.

Mao, L., Mian Akram, A., Chovanec, D., & Underwood, M. L. (2016). Embracing the spiral: Researcher reflexivity in diverse critical methodologies. *International Journal of Qualitative Methods, 15*(1). https://doi.org/10.1177/1609406916681005.

Martin, K. (2012). Childhood, lifehood and relatedness: Aboriginal ways of being, knowing and doing. In J. Phillips & J. Lampert (Eds.), *Introductory Indigenous studies in education: Reflection and the importance of knowing* (2nd ed., pp. 27–40). Frenchs Forest, NSW: Pearson Australia.

Martin, K., & Mirraboopa, B. (2003). Ways of knowing, being and doing: A theoretical framework and methods for Indigenous and indigenist re-search. *Journal of Australian studies, 76,* 203–214.

Martin, K. L. (2008). *Please knock before you enter: Aboriginal regulation of outsiders and the implications for researchers.* Teneriffe, QLD: Post Pressed.

Matasci, D. (2017). Assessing needs, fostering development: UNESCO, illiteracy and the global politics of education (1945–1960). *Comparative Education, 53*(1), 35–53. https://doi.org/10.1080/03050068.2017.1254952.

McCarthy, C. (2008). Understanding the neoliberal context of race and schooling in the age of globalization. In *Transnational perspectives on culture, policy, and education: Redirecting cultural studies in neoliberal times* (pp. 319–340, Chapter 15). New York: Peter Lang.

McDonald, E., Cunningham, T., & Slavin, N. (2015). Evaluating a handwashing with soap program in Australian remote Aboriginal communities: A pre and post intervention study design health behavior, health promotion and society. *BMC Public Health, 15*(1). https://doi.org/10.1186/s12889-015-2503-x.

McKenzie-Mohr, D. (2000a). Fostering sustainable behavior through community-based social marketing. *American Psychologist, 55*(5), 531–537. https://doi.org/10.1037/0003-066X.55.5.531.

McKenzie-Mohr, D. (2000b). Promoting sustainable behavior: An introduction to community-based social marketing. *Journal of Social Issues, 56*(3), 543.

McLeod, G., Insch, A., & Henry, J. (2011). Reducing barriers to sun protection—Application of a holistic model for social marketing. *Australasian Marketing Journal (AMJ), 19*(3), 212–222. https://doi.org/10.1016/j.ausmj.2011.05.008.

McLeod, J., & Yates, L. (2006). *Making modern lives: Subjectivity, schooling, and social change.* New York: State University of New York.

McMahon, S., Harwood, V., & Hickey-Moody, A. (2016). 'Students that just hate school wouldn't go': Educationally disengaged and disadvantaged young people's talk about university education. *British Journal of Sociology of Education, 37*(8), 1109–1128. https://doi.org/10.1080/01425692.2015.1014546.

Merritt, R. K., Kamin, T., Hussenöder, F., & Huibregtsen, J. (2017). The history of social marketing in Europe: The story so far. *Social Marketing Quarterly, 23*(4), 291–301. https://doi.org/10.1177/1524500417732771.

Miller, K. (2014). Respectful listening and reflective communication from the heart and with the spirit. *Qualitative Social Work, 13*(6), 828–841. https://doi.org/10.1177/1473325013508596.

Miñana Blasco, C., & Arango Vargas, C. (2011). Educational policy, anthropology, and the state. In *A companion to the anthropology of education*. Malden: Wiley-Blackwell.

Mols, F., Haslam, S. A., Jetten, J., & Steffens, N. K. (2015). Why a nudge is not enough: A social identity critique of governance by stealth. *European Journal of Political Research, 54*(1), 81–98. https://doi.org/10.1111/1475-6765.12073.

Muncie, J. (2006). Critical research. In J. Muncie & E. McLaughlin (Eds.), *The Sage dictionary of criminology* (2nd ed., pp. 100–102). London: Sage.

Murray, N., & Harwood, V. (2016). *The importance of Aboriginal Protocols in promoting educational futures*. National Centre for Student Equity in Higher Education.

Murray, N., & Harwood, V. (2018). *Lead My Learning*. Retrieved from lead-mylearning.com.au.

National Social Marketing Centre (Ed.). (2011). *Big pocket guide to using social marketing for behaviour change*. London: NSMC.

National Social Marketing Centre, Blair-Stevens, C., Slater, & French, J. (2006). *Social marketing benchmark criteria*. Retrieved from www.thensmc.com/file/244/download?token=S74a2YN9.

Newton, J. D., Newton, F. J., Turk, T., & Ewing, M. T. (2013). Ethical evaluation of audience segmentation in social marketing. *European Journal of Marketing, 47*(9), 1421–1438. https://doi.org/10.1108/EJM-09-2011-0515.

Nigg, C. R., Allegrante, J. P., & Ory, M. (2002). Theory-comparison and multiple-behavior research: Common themes advancing health behavior research. *Health Education Research, 17*(5), 670–679.

Norões, K., & McCowan, T. (2015). The challenge of widening participation to higher education in Brazil: Injustices, innovations, and outcomes. In M. Shah, A. Bennett, & E. Southgate (Eds.), *Widening higher education participation: A global perspective* (pp. 63–80). Waltham, MA: Chandos Publishing.

Obama, M. (2018). *Becoming*. New York: Viking.

Ong, D., & Blair-Stevens, C. (2009). The total process planning (TPP) framework. In J. French & C. Blair-Stevens, D. McVey, & R. Merritt (Eds.), *Social marketing and public health: Theory and practice*. Oxford: Oxford University Press.

Opel, D., Diekema, D. S., Lee, N. R., & Marcuse, E. K. (2009). Social marketing as a strategy to increase immunization rates. *JAMA Pediatrics, 163*(5), 432–437.

Ortner, S. B. (1989). *High religion: A cultural and political history of Sherpa Buddhism*. Princeton, NJ: Princeton University Press.

O'Shea, S., May, J., Stone, C., & Delahunty, J. (2017). *First-in-family students, university experience and family life motivations, transitions and participation*. London: Palgrave Macmillan.

O'Shea, S., & Stone, C. (2011). Transformations and self-discovery: Mature-age women's reflections on returning to university study. *Studies in Continuing Education, 33*(3), 273–288. https://doi.org/10.1080/0158037X.2011.565046.

Ou, S.-R., & Reynolds, A. J. (2014). Early determinants of postsecondary education participation and degree attainment: Findings from an inner-city minority cohort. *Education and Urban Society, 46*(4), 474–504. https://doi.org/10.1177/0013124512447810.

Oxford English Dictionary. (2018). *Promotion, n*. Oxford: Oxford University Press.

Paniagua, A. (2017). The intersection of cultural diversity and special education in Catalonia: The subtle production of exclusion through classroom routines. *Anthropology & Education Quarterly, 48*(2), 141–158. https://doi.org/10.1111/aeq.12190.

Peattie, K., & Peattie, S. (2011). The social marketing mix: A critical review. In G. Hastings, K. Angus, & C. Bryant (Eds.), *The SAGE handbook of social marketing* (pp. 152–166). London: Sage.

Perry, M., Fantuzzo, J., & Munis, P. (2002). *Manual—Family involvement questionnaire*. Philadelphia: University of Pennsylvania.

Potter, S. J., & Stapleton, J. G. (2012). Translating sexual assault prevention from a college campus to a United States military installation: Piloting the know-your-power bystander social marketing campaign. *Journal of Interpersonal Violence, 27*(8), 1593–1621. https://doi.org/10.1177/0886260511425795.

Povinelli, E. A. (1995). Do rocks listen—The cultural polities of apprehending Australian Aboriginal labor. *American Anthropologist, 97*(3), 505–518.

Povinelli, E. A. (2011). *Economies of abandonment: Social belonging and endurance in late liberalism*. Durham, NC: Duke University Press.

Povinelli, E. A. (2016). *Geontologies: A requiem to late liberalism*. Durham: Duke University Press.

Prime Minister and Cabinet. (2019). *Closing the gap, report 2019*. Canberra.

Prochaska, J. O., & DiClemente, C. C. (1983). Stages and processes of self-change of smoking: Toward an integrative model of change. *Journal of Consulting and Clinical Psychology, 51*(3), 390–395. https://doi.org/10.1037/0022-006X.51.3.390.

Pykett, J., Jones, R., Welsh, M., & Whitehead, M. (2014). The art of choosing and the politics of social marketing. *Policy Studies, 35*(2), 97–114. https://doi.org/10.1080/01442872.2013.875141.

Raco, M. (2009). From expectations to aspirations: State modernisation, urban policy, and the existential politics of welfare in the UK, *Political Geography, 28*, 436–454.

Reay, D. (1995). The employ cleaners to do that: Habitus in the primary classroom. *British Journal of Sociology of Education, 16*, 353–371.

Robinson-Maynard, A., Meaton, J., & Lowry, R. (2013). Identifying key criteria as predictors of success in social marketing: Establishing an evaluation template and grid (ETG). In K. Kubacki & S. Rundle-Thiele (Eds.), *Contemporary issues in social marketing* (pp. 41–58). Newcastle upon Tyne: Cambridge Scholars Publishing.

Rogoff, B. (2014). *Learning by observing and pitching in overview.* Retrieved from http://www.learningbyobservingandpitchingin.com/icp-overview-english. 5 October, 2019.

Rogoff, B. (2014). Learning by observing and pitching in to family and community endeavours. *Human Development, 57*, 69–81.

Rogoff, B. (2016). Culture and participation: A paradigm shift. *Current Opinion in Psychology, 8*, 182–189. https://doi.org/10.1016/j.copsyc.2015.12.002.

Rogoff, B., Coppens, A. D., Alcalá, L., Aceves-Azuara, I., Ruvalcaba, O., López, A., & Dayton, A. (2017). Noticing learners' strengths through cultural research. *Perspectives on Psychological Science, 12*(5), 876–888. https://doi.org/10.1177/1745691617718355.

Rosaldo, R. (1993). *Culture and truth: The remaking of social analysis.* Boston: Beacon Press.

Rosenstock, I. M., Strecher, V. J., & Becker, M. H. (1988). Social learning theory and the health belief model. *Health Education Quarterly, 15*(2), 175–183. https://doi.org/10.1177/109019818801500203.

Rothman, A. J. (2000). Toward a theory-based analysis of behavioral maintenance. *Health Psychology: Official Journal of the Division of Health Psychology, American Psychological Association, 19*(1S), 64–69. https://doi.org/10.1037/0278-6133.19.Suppl1.64.

Rundle-Thiele, S. (2015). Looking back and moving forwards: An agenda for social marketing research. *Recherche et Applications en Marketing (English Edition), 30*(3), 128–133. https://doi.org/10.1177/2051570715599338.

Russell-Bennet, R., Drenan, J., & Raciti, M. (2016). *Social marketing strategy for LSES communities: Research and strategy phase.*

Retrieved from https://research.qut.edu.au/servicesocialmarketing/research-projects/widening-participation-in-the-tertiary-education-sector/.

Sarra, C. (2011). *Strong and smart: Towards a pedagogy for emancipation, education for first peoples.* New York, NY: Routledge.

Saunders, R. P., Evans, M. H., & Joshi, P. (2005). Developing a process-evaluation plan for assessing health promotion program implementation: A how-to guide. *Health promotion practice, 6*(2), 134–147.

Saunders, S. G., Barrington, D. J., & Sridharan, S. (2015). Redefining social marketing: Beyond behavioural change. *Journal of Social Marketing, 5*(2), 160–168. https://doi.org/10.1108/JSOCM-03-2014-0021.

Sellar, S., Gale, T., & Parker, S. (2011). Appreciating aspriations in Australian higher education. *Cambridge Journal of Education, 41*(1), 37–52.

Sen, A. K. (1999). *Development as freedom.* Oxford: Oxford University Press.

Sewak, A., & Singh, G. (2017). Integrating social marketing into Fijian HIV/AIDS prevention programs: Lessons from systematic review. *Health Communication, 32*(1), 32–40. https://doi.org/10.1080/10410236.2015.1099500.

Shah, M., Bennett, A., & Southgate, E. (2016). *Widening higher education participation: A global perspective.* Waltham, MA: Chandos Publishing.

Shah, M., & Whiteford, G. (2017). *Bridges, pathways and transitions: International innovations in widening participation.* Cambridge, MA: Chandos Publishing.

Shavitt, Y., & Blossfield, H.-P. (Eds.). (1993). *Persistent inequality: Changing educational attainment in thirteen countries.* Boulder, CO: Westview Press.

Sherwood, J., & Kendall, S. (2013). Reframing spaces by building relationships: Community collaborative participatory action research with Aboriginal mothers in prison. *Contemporary Nurse, 46*(1), 83–94. https://doi.org/10.5172/conu.2013.46.1.83.

Slee, R. (1994). Finding a student voice in school reform: Student disaffection, pathologies of disruption and educational control. *International Studies in Sociology of Education, 4*(2), 147–172.

Smith, L. T. (2012). *Decolonizing methodologies: Research and Indigenous peoples* (2nd ed.). London: Zed Books.

Smyth, J. (2004). Social capital and the 'socially just school'. *British Journal of Sociology of Education, 25*(1), 19–33.

Society for Promoting the Education of the Poor in Ireland. (1820). *Eighth report of the Society for Promoting the Education of the Poor of Ireland.* Dublin.

Sommer, T. E., Chase-Lansdale, P. L., Brooks-Gunn, J., Gardner, M., Rauneer, D. M., & Freel, K. (2012). Early childhood education centers and mothers' postsecondary attainment: A new conceptual framework for a dual-generation education intervention. *Teachers College Record, 114*(100305), 1-40. Retrieved from https://www.tcrecord.org, Date Accessed: 8 October 2019.

Stahl, G. (2018). *Ethnography of a neo-liberal school: Cultures of success.* Oxford: Routledge.

Stead, M., McDermott, L., & Hastings, G. (2007). Towards evidence-based marketing: The case of childhood obesity. *Marketing Theory, 7*(4), 379–406. https://doi.org/10.1177/1470593107083163.

Steckler, A., & Linnan, L. (2000). Process evaluation for public health interventions and research. In A. Steckler & L. Linnan (Eds.), *Process evaluation for public health interventions and research* (pp. 1–23). San Francisco: Jossey-Bass.

Suarez-Almazor, M. E. (2011). Changing health behaviors with social marketing. *Osteoporosis international: A Journal Established as Result of Cooperation Between the European Foundation for Osteoporosis and the National Osteoporosis Foundation of the USA, 22*(Suppl. 3), 461–463. https://doi.org/10.1007/s00198-011-1699-6.

Tanaka, G. (2009). The elephant in the living room that no one wants to talk about: Why U.S. anthropologists are unable to acknowledge the end of culture. *Anthropology & Education Quarterly, 40*(1), 82–95. https://doi.org/10.1111/j.1548-1492.2009.01029.x.

Tapp, A., & Spotswood, F. (2013). Beyond persuasion: A cultural perspective of behaviour. *Journal of Social Marketing, 3*(3), 275–294. https://doi.org/10.1108/JSOCM-01-2013-0006.

Taylor, C. L., Clayton, D. J., & Rowley, J. S. (2004). Academic socialization: Understanding parental influences on children's school-related development in the early years. *Review of General Psychology, 8*(3), 163–178. https://doi.org/10.1037/1089-2680.8.3.163.

Thomson, P. (2000). Against the odds: Developing school programmes that make a difference for students and families in communities placed at risk. *Childrenz Issues, 3*(1), 7–13.

Thrasher, J. F., Huang, L., Perez-Hernandez, R., Niederdeppe, J., Arillo-Santillan, E., & Alday, J. (2011). Evaluation of a social marketing campaign to support Mexico City's comprehensive smoke-free law (Research and Practice) (Author abstract) (Report). *The American Journal of Public Health, 101*(2), 328. https://doi.org/10.2105/AJPH.2009.189704.

Towney, L. M. (2005). The power of healing in the yarns: Working with Aboriginal men. *International Journal of Narrative Therapy & Community Work, 2005*(1), 39–43. Peer Reviewed Full content available at https://search.informit.com.au/documentSummary;dn=244322186941673;res=IELFSC.

Truong, V. D. (2014). Social marketing: A systematic review of research 1998–2012. *Social Marketing Quarterly, 20*(1), 15–34. https://doi.org/10. 1177/1524500413517666.

Turner, T. (1993). Anthropology and multiculturalism: What is anthropology that multiculturalists should be mindful of it? *Cultural Anthropology, 8*(4), 411–429. https://doi.org/10.1525/can.1993.8.4.02a00010.

Ungunmerr, M.-R. (2017). To be listened to in her teaching: Dadirri: Inner deep listening and quiet still awareness. *EarthSong Journal: Perspectives in Ecology, Spirituality and Education, 3*, 14–15.

Universities Australia. (2008). *Advancing equity and participation in Australian higher education: Action to address participation and equity levels in higher education of people from low socioeconomic backgrounds and Indigenous people*. Canberra.

Urrieta, L. J. (2015). Learning by observing and pitching in and the connections to native and Indigenous knowledge systems. In M. Correa-Chevaz, R. Mejia-Arauz, & B. Rogoff (Eds.), *Children learn by observing and contributing to family and community endeavours: A cultural paradigm* (pp. 357–380). Waltham, MA: Elsevier.

Van Laere, K., Vandenbroeck, M., Roets, G., & Peeters, J. (2014). Challenging the feminisation of the workforce: Rethinking the mind–body dualism in early childhood education and care. *Gender and Education, 26*(3), 1–14. https://doi.org/10.1080/09540253.2014.901721.

Viadro, C., Earp, J. A. L., & Altpeter, M. (1997). Designing a process evaluation for a comprehensive breast cancer screening intervention: Challenges and opportunities. *Evaluation and Program Planning, 20*(3), 237–249.

Vincent, C., & Ball, S. J. (2007). 'Making up' the middle class child: Families, activities and class dispositions. *Sociology, 41*(6), 1061–1077.

Walker, M., Fredericks, B., Mills, K., & Anderson, D. (2013). "Yarning" as a method for community-based health research with Indigenous women: The Indigenous women's wellness research program. *Health Care for Women International, 35*(10), 1216–1226. https://doi.org/10.1080/07399332.2013. 815754.

Walsh, D., Rudd, R., Moeykens, B., & Moloney, T. (1993). Social marketing for public health. *Health Affairs, 12*(2), 104–119.

Walter, M., Martin, K., L., & Bodkin-Andrews, G. (Eds.). (2017). *Indigenous children growing up strong a longitudinal study of Aboriginal and Torres Strait Islander families*. London: Palgrave Macmillan.

Wasan, P. G., & Tripathi, G. (2014). Revisiting social marketing mix: A socio-cultural perspective. *Journal of Services Research, 14*(2), 127.

Waters, B. S. (2016). *We can speak for ourselves parent involvement and ideologies of Black mothers in Chicago.* Rotterdam: Sense Publishers.

Watson, I. (2014). Re-centring first nations knowledge and places in a Terra nullius space. *AlterNative: An International Journal of Indigenous Peoples, 10*(5), 508–520. https://doi.org/10.1177/117718011401000506.

Weinreich, N. K. (2011). *Hands-on social marketing a step-by-step guide to designing change for good* (2nd ed.). Los Angeles, CA: Sage.

West, R., Stewart, L., Foster, K., & Usher, K. (2013). Through a critical lens: Indigenist research and the Dadirri method (Vol. 22, pp. 1582, 2012). *Qualitative Health Research, 23*(12), 1708. https://doi.org/10.1177/1049732312467610.

Wettstein, D., & Suggs, L. S. (2016). Is it social marketing? The benchmarks meet the social marketing indicator. *Journal of Social Marketing, 6*(1), 2–17. https://doi.org/10.1108/jsocm-05-2014-0034.

Wettstein, D., Suzanne Suggs, L., & Lellig, C. (2012). Social marketing and alcohol misuse prevention in German-speaking countries. *Journal of Social Marketing, 2*(3), 187–206. https://doi.org/10.1108/20426761211265186.

White, L. (2015). *Free to be Mohawk: Indigenous education at the Akwesasne freedom school.* Norman, OK: University of Oklahoma Press.

Whiteford, L. (2015). Global health, medical anthropology, and social marketing: Steps to the ecology of collaboration. *Collegium Antropologicum, 39*(2), 285.

Wiebe, G. (1951). Merchandising commodities and citizenship on television. *The Public Opinion Quarterly, 15*(4), 679–691.

Wilkie, W. L., & Moore, E. S. (2003). Scholarly research in marketing: Exploring the "4 eras" of thought development. *Journal of Public Policy & Marketing, 22*(2), 116–146. https://doi.org/10.1509/jppm.22.2.116.17639.

Willis, P. (1977). *Learning to labour.* Farmborough: Saxon House.

Wilson-Strydom, M. (2015). *University access and success: Capabilities, diversity and social justice.* Oxford: Routledge.

Winkworth, G., McArthur, M., Layton, M., & Thompson, L. (2010). Someone to check in on me: Social capital, social support and vulnerable parents with very young children in the Australian Capital Territory. *Child and Family Social Work, 15,* 206–215.

Wolff, J., & De-Shalit, A. (2007). *Disadvantage.* Oxford: Oxford University Press.

Wong, M. L. (2002). Can social marketing be applied to leprosy programmes? *Leprosy Review, 73*(4), 308–318.

Wright, J., & Harwood, V. (Eds.). (2009). *Biopolitics and the 'obesity epidemic': Governing bodies.* New York: Routledge.

Youdell, D. (2011). *School trouble: Identity, power and politics in education.* Oxford: Routledge.

Zambon, F., Hyder, A., & Peden, M. (2012). Increasing seat belt use in the Russian context: Tailored social marketing campaign and concerted strengthened enforcement. *Injury Prevention, 18*(Suppl. 1), A245–A245. https://doi.org/10.1136/injuryprev-2012-040590w.69.

Zembylas, M. (2002). Structures of feelings. *Educational Theory, 52*(2), 187–208.

Index

The manufacturer's authorised representative in the EU is Springer
Nature Customer Service Centre GmbH, Europaplatz 3, 69115 Heidelberg,
Germany. If you have any concerns regarding our products, please
contact ProductSafety@springernature.com

Printed and bound by CPI Group (UK) Ltd, Croydon, CR0 4YY
29/04/2026
02099459-0001